Salvation As a Mechanical Process

Salvation As a Mechanical Process

Do Christians Need to Believe that
Jesus Died for Their Sins?

by Richard E. Davies

WIPF & STOCK · Eugene, Oregon

SALVATION AS A MECHANICAL PROCESS
Do Christians Need to Believe that Jesus Died for Their Sins?

Copyright © 2020 Richard E. Davies. All rights reserved. Except for brief quotations in critical publications or reviews, no part of this book may be reproduced in any manner without prior written permission from the publisher. Write: Permissions, Wipf and Stock Publishers, 199 W. 8th Ave., Suite 3, Eugene, OR 97401.

Wipf & Stock
An Imprint of Wipf and Stock Publishers
199 W. 8th Ave., Suite 3
Eugene, OR 97401

www.wipfandstock.com

PAPERBACK ISBN: 978-1-5326-9453-0
HARDCOVER ISBN: 978-1-5326-9454-7
EBOOK ISBN: 978-1-5326-9455-4

Manufactured in the U.S.A.   JANUARY 30, 2020

Unless otherwise noted, all photographs and illustrations are by the author and are included in the copyright claim.

Biblical quotations identified as NRSV as well as those not otherwise identified are from the NRSV: New Revised Standard Version Bible, copyright © 1989 National Council of the Churches of Christ in the United States of America. Used by permission. All rights reserved worldwide.

Scripture quotations marked (NIV) are taken from the Holy Bible, New International Version®, NIV®. Copyright © 1973, 1978, 1984, 2011 by Biblica, Inc.™ Used by permission of Zondervan. All rights reserved worldwide. www.zondervan.com. The "NIV" and "New International Version" are trademarks registered in the United States Patent and Trademark Office by Biblica, Inc.™

Contents

List of Illustrations | vii
Acknowledgments | ix
List of Abbreviations | xi
Introduction | xv

1. Singing God's Song | 1
2. Sacrifice in the Ancient World | 13
3. The Perfection of Pagan Gods, God Almighty, and the Blessed Virgin | 28
4. Blood Proves Jesus Christ Is Human | 44
5. Eucharist as Sacrifice and Participation | 60
6. The Eucharist in the Early Centuries | 78
7. Searching the Bible | 86
8. Alternatives to Sacrificial Blood Atonement | 113
9. Where Do We Go from Here? How to Sing a Different Song | 138

Appendix I—Thirty Pieces of Silver in Our World | 155
Appendix II—Love as Emotion | 158
Appendix III—A List of Comparisons between Hercules and Christ | 164
Appendix IV—Blood Atonement Is Not Confirmed by Chains of Biblical References | 167
Bibliography | 173
Index of Subjects | 179
Iidex of Scripture | 185

List of Illustrations

Timeline of scientists and Wesley | 6
Apollo with grain offering and libation pan | 16
Bull being brought to sacrifice | 17
Sacrificial recordkeeping | 17
Bull being examined after having been sacrificed | 18
Small terra cotta votive model bovine decorated for sacrifice | 24
Egyptian god Ra emanating rays in the form of flowers | 34
Greek interpretation of Danaë receiving the Golden Shower from Zeus | 41
Picture of Macedonian coin identifying Herakles as "soter" (savior) | 51
Timeline of Gospel composition | 61
Bringing gifts to a deceased person | 74
Lar pouring a libation and a pan specifically intended for libations | 101
Lamp cover featuring entwined snakes | 106
Crucifixion (detail) by Lippo Memmi, 1340 | 121
Schematic of the *Anastasis* icon | 131
Icon remembering the Melanesian martyrs | 148
Ancient depiction of facial expression of emotion | 159
Case study of ancient emotional depiction | 160

Acknowledgments

I SHOULD thank my teachers from long ago, Samuel Laeuchli and Paul Hessert, for giving me the tools with which I might write a book such as this. I am definitely not suggesting that they would support my contentions in this book, but they were both wonderful teachers.

Thanks to good friends Gary Vencill, Warren Lewis, and Adam Bartholomew for reading and critiquing a draft of this book. Again, this is not to say that they agree with me, but they are good enough friends to patiently critique and contend.

And thanks to my wife and daughter who read, commented, and encouraged.

—Richard Davies

List of Abbreviations

Aen. Virgil. *Aeneid*. Two translations are available at http://www.perseus.tufts.edu/hopper/searchresults?q=Aeneid.

ANF Roberts, Alexander, and James Donaldson, eds. *Ante-Nicene Fathers*. 10 vols. Buffalo: Christian Literature, 1885–97. https://www.ccel.org/ccel/schaff/anf01.i.html.

Apoc. Pet. "Apocalypse of Peter." In *The Nag Hammadi Scriptures: The International Edition*, edited by Marvin Meyer, 749–54. New York: HarperOne, 2007.

1 Apol. Justin Martyr. *First Apology*. In *ANF*, edited by Alexander Roberts and James Donaldson, 1:163–86. Buffalo: Christian Literature, 1885–97.

2 Apol. Justin Martyr. *Second Apology*. In *ANF*, edited by Alexander Roberts and James Donaldson, 1:188–93. Buffalo: Christian Literature, 1885–97.

CCLI Christian Copyright Licensing International

Cels. Origen. *Against Celsus*. In *ANF*, edited by Alexander Roberts and James Donaldson, 4:395–669. Buffalo: Christian Literature, 1885–97.

Civ. Augustine. *City of God*. In *NPNF1*, edited by Philip Schaff, translated by Marcus Dods, 2:1–511. Edinburgh: T. & T. Clark, 1886.

De or. Cicero. *De oratore*.

LIST OF ABBREVIATIONS

Descr.   Pausanias. *Description of Greece.* http://www.perseus.tufts.edu/hopper/text?doc=Perseus:text:1999.01.0160.

Dial.   Justin Martyr. *Dialogue with Trypho.* In *ANF*, edited by Alexander Roberts and James Donaldson, 1:194–270. Buffalo: Christian Literature, 1885–97.

Did.   *Didache* (or *Teaching of the Twelve Apostles*). In *The Apostolic Fathers*, translated by Kirsopp Lake, 1:305–33. Cambridge: Harvard University Press, 1912.

Diogn.   "The Epistle to Diognetus." In *The Apostolic Fathers*, translated by Kirsopp Lake, 2:347–75. Cambridge: Harvard University Press, 1912.

FC   Fathers of the Church Patristic Series, Catholic University of America Press, 1999.

Flacc.   Philo of Alexandria. *Against Flaccus.* http://www.earlychristianwritings.com/yonge/book36.html.

Haer.   Irenaeus. *Against Heresies.* In *ANF*, edited by Alexander Roberts and James Donaldson, 1:316–567. Buffalo: Christian Literature, 1885–97.

Hist.   Livy. *The History of Rome.* Various translations available at http://www.perseus.tufts.edu/hopper/searchresults?q=livy.

Hist. eccl.   Eusebius. *Church History.*

Ign. Eph.   Ignatius. "Epistle to the Ephesians." In *The Apostolic Fathers*, translated by Kirsopp Lake, 1:173–97. Cambridge: Harvard University Press, 1912. Also in *ANF*, edited by Alexander Roberts and James Donaldson, 1:49–58. Buffalo: Christian Literature, 1885–97.

Ign. Rom.   Ignatius. "Epistle to the Romans." In *The Apostolic Fathers*, translated by Kirsopp Lake, 1:225–38. Cambridge: Harvard University Press, 1912.

Ign. Phld.   Ignatius. "Epistle to the Philadelphians." In *The Apostolic Fathers*, translated by Kirsopp Lake, 1:238–51. Cambridge: Harvard University Press, 1912.

Ign. Smyrn.   Ignatius. "Epistle to the Smyrnaeans." In *The Apostolic Fathers*, translated by Kirsopp Lake, 1:251–67. Cambridge: Harvard University Press, 1912. Also in *ANF*, edited by Alexander Roberts and James Donaldson, 1:86–93. Buffalo: Christian Literature, 1885–97.

Il.   Homer, *Iliad*.

Marc.   Tertullian. *Against Marcion*. In *ANF*, edited by Alexander Roberts and James Donaldson, 3:269–479. Buffalo: Christian Literature, 1885–97.

Nat.   Pliny the Elder. *Natural History*. http://www.perseus.tufts.edu/hopper/text?doc=Perseus:text:1999.02.0137.

Nat.   Tertullian. *Ad Nationes* [*To the Heathen*]. In *ANF*, edited by Alexander Roberts and James Donaldson, 3:109–49. Buffalo: Christian Literature, 1885–97.

Nem.   Pindar. *Nemean Odes*. http://www.perseus.tufts.edu/hopper/text?doc=Perseus%3Atext%3A1999.01.0162%3Abook%3DN.%3Apoem%3D1.

NPNF1   Schaff, Philip, ed. *A Select Library of the Nicene and Post-Nicene Fathers of the Christian Church, First Series*. Translated by Marcus Dods. Edinburgh: T. & T. Clark, 1886.

NPNF2   Schaff, Philip, and Henry Wace, eds. *A Select Library of the Nicene and Post-Nicene Fathers of the Christian Church, Second Series*. 7 vols. Edinburgh: T. & T. Clark, 1892.

Od.   Homer. *Odyssey*. Two translations are available at http://www.perseus.tufts.edu/hopper/searchresults?q=Odyssey.

Or.   Tertullian. "De oratione" ("On prayer"). In *ANF*, edited by Alexander Roberts and James Donaldson, 3:681–91. Buffalo: Christian Literature, 1885–97.

LIST OF ABBREVIATIONS

Pracscr.   Tertullian. *Prescription Against Heretics.* In *ANF*, edited by Alexander Roberts and James Donaldson, 3:243–66. Buffalo: Christian Literature, 1885–97.

Praep. Ev.   Eusebius of Caesarea, *Praeparatio Evangelica.*

Prax.   Tertullian. *Against Praxeas.* In *ANF*, edited by Alexander Roberts and James Donaldson, 3:597–629. Buffalo: Christian Literature, 1885–97.

Protr.   Clement of Alexandria. "Exhortation to the Heathen." In *ANF*, edited by Alexander Roberts and James Donaldson, 2:171–206. Buffalo: Christian Literature, 1885–97.

Rom.   Cassius Dio. *Historiae Romanae* or *Romaika* [*History of Rome*].

Strom.   Clement of Alexandria. *Stromata* [*Miscellanies*]. In *ANF*, edited by Alexander Roberts and James Donaldson, 2:299–346. Buffalo: Christian Literature, 1885–97.

TDNTA   Bromiley, Geoffrey W. *Theological Dictionary of the New Testament Abridged in One Volume.* Edited by Gerhard Kittel and Gerhard Friedrich. Translated by Geoffrey W. Bromiley. Grand Rapids: Eerdmans, 1985.

Theog.   Hesiod. *Theogony.* http://www.perseus.tufts.edu/hopper/text?doc=Perseus:text:1999.01.0130.

Vesp.   Suetonius. *Life of Vespasian.*

Vit. Apoll.   Philostratus. *Life of Apollonius of Tyana.*

Introduction

A GOSPEL tract says, "Just as there are physical laws that govern the physical universe, so there are spiritual laws that govern your relationship with God."

This leads directly to what many (or most) Christians have been taught about the Roman judicial execution of Jesus, commonly called the crucifixion.

Christians have been taught that Jesus died on the cross to pay a fine or ransom to expiate or atone for our sins. Furthermore, they have been taught that the death of Jesus is the only way individuals can receive eternal salvation. In general, this notion is called the "doctrine of blood atonement" or "penal substitution" or some similar name. We are not concerned about the arguments on behalf of one or another name. We are concerned about the fact that there are ways to understand the cosmic significance of the execution of Jesus other than as a sacrifice, or "blood atonement." (Many Christians have been led to believe that crucifixion was a special form of execution for Jesus, although it was a common method used to execute ordinary criminals.)

I know that there are lay Christians who are concerned about accusations that Christians worship a cruel, bloodthirsty God. I know that there are seminary students who are trying to figure out the somewhat strange theological arguments that swirl around the Doctrine of the Atonement. I hope that this book will be interesting and useful for both groups.

Why is "blood atonement" the only explanation of Jesus's death that most Christians know how to discuss? I suggest that the reason is tied to the opening statement in that tract: we want a mechanical explanation for salvation. We want to know how God makes salvation happen. The notion of "blood atonement" can be simply understood as a series of cause-effect events that depend on eternal laws that are as certain as the law of gravity.

Generally the death of Jesus is explained something like this: There is a cosmic law against sin. Just as the law of gravity cannot be repealed, neither can the law against sin. We commit sin. The cosmic law says we must be punished. That means we must go to hell. But God, our creator, loves us and does not want us to go to hell. There is another cosmic law to the effect that penalties can be paid in a variety of ways. For example, if person A is a lawbreaker, it is permissible for person B to pay the fine. God, our creator, in the form of Jesus (his son), decided to pay everyone's fine by coming to earth and being crucified. If we accept his payment of the fine, we will be released from hell.

We like mechanical explanations of things. This is one reason why we have accepted the "blood atonement" explanation of salvation. We can use our logic to start with these two cosmic laws and construct a series of cause-effect events that work together like a machine. This book presumes that God Almighty, who created everything by simply speaking, doesn't need a machine, or even an instrument or tool.

Beyond that, as we shall see in this book, the culture of the Roman Empire in which Christianity was nurtured "forced" Christians into a thought pattern that led to formation of the notion of "blood atonement" as an explanation for the execution of Jesus.

Today, many Christians would be surprised to learn that there have been several other well-founded explanations for the cosmic significance of Jesus's execution. None of these other options is mechanical. Some depend on a certain understanding of psychology, and some are mystical. All the other options depend on a radical surrender to the profound grace of God. In other words, they leave God in control rather than turning salvation over to a mechanical process.

We will tease out the options throughout this book, but here is a brief summary:

First, in the New Testament, a major alternative (set forth by the apostle Paul) is "spiritual sacrifice." Students of Bible and theology speak of Paul's "Theology of the Cross," but they often overlook the fact that he also spoke extensively of the relation between daily life and sacrifice. In these teachings he always had in mind that "sacrifice" was an offering made by people to a deity. His "Theology of the Cross" did not express the limits of our responsibility to God. Paul didn't tie salvation exclusively to the death of Jesus. (It is worth remembering that "Theology of the Cross" is a title imposed on his writings by later theologians.)

Second, two early Christians, Irenaeus (about a century after Saint Paul) and Athanasius (about two centuries after Irenaeus) spoke metaphysically about Christ, who was both divine and human, suggesting that Christ was able to take our human substance and replace it with the substance of God. (Irenaeus is often quoted as having said, "Jesus Christ became what we are so that we might become what He is.") If we can accept this notion, and not demand that God must use "instruments" or "tools" when replacing our substance, this ancient explanation is not mechanical.

Third, most Christians do not know that the doctrine of blood atonement was not the default explanation for the cosmic significance of the crucifixion until the twelfth century when a monk named Anselm set it forth in detail. At the same time as Anselm, another monk named Abelard argued that the crucial factor is the gift that we humans have received. Abelard argued that any true Christian should feel overwhelmed by the gracious gift of God and respond with deep thankfulness. Abelard did not suggest that there is a mechanical process to accomplish salvation. Grace is the only factor.

Finally in this book, we review the strange Roman folkloric custom of *devotio*. Romans were taught that some military generals had achieved battlefield victory by intentionally sacrificing their own lives. In folklore, this practice depended on prayers to some of the most disreputable pagan deities, and these are certainly deities that we, in the twenty-first century, neither know nor respect. Even so, Saint Augustine appealed to these traditions when he encouraged Christians to be better than pagans. In our time we have our own folklore about leaders who inspire their followers by surrendering themselves. Is this a good way to think about the crucifixion of Jesus? We will discuss this question at length.

None of these four alternative explanations for the cosmic significance of the crucifixion of Jesus is theologically adequate, but we ask how our understanding of Christian salvation would be different if, for the past thousand or fifteen hundred years theologians had debated vigorously about any of these alternative explanations.

As a matter of fact, in the late twentieth century and early twenty-first century, the proposal of Irenaeus/Athanasius has attracted the attention of academic theologians, and perhaps someday it will be seen as a better explanation than sacrificial blood atonement.

INTRODUCTION

In the concluding chapter we say, "It is the presumption of this book that not only is blood sacrifice an artifact of ancient history that no longer makes sense, but also that we don't need to understand the mechanics of salvation." This book is about "unpacking" this presumption.

1

Singing God's Song

> There is but one thing man can be assured of regarding God's nature, to know and perceive that nothing can be revealed in human language concerning God.
>
> —ARNOBIUS[1]

AMONG many Christians the blood of Jesus is seen as an economic symbol. Consider the twentieth-century gospel song, "Victory in Jesus," which affirms that Jesus "bought me with his redeeming blood." It is a rousing "upbeat" song that is fun to sing. We find it in several Baptist hymnals, the *United Methodist Hymnal, Hymns for a Pilgrim People* (congregational), and a number of non-denominational hymnals. The CCLI licensing agency lists it among its top one hundred hymns. In other words, it is widely known. In the one phrase "bought me with his redeeming blood," the song accurately summarizes the doctrine of sacrificial blood atonement, a Christian doctrine that is vigorously expounded and defended by some, ignored by others, but questioned by few. Even those who ignore this doctrine are influenced by it, so it is worth looking into the background of something that is really a strange statement of belief.

While I was writing this book, I received in the mail a brochure quoting Franklin Graham, son of evangelist Billy Graham: "The most important thing my father taught me is that Jesus Christ is God's Son who took your sins and mine to the cross, shed His blood for our sins, died in our place, and

---

1. Arnobius, *Apology* (or *Against Heretics*) 3.19.

God raised him to life. He taught me that we needed to preach that message with urgency until Christ returns." I have no evidence that this quotation is truly from Franklin Graham, but it is certain that the organization issuing the brochure accepts the notion that the essence of Christianity is found in the Roman execution of Jesus, seen as sacrificial blood atonement.

We will see that the doctrine of blood atonement is as old as Christianity, and we will also see how this doctrine came about. Ancient Roman cultural presumptions made this doctrine logically inevitable, even though by the end of the first millennium logical paradoxes inherent in this doctrine were causing problems for Christian thinkers. The question by which people justify the doctrine is, "How can we reconcile God's justice with God's mercy?" If God is just, then there is no hope that God will admit sinners such as us into heaven. We have to hope that God is merciful, but if God is merciful, how can God be just?[2] The basic solution to this paradox has been that Jesus Christ paid a ransom for our souls when he was crucified. This economic transaction settled the question of justice and allowed God to mercifully admit us to heaven. However, as we shall see, there are further logical problems to be solved, there are alternatives for understanding God's mercy, and the development of the doctrine was not simply a response to the economic question but a response to ancient culture and philosophy.

The notion that the execution of Jesus was a blood sacrifice to God Almighty and was accepted by God as atonement for human sin was not immediately obvious to Christians. A later chapter in this book will be a brief survey of the New Testament with respect to blood atonement. The notion of sacrificial blood atonement was clearly taught by some New Testament authors, but not by all. Some of the New Testament passages quoted by some Christians in order to sanctify this notion can easily be read differently. It will be interesting to see that Saint Paul, who speaks clearly about Christ being a sacrifice, also speaks about atonement and salvation through other means. Sometimes our interpretation of the New Testament depends on the assumptions we bring when reading.

Among the Christian writers belonging to the second, third, and fourth generation of Christians, all are concerned about morality, teaching that those who are good will go to heaven while those who are bad will go to hell. Among them there is little discussion of atonement, sacrificial or

---

2. The Venerable Bede, in the seventh or eighth century, had a well-known sermon on this topic. Brewer, *World's Best Orations*, 340–43.

otherwise. Among those that speak of atonement, teaching about whether the execution of Jesus constituted a sacrifice is divided.

Among the early witnesses affirming the notion of blood atonement, the *Letter to Diognetus*, probably written between 130 and 200 (about a century and a half after the first Easter) says that Jesus was a sacrifice to God: "Himself in pity took our sin, himself gave his own Son as ransom for us, the Holy for the wicked, the innocent for the guilty, the just for the unjust, the incorruptible for the corruptible, the immortal for the mortal. For what else could cover our sins but his righteousness?"[3] This was clearly influenced by the "servant songs" of Isaiah, which were understood as a prophecy of the coming of Christ (e.g., Isa 53:5) and it is as straightforward a statement of blood atonement as we are likely to encounter.

Later, Origen (184–253) agreed with Paul's comment that Jesus was like a Levitical sin offering (Rom 8:3), which is another affirmation of blood atonement. One of the servant songs, Isaiah 53:10 (in the Greek Septuagint version), even refers to the servant as a "sin offering," using the same term Saint Paul used in Romans 8:3, so it is not surprising that a textual scholar such as Origen would be in full agreement.[4]

In contrast, Clement of Alexandria (who may have been one of Origen's teachers, although this is not certain) apparently found no need for an atoning sacrifice. His understanding was that God's grace is simply available to all who have faith. He presents a long chapter about the cruelty of pagan deities who demand human sacrifice and does not mention the death of Jesus as a sacrifice. A little later he devotes a long chapter to an exhortation to accept Christian salvation. In this chapter he quotes several New Testament passages and emphasizes faith and wisdom, but never mentions sacrifice.[5] It appears that Clement (and by implication, those whom he taught) had no concern either for sacrifice in general or for a cosmic understanding of the death of Jesus. His exhortation is based on an underlying concern for sin, but his theology of saving grace does not require an atoning sacrifice.

As we have said, few of the early Christian writers addressed the cosmic reason for the execution of Jesus. Although it is dangerous to argue

---

3. *Diogn.* 9.2–3
4. Sandy and Headlam, *Romans*, 193.
5. Clement of Alexandria, *Protr.* 3, 9. Ensor, "Clement of Alexandria," defended the notion that Clement actually presumed blood atonement as the significance of the crucifixion, even though Clement didn't mention it.

from silence, it doesn't appear that the execution of Jesus was widely seen as a sacrifice. Humans require generations and centuries in coming to terms with profound intellectual notions such as the Atoning Sacrifice.

Why did the notion of sacrificial blood atonement become the standard interpretation of the execution of Jesus Christ? In this book we suggest that sacrificial blood atonement was compatible with a number of nonbiblical assumptions, some inherited from ancient pagan culture and some inherited from the speculations of Plato and Aristotle. When the age of persecution was over and Christian leaders began assembling in the great councils of the church to give definition to the faith, tacit nonbiblical assumptions controlled the decision-making. Why did these assumptions prevail? Primarily because of a human desire to understand "how" anything happens. Humans are tool-makers, mechanics. Humans always seek a mechanical explanation for phenomena.

Even among preindustrial people the "mechanical" explanation prevails. When primitive people attribute a "spirit" to a rock, saying that the spirit willed the rock to fall, they are seeking a "mechanical" cause and effect explanation. In a similar way, the idea of blood atonement is a "mechanical" explanation of how God can offer salvation to people. Should we put the word "mechanical" in quotation marks? Maybe not, because the early bishop of Antioch, Ignatius, spoke in explicitly mechanical terms: "[You are] carried up to the heights by the engine of Jesus Christ, that is the cross, and using as a rope the Holy Spirit. And your faith is your windlass and love is the road which leads up to God."[6] The cross is an engine! This explanation is no doubt inspired either by construction cranes (much monumental construction was being done across the Roman Empire) or by the devices used in ancient drama to bring deities "magically" onto the set, the devices that gave rise to the Latin phrase *Deus ex machina*, or "God from the machine."[7]

The demand for a "mechanical" explanation of salvation increased at the end of the Middle Ages, and later in the eighteenth century when it became apparent that the physical world is governed by precise physical laws. Blood atonement was simple in the same way that Newton's laws were simple, so blood atonement became the primary explanation of salvation.

6. Ignatius, *Eph.* 9.1.

7. For a diagram of a Roman construction crane, see Hodges, *Technology in the Ancient World*, 223. Also see the mosaic illustration of the construction of the Tower of Babel in Magness et al., "Inside the Huqoq Synagogue," 37. For an example of the sudden appearance of a deity, see the end of "Hippolytus" by Euripides, starting with line 1283.

Most of this book will examine the ancient origins of the doctrine, but for the moment we want to look at the doctrine in more recent times. The point is that this doctrine, however understood, is not irrelevant intellectual baggage left over from ancient history.

In the fifteenth/sixteenth century, Nicolaus Copernicus (1473–1543) initiated a major change in the way we ask and answer questions about the world when he proposed that the earth travels around the sun.[8] Galileo Galilei (1564–1642) demonstrated the reality of Copernicus's theory. Then Johannes Kepler (1571–1630) specified the physical laws that specify how the earth travels around the sun. This discovery and specification of physical laws was not confined to heavenly bodies. Galileo had also specified several physical laws that govern our daily experience of the world, and in the tradition set up by Galileo, Robert Boyle (1627–91) specified physical laws related to gas in a container (think about air in a tire). Isaac Newton (1642–1727) specified physical laws governing motion of objects on earth and specified the gravitational force binding the earth to the sun, to the moon, etc. He and Gottfried Leibniz (1646–1716) independently developed a mathematical technique, calculus, to handle some of the physical laws being specified. The chain of distinguished researchers continues: Daniel Bernoulli (1700–82) specified physical laws governing the flow of a fluid (including water and air). Electricity was the focus of study by Alessandro Volta (1745–1827), Andre-Marié Ampère (1775–1836) and Georg Simon Ohm (1789–1854).[9]

---

8. There is a valid scholarly debate as to how much of an intellectual break there was between the sixteenth-century scientific investigators and their predecessors, but the accumulation of mathematically certain physical laws clearly influenced the popular imagination from the sixteenth century until now. For an old, but still useful, bibliographic essay on whether or not there was an intellectual break, see Grant, *Physical Science in the Middle Ages*, 114–15.

9. Heisenberg, *Physics and Philosophy*, 94, speaks about the connection among all these scientific discoveries, then describes at some length the limitation of this connection. His point is that these combined discoveries cannot fully describe the world. His summary statement is on page 108: "But even if complete clarity has been achieved . . . it is not known how accurately the set of concepts describes reality." In the twentieth century, scientists began to understand the shortcomings of the presuppositions of the preceding centuries. The description of the world provided by these scientists is accurate when applied to everyday experience, but their mechanical presuppositions cannot fully describe reality.

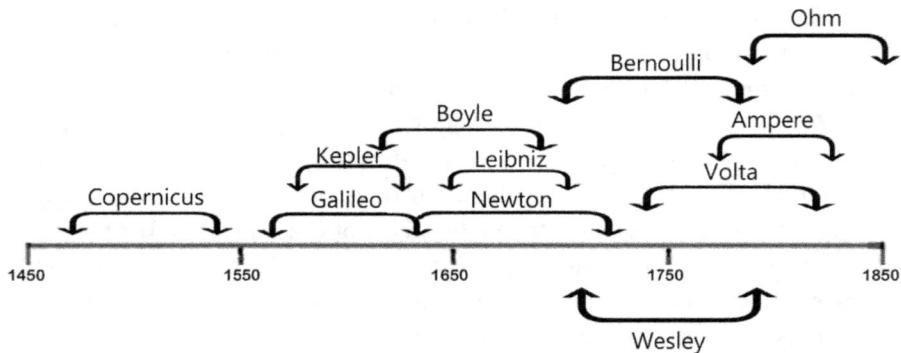

Timeline of scientists and Wesley.

For our purposes, the dates in this list of scientists are more important than the names. Each of these people was responsible for discoveries that impact our lives on a daily basis, and there are other similarly important scientists not on this list, but notice also that this list is a continuous chronological sequence from the fifteenth century to the nineteenth century. As the years, decades, and centuries went by, it became more and more evident that the physical world is governed by laws that we can specify mathematically and explain discursively. If the physical world, which God created, is subject to such specification, maybe there are analogous laws for all of God's activity. This is not to say that we can write mathematical formulas to specify everything God does, but people got the sense that we should be able to talk about all of God's activity in the same way we talk about the mechanism of God's physical world.

This scientific activity was both derived from and led to a great interest in "natural theology," an attempt to prove that God exists by observing the natural world.[10] Most of the scientists we have mentioned were interested in the theological implications of their work.[11]

---

10. An early work was John Ray's *The Wisdom of God Manifested in the Works of the Creation* (1691). Ray made significant contributions to biological science. William Paley's *Natural Theology*, first published in 1802, went through many editions and was widely read throughout much of the nineteenth century.

11. Copernicus was canon of the Cathedral of Frauenberg (or Frombork) in East Prussia (modern Poland). In 1733 Newton wrote *Observations on the Prophecies of Daniel and the Apocalypse of St. John*, which he considered to be among his most important works. These two exemplify the broad theological concern among these scientists. They considered the discovery of God's laws to be an act of devotion. See Kline, *Mathematics*,

One result of this line of thinking was the mechanical philosophy called Deism, a loosely defined philosophical approach to religion. If we don't define "reason" too closely, Deists agreed among themselves that religion should conform to "reason," that is, conform to those things humans can understand. The implications of this were not consistent among Deists. (One cannot find a single work that defines Deism, nor can one identify a belief to which all Deists agreed.) Generally they taught that there are no miracles because a miracle would violate the laws with which God guides the physical world. Also, they generally taught that God does not provide direct revelation or otherwise intervene in the physical world. Deist thinkers had no consistent notion of life after death, so no consistent notion of eternal reward or punishment, so no consistent concern for atonement.

Even though the Deists supported no institutions such as churches, John Wesley (1703–91) saw this loose philosophical movement as a threat. The question, in the presence of great scientific advances, was what should be the role of loyalty to Jesus Christ in our lives? Jesus was a great teacher of morality, but there have been many great teachers of morality. What is special about Jesus Christ? Wesley's answer: the sacrificial blood atonement. He provided this answer with explicit reference to Deism: "Indeed, nothing in the Christian system is of greater consequence than the doctrine of Atonement. It is properly the distinguishing point between Deism and Christianity. 'The scriptural scheme of morality,' said Lord Huntingdon, 'is what everyone must admire; but the doctrine of Atonement I cannot comprehend.' Here, then, we divide. Give up the Atonement, and the Deists are agreed with us."[12]

John Wesley, as a young priest in the Church of England, had a direct personal experience of encountering God. This was so specific that we have a date for it, May 24, 1738. He described it in his journal with the famous phrase, "My heart was strangely warmed." Since Wesley had experienced God's presence directly, he knew that the Deist teaching that God does not enter the world was absurd. Furthermore, if God doesn't enter the world, Jesus could not be the Son of God. We shall see that the Christians of the first three centuries had connected the status of Jesus as Son of God with God's direct involvement in our world. (We shall also see that the doctrine

---

especially 39–79. Theologians sought to honor God in the same way, that is, by discovering the mechanical laws of God.

12. *The Letters of John Wesley*, VI, 297f. (February 7, 1778). Quoted in Lindström, *Wesley and Sanctification*, 71, fn. 1.

of the Virgin Birth came from this concern: Mary, the perfect woman, was the necessary connection between the transcendent God of eternal perfection and the sinful world.) Did the possibility of God having a direct connection with this world necessarily imply that everyone must have a mystical experience such as Wesley's or Saint Paul's (Acts 9:1–30)? Many of Wesley's contemporaries denied it. The Methodist emphasis on experience was quite controversial in Wesley's day.

How does a person become Christian? In our time the emphasis on personal experience has become normative so that today many (or most) would say that the first essential is having a personal encounter with God (or "God in Christ"). Many today would be surprised (and troubled) to find that there are alternatives that we can find in the study of Christian history. One alternative is that a person becomes Christian when the head of the family or the head of the clan becomes Christian. Throughout history most Christians have affiliated with the faith simply because of membership in family, clan, or nation. In the New Testament book of Acts we find both models for becoming Christian in successive chapters. Acts 9 tells us about Saint Paul's personal vision of Christ, a vision which none of his traveling companions shared. Acts 10 tells us about a high-ranking Roman army officer bringing his entire household (which would include family and slaves) into the faith.

As it happens, the "individual experience" approach to Christianity has also laid claim to the doctrine of sacrificial blood atonement. The connection between personal experience and blood atonement is not one of logical necessity, but of historical accident. By the eighteenth century, anyone who had any theological curiosity was seeking a mechanical explanation for Christian salvation. For anti-Deists the sacrificial death of Christ on the cross was seen as the mechanism.

We can see this especially clearly in eighteenth- and nineteenth-century hymns and gospel songs. Consider as an example a much earlier hymn that, significantly, was translated from Latin into English in the eighteenth century:

> Of Him who did salvation bring,
> I could forever think and sing:
> Arise, ye needy, He'll relieve;
> Arise, ye guilty, He'll forgive.

> To shame our sins He blushed in blood;
> He closed his eyes to show us God:
> Let all the world fall down and know
> That none but God such love can show.[13]

This medieval hymn demonstrates that the middle ages shared a sense of personal experience and trust in blood atonement with the eighteenth century. This combination of pietism and the blood atonement was not normative in the middle ages, but was one way of understanding God's work of salvation. As we now have it, this hymn was translated and modified in the eighteenth century by Anthony W. Boehm and John C. Jacobi. It was published in the United States in every edition of the Methodist Episcopal Hymnal from 1836 to 1939.[14] In other words, even though it was a medieval hymn, it was preserved because it fit the theological tenor of a time to come 600, 700 or 800 years later.

Isaac Watts was one of the great eighteenth-century hymn writers. His hymns were rousing and memorable, and they remain popular:

> Alas! And did my Savior bleed,
> And did my sovereign die?
> Would He devote his sacred head
> For sinners such as I?
>
> Was it for sins that I have done,
> He suffered on the tree?
> Amazing pity! Grace unknown!
> And love beyond degree![15]

Charles Wesley, brother of John, was a prolific hymn writer who didn't seem to be able to express himself except in verse. One of his best known hymns, "O For a Thousand Tongues to Sing," an epic exposition of Christian theology, includes the stanza:

> He breaks the pow'r of canceled sin,
> He sets the pris'nor free;

---

13. Bernard of Clairvaux, ~1100 CE.
14. Number 188 in the 1939 hymnal. These stanzas are not in the 1964 or 1989 editions of the hymnal.
15. Isaac Watts (1674–1748), "Alas! And Did My Savior Bleed?," stanzas 1–2.

His blood can make the foulest clean;
His blood availed for me.[16]

A bedrock of any system of theology is the notion that no god/God can owe anything to a human being. If this is the case then our "business psyche" can ask why Christ would die for humanity. Christ doesn't owe any debt to humanity. The death of Christ as atonement must be an absolute gift. Charles Wesley marveled at this and used a metaphor from the banking industry:

And can it be, that I should gain
An interest in the Savior's blood?
Died he for me, who caused his pain?
For me? Who him to death pursued?
Amazing love! How can it be
That thou, my God, shouldst die for me?[17]

In this stanza we see Jesus's crucifixion as the key to eternal salvation linked with the personal/pietistic focus. Notice the word "interest." It is used the way we now use that word in legal discussions. One who has an "interest" in property has a legal share or ownership of the property. The question posed is, "How can I have a right to receive the blood?" The answer here is that the blood is a gift from God. Jesus did "die for me." There is a sense in which I "own" the blood of Jesus.

There is a vast number of hymns and songs celebrating the atonement. Let's look at a few from British and American pietism of the nineteenth century. By the nineteenth century the blood atonement was often in the assumed background, an implicit message. For example, "Spirit of God, Descend upon My Heart" (by George Croly, 1867) is a meditative prayer-hymn calling on God to inspire the singer with God's Holy Spirit. Central to this hymn is this stanza:

Hast thou not bid me love thee, God and King?
All, all thine own, soul, heart and strength and mind.
I see thy cross; there teach my heart to cling.
O let me seek thee, and O let me find!

---

16. Charles Wesley, "O For a Thousand Tongues to Sing," stanza 4. The full poem includes eighteen stanzas. For a brief review of the poem's complicated history, see United Methodist Church, *United Methodist Hymnal*, 56.

17. Charles Wesley, "O For a Thousand Tongues to Sing," stanza 1.

The message is that the secret to obtaining mystical harmony with God is to find it in the execution of Jesus, perhaps by meditating on his execution. His execution can unite me with God. His execution is the source of atonement. (We shall see in chapter 7 how this is from a notion set forth by the apostle Paul.)

Likewise a rousing and popular nineteenth-century hymn of commitment, "Lead on, O King Eternal" (by Ernest W. Shurtleff, 1887) subtly invokes the blood atonement in its final stanza:

> Lead on, O King eternal, we follow, not with fears,
> For gladness breaks like morning where-e'er thy face appears.
> Thy cross is lifted o'er us, we journey in its light;
> The crown awaits the conquest; lead on, O God of might.

Is the reference to the "cross" in this stanza simply a way of speaking of the leadership and example of Jesus, or is it a subtle reference to the blood atonement? When we look at the last line, a reference to heavenly salvation, we see the usual theology of blood atonement connecting the crucifixion with salvation for the believer. In the first century anyone who was "successful" had a gold crown to wear to dinner parties, and in this sense anyone who gets to heaven will have a crown (Rev 4:4), while "conquest" reflects a romantic notion of the medieval crusades.

Here are two other examples that simply presume the authority of the doctrine of sacrificial blood atonement:

> I love Thy kingdom, Lord,
> The house of Thine abode,
> The Church our blest Redeemer saved
> With His own precious blood.[18]

> Here I'll raise my Ebenezer
> Hither by Thy help I'll come;
> And I hope, by Thy good pleasure,
> Safely to arrive at home.
> Jesus sought me when a stranger,
> Wand'ring from the fold of God;
> He, to rescue me from danger,
> Interposed his precious blood.[19]

---

18. Timothy Dwight, "I Love Thy Kingdom, Lord," stanza 1.
19. Robert Robinson, "Come, Thou Fount of Every Blessing," stanza 2.

Meanwhile the late nineteenth and early twentieth centuries saw the development of an extensive gospel music industry, with professional song writers often writing a new song every day. Among the most famous of these writers was Fanny Crosby, famous partly because she was blind, but also famous for a talent approaching genius. She was firmly convinced of the truth of atonement. For example, "I Am Thine, O Lord" is about ethical commitment ("consecrate me now to Thy service"), but the refrain presumes the need for sacrificial blood atonement as a required condition for an ethical life:

> Draw me nearer, nearer blessed Lord,
> To the cross where thou hast died.
> Draw me nearer, nearer blessed Lord,
> To thy precious bleeding side.[20]

It is not difficult to find additional hymns and gospel songs that exemplify the presumption that sacrificial blood atonement is the primary doctrine of the Christian faith, and the fact that this doctrine is both expounded and presumed in congregational singing is simply testimony to the pervasiveness of this doctrine in Christian understanding of God's work.

A moment's thought should convince anyone that this is a really strange doctrine. The crucifixion is a fact of history, but is this fact best interpreted as an expression of God's mercy? Let's admit that we are sinful and need "atonement," that is, we need help in coming to a personal, forgiving relationship with God. What does the crucifixion of Jesus have to do with the forgiveness of our sins?[21] Are there ways to understand eternal salvation other than through the doctrine of sacrificial blood atonement? We will consider this question in the final two chapters. Now we will examine the circumstances within the culture of the Roman Empire that made the doctrine an essential part of the new religion called Christianity.

---

20. Fanny J. Crosby, refrain to "I Am Thine, O Lord."

21. Theological scholars in the early to mid-twentieth century, led by Rudolph Bultmann, emphasized the importance of the cross because they rejected what they called "mythology," that is, the seemingly fantastic parts of the New Testament story. In contrast, the crucifixion of Jesus could be accepted as purely historical. See Bultmann, "New Testament and Mythology," 34–36.

2

Sacrifice in the Ancient World

> But thou, stand thou up from among those who are lying on the earth and caressing stones, and giving their substance as food for the fire, and offering their raiment to idols . . . if thou follow after evil, thou shall be condemned for thy evil deeds; but, if after goodness, thou shall receive from Him abundant good, together with immortal life forever.
>
> —MELITO OF SARDIS.[1]

IN the ancient world, sacrifice was the essence of religion. All religion had sacrifice, and if there was no sacrifice, then the organization or activity wasn't religion.[2] The only differences between Jewish sacrifice and pagan sacrifice were that Jewish sacrifice had to be offered (practically speaking) at only one location (the temple in Jerusalem) and anyone making offerings to the God of the Jews was not allowed to offer sacrifice to any other deity.[3]

---

1. Melito of Sardis, *Apology* (delivered to Antonius Caesar), in Roberts and Donaldson, *Ante-Nicene Fathers*, 8:754.

2. The Roman historian Livy tells us that when the authorities wanted to ban unauthorized religion, they burned the ritual books (since sacrifice had to be accompanied by precise ritual) and banned the sacrifices of that religion: "no one should sacrifice in a public or consecrated place according to a strange or foreign rite." Livy, *Hist.* 25.1.11–12.

3. Various documents suggest the possibility of Jewish temples in locations outside of Jerusalem. The evidence is equivocal and if they were actual temples, they were almost all gone by the Christian era. (Runesson, *Ancient Synagogue*, 274–94.) There was a Jewish temple at Elephantine in the far south of Egypt. Sacrifices were offered there, but after

Just like with pagan religion, Jewish sacrifice was offered outside the temple building. The temple itself was the dwelling of God, not a place for congregational worship. In contrast, synagogue (congregational) worship developed during the Babylonian exile when it became impossible to make temple sacrifices, and over a period of five hundred years or so, synagogue worship became the norm for most Jews, who had been dispersed throughout the Roman Empire and beyond. Even so, the great dream of every observant Jew was still that they might go, at least once, to Jerusalem to participate in temple sacrifice, especially at Passover.

The general purpose of sacrifice is clear: it connects a deity (or sometimes a hero) with the person making the sacrifice. Even though we know this general purpose, we still don't know exactly why sacrifices were offered. Was it a way to praise and thank the deity? Was it an attempt to get the deity to do good things for the worshiper? Was it an attempt to persuade the deity not to do bad things to the worshiper? Was it simply something expected within the ancient culture?[4]

Even though we can't be sure about any particular sacrifice, we can be quite certain that most sacrifice was offered as a *quid pro quo*, an attempt to persuade the deity to do good things or refrain from doing bad things.[5] Consider an example portrayed in a mime drama. "Mimes" were short dramas that were very popular in the Roman Empire. Unlike modern mimes, ancient mime dramas had spoken dialogue and in one such mime,

---

410 BCE sacrifices were restricted to incense and grain. (Stevens, *Temples, Tithes, and Taxes*, 63, has published the relevant document. For more on this temple, see Rosenberg, "Jewish Temple at Elephantine.") In the Christian era there was the Samaritan temple on Mount Gerizim (John 4:20) which some might count as a "Jewish" temple outside of Jerusalem, but cannot be so considered for our purposes. There was a Jewish temple at Leontopolis in Egypt which was destroyed around 74 CE (shortly after the destruction of the Jerusalem temple in 70 CE). It seems likely that this temple represented a schismatic group opposed to Jerusalem. (Bohak, *Joseph and Aseneth*. Bohak has also presented the basic thesis in several articles.) We note that even if they had been legitimate, none of the alternative temples were as accessible to most Jews in the Roman Empire as the Jerusalem temple. In contrast with pagan religions, each of which was represented by hundreds of temples, we can easily say that Jews were restricted to sacrifice in only one temple.

4. Eisenbaum ("Remedy for Having Been Born," 678–80, 698) advocates for the notion that sacrifice sought expiation (forgiveness/atonement) for sin, or cleansing from pollution, which was presumably the result of sin. This was especially true in sacrifice after childbirth. She makes it clear that this is the case in both the pagan world and the Jewish world. This seems to be simply a particular instance of persuading the deity not to do bad things.

5. *Quid pro quo* is obvious in the case of *ver sacrum*. Schmitz, "Ver Sacrum."

about two women bringing an offering to a temple, the priest proclaims to them, "Ladies! Your meat offerings are simply perfect, and they certainly guarantee good fortune for both of you." This proclamation affirms the *quid pro quo* aspect of sacrifice and it also indicates something about the kind of offering acceptable. Mimes were usually satire, and in this drama the women have simply brought a rooster, claiming they could not afford more. One of them says to the god, "we would gladly have brought an ox or a good fat sow" if we could afford it. This is humorous because we have reason to doubt the sincerity of these women. The priest's praise of the rooster was certainly part of the humor in this short skit, and was probably sarcastic, but it also reflected reality. Sacrifice was necessary and whatever one could afford was acceptable.[6]

The common assumption was that no deity could be approached or expected to look favorably on a worshiper unless the worshiper offered a sacrifice. No prayer would be answered unless it was accompanied by a sacrifice. Although it may sound strange, this has to do with why Mary and Joseph made an offering of "a pair of doves or two young pigeons" (Luke 1:24; Lev 12:8). With this sacrifice, Joseph (as we shall see in chapters 5 and 7) accepted Jesus as his son and made a formal prayer, probably asking that Jesus would survive through childhood and become a strong, productive adult. Did Joseph and Mary actually believe in the magic of the sacrifice as a way of getting God's attention to the prayer? Maybe not, but so many people believed in sacrificial magic that it was socially unacceptable to avoid the practice. Cultural norms constituted one reason for offering sacrifice.

It is interesting that the Greek/Roman gods and goddesses also offered sacrifices. We have many pictures of them pouring libations: pictures on vases, on monuments, on coins, in the form of statues, in mosaics and frescoes, and engraved on jewelry. Maybe this reflected the hierarchy among the deities, or maybe it was teaching by example: if the deities can be pious, I should also be pious.

---

6. Herondas (or Herodas), mime IV, in Grant, *Hellenistic Religions*, 4–6.

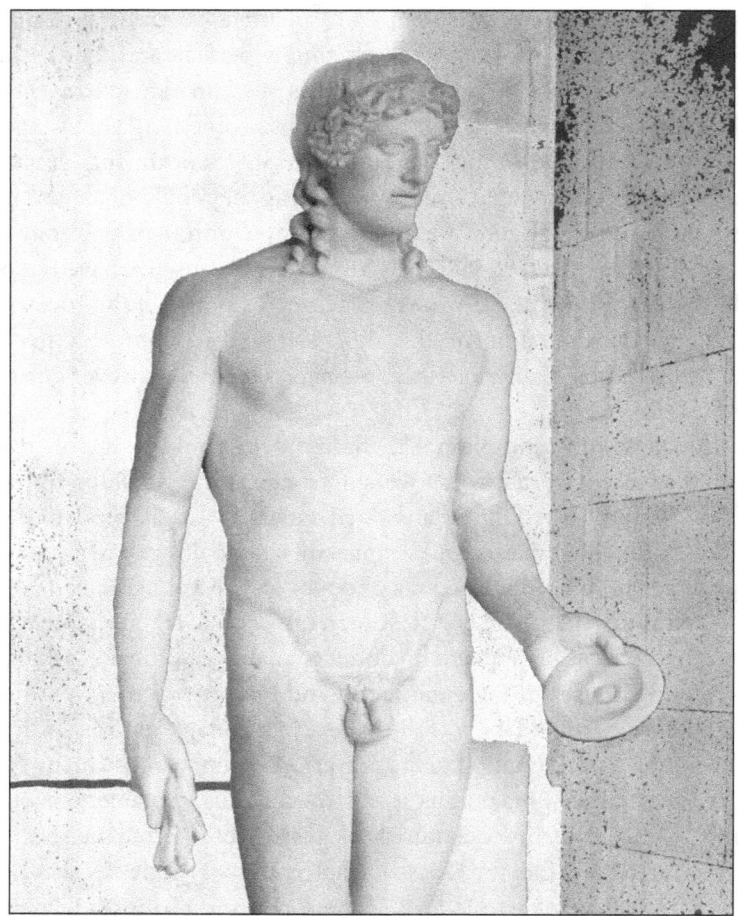

Apollo with grain offering and libation pan. Roman copy of Greek original, second century CE. Louvre Ma884.

Not everyone offered sacrifices every week or every month (unlike Christians attending worship weekly and participating in Eucharist weekly or on some other regular schedule), but there were enough people offering sacrifices at any time that there was a "sacrifice industry" that was quite important to the overall economy. There were farmers who specialized in raising sacrificial animals, and there were farmers who raised grain to feed the animals. When an animal was led to sacrifice it was bedecked with flower garlands, as were the worshipers bringing the animal to the altar, so weaving garlands was a profession. There were accountants who kept track of the animals being offered and of those who offered them. There were specialists in efficient killing. There were butchers skilled in separating those parts of the animal pleasing to the deity from those parts reserved for human consumption. There were those who tended the fire. And of course there were priests and priestesses who knew the words and melodies for the sacrificial rituals.

Bull being brought to sacrifice. Glyptothek, Munich. There is an almost-identical frieze on display in the Louvre, P231.

Sacrificial recordkeeping, part of the above frieze.

Bull being examined after having been sacrificed. Rome, ca. 100 CE. Louvre, Ma978.

We get glimpses of this industry in various odd places. For example, in the Temple of Demeter and Persephone outside of ancient Corinth, archaeologists have found three "curse tablets" directed against a particular young woman. Curse tablets were common in the ancient world. If you had a dispute with someone, possibly a legal dispute, possibly an upcoming sports contest, possibly involving a love triangle, you could go to a temple and have a petition written (on lead or gold for durability) asking the deity to disable your opponent. The woman named Karpile Babbia must have been quite a vamp, because all three curse tablets directed against her are to prevent her from stealing the boyfriends of other women. The pertinent point for us is that these tablets specified her profession: she was a "weaver of garlands," and of course the garlands would have been used to decorate sacrifices.[7]

We get a real sense of the importance of the sacrifice industry to the overall economy in the famous letter that Pliny the Younger sent to Emperor Trajan sometime between 111 and 113 CE, the earliest secular reference to Christians we have. Pliny was serving as governor in Bithynia, on the southern shore of the Black Sea. Interestingly, this is a place Saint

---

7. Bookidis and Stroud, *Demeter and Persephone*, 30.

Paul never visited, so Christianity there resulted from the work of unknown evangelists. Pliny was governor about eighty years after the first Easter, and he notes in his letter that some Christians had been part of the faith for twenty-five years. This implies that Christianity had been introduced to Bithynia about twenty years after Staint Paul's death. Pliny seeks advice from the emperor regarding these Christians. The Christians came to his attention because they were upsetting the economy and he assures the emperor that he has taken actions against the Christians: "It is certainly quite clear that the temples, which had been almost deserted, have begun to be frequented, that the established religious rites, long neglected, are being resumed, and that from everywhere sacrificial animals are coming, for which until now very few purchasers could be found."[8] Melito of Sardis also observed that the empire had a financial interest in the sacrifice industry: "[From the worship of the Cæsars,] both *pecuniary* tribute and produce accrue to Cæsar, as to one who is greater than they [those who worship]. On this account, those who despise them, and *so* cause Cæsar's revenue to fall short, are put to death."[9]

Even though poor people would offer whatever they could afford (such as "two young pigeons" or a rooster), there was a clear belief that a rich offering would result in greater blessings than a poor offering, and the sacrifice industry, including farmers, weavers of garlands, and many others, provided the opportunity to make a rich offering.

About three hundred years before Christ, Alexander the Great got into a dispute with his tutor, Leonidas, about how much one should offer. Alexander argued that one should be generous with the gods, and after he began his conquest of the entire world, he sent Leonidas sixteen tons of frankincense from the ancient city of Gaza so that Leonidas could indeed be generous. Much later, after he had waged war in India and sailed down the Indus into the Arabian Sea he sacrificed bulls to Poseidon and threw them overboard. He then poured a libation from a golden cup into the sea, followed by throwing the cup and some golden bowls overboard. This could be thanksgiving for safe travel to the sea or petition for a safe journey as he continued his journey on the sea. In either case it is clearly a

---

8. This letter is found in many publications as well as on many web sites. One source is: http://www.earlychurchtexts.com/public/pliny_letter_to_trajan_about_christians.htm.

9. Melito of Sardis, *Apology* (delivered to Antonius Caesar), Roberts and Donaldson, *Ante-Nicene Fathers*, 8:752.

business transaction between the worshiper and the deity. Alexander was never parsimonious when dealing with the deities.[10]

Alexander was not alone in attempting to bribe the deities with lavish offerings. In the civil war following the assassination of Julius Caesar, an opponent of Octavian threw horses into the sea (because Poseidon/Neptune was god of horses as well as god of the sea). Octavian himself boasted on *Res Gesta* about donating silver statues of himself to Apollo.[11]

The point of all this is to show how firmly sacrifice was rooted in the culture. We should not be surprised that Christians felt the need for their religion to also have a sacrifice.

What Might a Deity Need from Sacrifice?

Ancient people offered various explanations of what a god or goddess might hope to get from a sacrifice. We find one answer in Hesiod's account of mythology, the *Theogony*.[12] We are told that after the creation of humanity, gods and humans met to negotiate about animal sacrifice. The heavenly trickster, Prometheus, slaughtered a great ox, butchered it, and divided it into two piles. One pile consisted of good meat, the other pile consisted of bones and fat. The bones and fat he covered with the animal's beautiful hide, but he put the meat into the animal's stomach, which didn't look very good. Prometheus then offered Zeus a choice between the two piles, and Zeus chose the bones, an eternal decision. Consequently a sacrifice provided good meat for the person making the offering as well as for priests and priestesses and sometimes a banquet for the public. (God Almighty also permitted this. See Leviticus 21:22 and context.)

In the mime we quoted above, the women leave a drumstick for the priest and take the rest of their sacrificial rooster to eat at home. (They also leave something for the temple's resident snake to eat.) The audience probably had a real laugh as the dejected priest accepted the rooster's leg. (Priests were not always held in high esteem.)

This pagan understanding that meat should be used for human consumption has a formal similarity with the Jewish practice of dedication. The Torah directed that any slaughtered animal had to be brought to the

---

10. Rogers, *Alexander*, 86, 225.

11. Zanker, *Power of Images*, 40, 86. Zanker has an interesting critique of Octavian's donation of statues, suggesting it was a calculated political maneuver.

12. Hesiod, *Theog.* 535–57.

tent of meeting as an offering to the Lord (Lev 17:3–4, see 19:5–6). The purpose of this offering was not to provide flesh for God to eat but to make sure the slaughtered animal was not offered to a pagan deity (Lev 17:7). Even though God Almighty didn't want any part of the animal, an outsider watching the similar practice of pagans and Jews with respect to temple sacrifice would have a difficult time distinguishing between them.

This, however, doesn't mean that the deities really want bones and fat. When Zeus discovered what was in the pile he had chosen, he decided to punish humanity by taking away fire. That's when Prometheus surreptitiously restored the fire, resulting in Prometheus's well-known punishment on the mountain.

The Role of Blood

So what do gods and goddesses want? Is there anything we can provide for them? Homer had said, "No." In the *Iliad* he described battle injuries received by deities, and noted in passing that gods and goddesses have no blood and don't eat human food. Something called *ichor* takes the place of blood:

> Blood follow'd, but immortal: ichor pure,
> Such as the blest inhabitants of heav'n
> May bleed; nectareous: *for the Gods eat not*
> *Man's food, nor slake as he with sable wine*
> *Their thirst*, thence bloodless and from death exempt.[13]

If deities don't eat or drink anything that humans eat or drink and don't have blood, they don't need blood sacrifices.

What Homer said corresponds to the Christian answer which Justin Martyr gave quite simply: "And neither do we honor with many sacrifices and garlands of flowers such deities as men have formed . . . God does not need the material offerings which men can give, seeing, indeed, that He Himself is the provider of all things." Justin also writes that sacrifice is not ethical, because it wastes the God-given food that people need for sustenance. Furthermore, God requires justice, not sacrifice (recalling the Hebrew prophets, e.g., Amos 5:23–24).[14] Maybe the sacrifices are good for demons. Justin said that demons convinced humans to worship them

13. Homer, *Il.* 5.391–95 (italics added). For context see 359–441.
14. Justin, *1 Apol.* 9, 10, 13, 37.

simply because *they* need sacrifices and libations for survival.[15] Maybe Justin was being sarcastic. Sarcastic or serious, he wrote an entire book on demons, now lost to us.[16]

There is little evidence of blood as an important element in pagan animal sacrifice.[17] As we have seen, food for the pagan deities was "ambrosia" and/or "nectar." We shall have much more to say about *ichor*.[18] We will discuss ichor and blood in pagan belief and ritual in chapter 4.

When we think about Jewish sacrifice, obviously God Almighty, who is not human in form, has no blood or even veins to contain the blood, and does not need blood for sustenance. However if God didn't eat the blood, neither did the people (Lev 17:10–14; 19:26). A slaughtered animal was to be bled out, and if someone (perhaps out of necessity) ate from a carcass resulting from a predator attack or natural death, thus eating the blood, a cleansing ritual was required (Lev 17:15–16; see Deut 14:21).

Blood is part of a Jewish ritual of atonement that is separate from the regular offering of slaughtered animals. The ritual of atonement involved both a live goat that was released into the wild (the "scapegoat") and animals that were slaughtered as sacrifice. The blood was taken from these sacrificial animals and used ritually to cleanse the altar and tent of meeting. The people were cleansed when the (live) scapegoat carried their sins into the wilderness, not by the blood (Lev 16:6–28, also similar references throughout Lev and in Exod 29 and Num 18–19, as well as a later interpretation, Ezek 43:18–27).

We emphasize that, in Israel's tradition, blood makes atonement for the sins of the altar, possibly reflecting the ritual pollution brought on the altar by unlawful sacrifices. In the Bible, blood seldom makes atonement for people. We find blood atonement for people only for Aaron and sons, i.e., the priests (Exod 29:21), and a leper (Lev 14:1–32).

---

15. Justin, 2 *Apol.* 5.

16. Eusebius, *Hist. eccl.* 4.18.

17. Aeneas, as part of an elaborate ritual in honor of his deceased father, poured libations of wine, milk, and bulls' blood on the ground. In the *Aeneid*, the wine was clearly for Bacchus, although it would seem more appropriate to pour it on the altar. As for the libations of blood, one would think they were offered to Anchises, the father of Aeneas, because the ancient literature consistently maintains that the dead desire blood. Otherwise, one would think the blood libation would be for one of the underworld (chthonic) deities. See *Aen.* 5.75–80. The best known account of the great desire for blood among the dead is Homer, *Od.* 11.1–2.

18. Clay, "Immortal and Ageless Forever," 112–17; Wright, "Food of the Gods," 4–6.

Interestingly, there are also records of blood being used to purify pagan altars. The preface to the life of Apollonius of Tyana (a Greek sage who was contemporary with Jesus) notes that Pythagoras (his master) refused to sprinkle the altar with blood (which was apparently the ritual custom).[19] Later in this biography, Apollonius observes what he saw among the Scythians: "It's not the scourging," he said, "but the sprinkling of the altar with human blood that is important, for the Scythians too held the altar to be worthy thereof."[20] We emphasize that blood was for purification of the altar, not for purification of the people.

Sacrifice as a Beautiful Occasion

Perhaps deities don't need what we have to offer, but have aesthetic appreciations for some of our offerings. Thus the Greek poet Sappho offers this advice: "But do you, Dica, let your dainty fingers twine a wreath of anise-sprays and bind your lovely locks; for it may well be that the blessed Graces, too, are more apt to look with favor on that which is adorned with flowers, whereas they turn away from all that goes ungarlanded."[21] Thus the opportunity for Kapille Babbia to earn a living weaving garlands.[22]

---

19. Philostratus, *Vit. Apoll.* 1.1.
20. Philostratus, *Vit. Apoll.* 6.20.
21. Edmonds, *Lyrica Graeca*, 265–67, epigram #117.
22. Christians continued the teaching that God prefers garlands. In the fourth century (eight centuries after Sappho) Ephrem the Syrian wrote a Christmas hymn that included the lines: "On this feast let everyone garland the door of his heart. May the Holy Spirit desire to enter in its door to dwell and sanctify." MacCulloch, *Christianity*, 183.

SALVATION AS A MECHANICAL PROCESS

Small terra cotta votive model bovine decorated for sacrifice. One wonders if such models could be used by poor people as surrogate sacrifices. First century CE. Antikensammlungen, Munich.

The opinion of Homer and Justin that the deities don't need anything from humans was unacceptable to the people of the Roman Empire. From earliest times there had been a sense that the deities needed something we had to offer. The *Epic of Gilgamesh* (perhaps 4,000 BCE) tells us that when the great flood subsided, famished deities came to the altar of sacrifice "like flies" because the extended lack of nourishing sacrificial smoke had left them hungry.[23] This was echoed in a much more refined fashion in the biblical account of Noah (Gen 8:21). This universal understanding about need for divine nourishment provides a basis for interpreting artifacts. An elaborate ceremonial bronze bucket (9 3/8 inches tall) from the archeological site of Vače, Slovenia, dated around 500 BCE, is inscribed with pictures apparently depicting living people in the act of feeding deities and/or deceased ancestors.[24]

23. Gardner and Maier, *Gilgamesh*, 239: Tablet III, column iv, ll. 155–61.

24. Near Litija, about forty miles west of the Italian border. See Srejović, *Museums of Yugoslavia*, 35.

The thought that deities need smoke from the sacrifice is archaic and no one in the days of the Roman Empire spoke about it. Once again we are left asking what the deities hoped to get from sacrifice. Not smoke, not blood, not meat. There was a sense that the deities liked sweet-smelling incense, which is why Alexander gave his tutor frankincense. (Of course the incense masked the slaughterhouse stench at the altar.) Maybe they were attracted by beauty, but if that is all, why not decorate the temples with flowers and let it be?

The answer to the question of what the deities wanted is "attitude." In a highly stratified society the deities were above everyone else (although they also had variations in status within their group). Deities wanted people to acknowledge godly superiority by giving up something they treasured. That is why Alexander threw bulls and gold into the sea. We are tempted to say that the deities wanted humility, but that's not really what most people thought. It was commonly thought that one could please a deity through ritual and expense regardless of one's humility or pride. (Jesus taught that humility is most important. Recall his comment, which was contrary to the common assumption, about the rich man and the tax collector in the temple in Luke 18:9–14.)

Was the Execution of Jesus a Sacrifice?

When we think about it, the execution of Jesus constituted an unlikely sacrifice. Sappho said that sacrificial victims should be pretty, but a crucifixion was intentionally ugly. Crucifixion was intended to do more than kill the criminal. It was also meant to degrade the criminal and, by its ugliness, to convince others to avoid behavior that would lead to crucifixion. (This was one of the reasons for the trilingual sign indicating that Jesus was "King of the Jews." Others would be dissuaded from claiming this subversive title [Matt 27:37; Mark 15:26; Luke 23:38; John 19:19–20].) It usually took a long time for a person to die on a cross, and normally the body was left on the cross for a long time after death. Finally the body was taken to the garbage dump. Not pretty at all.

The crucifixion was not even as pretty as our art makes it out to be. The "cross" was not necessarily an actual cross. If an appropriate tree was available, it would do. Good lumber was precious and was not used for every execution. But we know that Jesus was executed with others. The location was probably used so frequently for executions that posts had been raised for the purpose. The "cross" which Jesus (and Simon of Cyrene) carried to the site was the cross-bar placed on top of the post. Certainly the cross was not high, as it is often portrayed in our art. It was only as high as necessary, and probably low enough for dogs to feed on the flesh of the crucified criminals.

Suetonius, biographer of the Emperors, tells about various omens announcing that Vespasian should be Emperor. Among them is this: "Once when he was taking breakfast, a stray dog brought in a human hand from the cross-roads and dropped it under the table." The editor and translator, J. C. Rolfe, explains that this grisly event was an omen because the hand symbolized power (*manus* = *potestas*). More recently, Thayer, an internet editor, has suggested that such a thing would not have been unusual. Perhaps the hand was from a crucifixion, or perhaps from a rite sacred to Hecate. Either would probably have been located at a crossroad. Our point is that a crucifixion was definitely not pretty.[25]

In contrast with the execution of criminals, the history of human sacrifice shows that human sacrificial victims were dressed up, just like animal sacrifices were "dressed up." All sacrifice was supposed to be "pretty." We don't know of human sacrifice in the Roman Empire, but in Greek mythological tradition we are told about human sacrifices, quite possibly indicating that human sacrifice was practiced in more recent times and more civilized cultures than we would like to think. A good example is the mythological story of Iphigenia. She was the daughter of Agamemnon, a hero of the Trojan War. He was trying to get his fleet of ships to Troy, but they were becalmed, so he sent for his daughter, saying that he had promised her in marriage to Achilles. She didn't understand the lie her father told, and dressed as a beautiful bride. She was then taken to the altar for slaughter. There are two versions of how the story turned out. In one version, she simply died. In the other version (preserved for us in two dramas of Euripides) the goddess Artemis substituted a deer on the altar and whisked her away to (modern) Crimea to serve as a priestess (where she oversaw human sacrifice). Our point is simply that she was beautified prior to her scheduled role as sacrificial victim.

Incense was routinely used in sacrificial rituals (both pagan and Jewish). Everyone thought the deities liked sweet smells. In contrast, the crucifixion could not have smelled very good, and there was no incense

---

25. Suetonius, *Vesp.* 293. Thayer's website is found here: http://penelope.uchicago.edu/Thayer/E/HELP/projects.html.

burned as part of the execution to mask the stench of the place. Throughout the Christian Bible we are told that sacrifice is not valid unless it includes incense.[26]

There was a universal assumption that no deity would accept a sacrifice unless the sacrificial ritual was carried out in the prescribed manner. No deviation in the liturgy was permitted. That is a major reason for having priests: they know the rituals and can perform them flawlessly. When a criminal was crucified, no ritual was performed, flawless or not.[27]

In what sense could Jesus be considered a "sacrifice?" There is one possibility. An acceptable sacrifice should be expensive, or as expensive as the worshiper could afford. Was Jesus expensive? He was apparently "worth" thirty pieces of silver, and Appendix I shows that this was not necessarily "expensive." However, if Jesus is God's only Son, then Jesus is of incalculable worth to the Father. As we said in chapter 1, the notion of sacrificial blood atonement has been seen by people as an economic notion, assuming that God is some sort of profit/loss business person. Advocates for sacrificial blood atonement emphasize that a son is of incalculable value.

---

26. Exodus 30 gives extensive instructions on offering incense. Throughout the Old Testament there is a firm requirement that incense not be offered to pagan deities, showing us how important the offering of incense was as part of any sacrifice. It is interesting that Zechariah, father of John the Baptist, was offering incense when Gabriel promised him that Elizabeth would bear a son (Luke 1:9), and in Revelation we are told that offering incense is an important activity in heaven (Rev 8:3–4).

27. On flawless ritual: Pliny the Elder, *Nat.* 28.3.2 and Livy, *Hist.* 25.1.11–12.

3

The Perfection of Pagan Gods, God Almighty, and the Blessed Virgin

There is, people think, a friendship toward god . . . but here they are wrong. For friendship, we maintain, exists only where there can be a return of affection, but friendship toward god does not admit of love being returned, nor at all of loving. For it would be strange if one were to say that he loved Zeus. . . .
Therefore it is not love toward god of which we are in search.

—(PSEUDO-) ARISTOTLE[1]

GREEK/ROMAN culture was not satisfied with what the Jewish writings (both the Old Testament and other writings) had to say about God Almighty. In the Old Testament there is no attempt to give a philosophical explanation of God. Instead, the reality and importance of God is assumed. Genesis begins, "In the beginning God . . ." God Almighty is described in metaphor only, never with a precise philosophical description. The descriptions of God Almighty have to do with function, not form. Consider Psalm 18. Boman says: "No one has mentioned as many parts of Jahveh's body as the author of Psalm 18, but if we put together all the expressions that he uses, they do not give a uniform picture. A fire burned within him, a cloud of smoke arose from his nostrils, and bright flames poured forth from his mouth (v. 8) . . . the darkness which encircles Jahveh (v. 9) fits ill with the

---

1. Aristotle, *Mag. Mor.* 2.1208b.

fire (v. 8). . . . the references to bodily members are not to be construed as actual descriptions but as figurative expressions which describe his qualities with poetic license."[2]

Boman then gives us a long exposition about God's nostrils, which he says is "that part of God's body the mention of which jars us most."[3] He notes that the word which references "nostril" also references "wrath." The Old Testament is full of metaphorical references in which body parts and natural objects speak of God, even when there is no possible way that they make visual sense. For example, Isaiah speaks of trees clapping their hands (Isa 55:12). The point is that Hebrew culture had a very definite "image" of God, but it was not a visual image. "Their images of God were motor, dynamic, and auditive."[4]

There were two broad groups of the Roman populace for which the Jewish understanding of God Almighty didn't make sense. One group was the philosophers; the other was the common people.

As we know, most people in the Roman Empire thought about "gods," not about God. Almost all those in the Roman Empire who were not philosophers believed in a multiplicity of deities, with most deities concerned for some aspect of the natural world: Neptune with the sea (and also with horses), Artemis with wild animals, Apollo with the sun and his sister, Diana (who was also Artemis) with the moon, etc. Pagan deities were also concerned with human creativity: music, poetry, etc. None of the deities was concerned with morality or ethics, and none of them had any real concern for the well-being of humanity. In the pagan religious system, "sin" was defined as violating religious ritual and had nothing to do with morality or ethics. As we have said, the normal purpose of sacrifice was to get the deity to pay attention to the human and either do something good or abstain from doing harm. There was no connection between the ordinary pagan person's understanding of the gods and the Hebrew understanding of God Almighty.

In contrast, many philosophically inclined people didn't accept the family of gods and goddesses on Mount Olympus, and speculated about what a real God would be like. Several centuries before Jesus, Plato had led

2. Boman, *Hebrew Thought Compared with Greek*, 102–3.
3. Boman, *Hebrew Thought Compared with Greek*, 103.
4. Boman, *Hebrew Thought Compared with Greek*, 108. Barr, *Semantics of Biblical Language*, 46–88, argues forcefully that Boman overemphasizes the Hebrew focus on activity against the Greek focus on form. The point being made here is independent of this debate. We are not citing Boman from where he pushes his thesis to the limits.

the way in philosophical thought about God, and by the first Christian century Plato's thought, as interpreted by later philosophers, had permeated every province of the Roman Empire. Most people continued to worship a multiplicity of deities, but throughout the Roman Empire thoughtful, philosophical people agreed that there must be a single god behind this world who lived in a heaven, someplace above the stars.

They also thought that this god must be perfect. As we shall see, this ancient Greek idea of a "perfect" god is not the same as the idea of God taught in the Old Testament. God Almighty, as understood by the Jews, is morally perfect. God Almighty is the one who initiated the covenant of the Ten Commandments and who inspired the prophets to speak out against self-serving politicians and oligarchs. The perfection of God Almighty has to do with moral and ethical behavior.

The Old Testament teaches us that the morally perfect God is willing to talk with people and teach them. God appeared to and spoke with Adam and Eve in the garden of Eden. God appeared to Moses as a burning bush (Exod 3:1–6) and as an undefined "back" (Exod 33:23). God spoke with and inspired all of the Old Testament prophets. The appearances of God to people, as recorded in the Old Testament, would make a long list. God even bargains with Abraham in Genesis 18:22–33. We get the idea that God knew all along what the result of the bargaining would be: the only righteous people in Sodom were Lot and his family, but God didn't simply pronounce that fact to Abraham, instead letting Abraham learn through debate. The point is that the Jews understood God to be an active deity who interacted with people and was concerned with human morality and ethics.

According to the Greek/Roman philosophers, if God interacted with humanity in the way the Old Testament describes, then God is not perfect. Philosophers and followers of God Almighty both believed in the perfection of God, but their definitions of perfection were incompatible. Even so, since they both spoke of "perfection," there was a great opportunity for confusion. When the Christian Gospel went beyond its Jewish roots into the Roman Empire, it encountered people who understood the world in terms of Plato and Aristotle, and these people asked questions the Jewish writings didn't answer.

Some of those questions: (a) You say that God is love. But love is an emotion. Emotions are uncontrollable. How can a perfect God have emotion? (See Appendix II for brief discussion of love as emotion.) (b) How can a perfect God have anything to do with imperfect humanity? What possible point of connection is there? (c) You say that Jesus, a human, was/is God's son. How can a perfect God have a human son? Even though the philosophers taught about one god, the entire Christian narrative seemed odd to them.

According to the philosophers, "perfection" was not moral perfection. Their line of thinking about god led to problems, because if God is perfect and lives far away, there can't be any contact between God and us. The philosophical notion of perfection was static; we can think of a statue. (There were many thousands of statues of the pagan gods throughout the Roman Empire.) The primary quality of a statue is that it doesn't change.

To explain it another way: the philosophical notion was that if god is perfect and "moves," that movement will change the god and will reduce the perfection: god will no longer be perfect. ("Movement" was defined as any change, not limited to physical movement.) If, somehow, god changes and gets better, then god was imperfect before the change. The philosophers were concerned with a perfect state of being (an ontological perfection) and this is profoundly different from moral/ethical perfection. In Jewish theology "perfection" is dynamic, a quality seen in decision and action.

These two views of perfection are incompatible, but Christian writers got confused about this and spoke of the perfection of God both in terms of Jewish theology and Greek philosophy.

Plato didn't write many lectures in which he stated his position unequivocally, but his dialogue called "*Timaeus*" is primarily a lecture in the mouth of a man called Timaeus. No one in Plato's circle of friends disagrees with Timaeus, so his lecture gives us a good view of Plato's understanding of God. Let's be clear that this lecture is primarily about the human soul and body with an emphasis on bodily ailments, but the lecture begins by noting at length how humanity is the creation of god.

As Timaeus begins his lecture, he makes an opening statement that is very attractive to Christians. We will look at it and then make a couple of comments:

> Let me tell you then why the creator made this world of generation. He was good, and the good can never have any jealousy of anything. And being free from jealousy, he desired that all things should be as like himself as they could be. This is in the truest sense the origin of creation and of the world, as we shall do well in believing on the testimony of wise men: God desired that all things should be good and nothing bad, so far as this was attainable. Wherefore also finding the whole visible sphere not at rest,

> but moving in an irregular and disorderly fashion, out of disorder he brought order, considering that this was in every way better than the other. Now the deeds of the best could never be or have been other than the fairest; and the creator, reflecting on the things which are by nature visible, found that no unintelligent creature taken as a whole was fairer than the intelligent taken as a whole; and that intelligence could not be present in anything which was devoid of soul. For which reason, when he was framing the universe, he put intelligence in soul, and soul in body, that he might be the creator of a work which was by nature fairest and best. Wherefore, using the language of probability, we may say that the world became a living creature truly endowed with soul and intelligence by the providence of God. (29e–30b)

A quick, uncritical reading of this statement would lead one to conclude that it agrees with the Genesis understanding of God. *Timaeus* and Genesis agree that God is the creator. God is good. God desired to create humanity in God's own form. Before creation began, whatever "was" was unformed, disordered, chaotic. Creation brought formation to that which was "without form," order to that which was disordered. When God made humans, God breathed a soul into them. (The Greek word for "soul," *pseuche*, has a wide range of meaning, including "breath.") In addition to all of this agreement, Christians identified Christ with God's Word (John 1:1–2). In Greek that is *Logos*, and *logos* is another word with a wide range of meanings. In addition to "word," it also means "rationality" or "intelligence."

We can see why some of the early Christian writers said that Plato had studied Moses (who was considered to be the author of the first five books of the Old Testament).

In this opening statement there is only one thing that is at odds with the Old Testament, but it is crucial: "The good can never have any jealousy of anything." This statement sounds wonderful because we don't like jealousy. Furthermore, *Timaeus* uses this statement as the justification for God making humanity in God's image while the Old Testament doesn't give a reason for God making humanity in God's image. However good this statement about jealousy may sound, we need to look behind it. Why did *Timaeus* presume that God is not jealous? (At this point we can bypass God's own statement about being a "jealous God" [Exod 20:5; Deut 5:9], which, we would argue, deals with a different aspect of "jealousy.")

We can address the problem by looking at some other statements in Timaeus's lecture. Before he began the lecture itself he explained some notions about God, including that "the world has been framed in the likeness of that which is apprehended by reason and mind and is unchangeable" (29a). Later, during the lecture, he said that "motion never exists in what is uniform. For to conceive that anything can be moved without a mover is hard or indeed impossible . . . we must assign rest to uniformity and motion to the want of uniformity" (57e).

In our daily life we like the notion that God is unchangeable, that God is a rock, that God is our foundation. However, we don't normally think of unchangeability in the absolute sense that it meant for the Greek philosophers. Recall that the philosophers saw "perfection" as static, like a statue. If the statue came to life and moved, it would no longer be perfect, so a perfect God couldn't do anything. That is the sense in which they considered god to be unchangeable.

When the philosophers spoke of "movement," they meant much more than physical movement. "Movement" included emotions. The philosophers' god was limited to rational thought. This is why Plato's god is not "jealous." God's lack of jealousy is not a matter of self-control or decision. God is simply incapable of anything irrational, such as emotion. Of course love is also an emotion. The god of the Greek philosophers is incapable of jealousy, love, and any other emotion. In the TV series "Star Trek," Gene Roddenberry managed to make a thoroughly rational, unemotional character sympathetic. Mr. Spock was able to work well with his emotional human companions, but even Mr. Spock was not as perfectly rational as the god of the philosophers.

We will see that the great contradiction in developing Christian theology was between the morally perfect but active Jewish understanding of God and the ontologically perfect and inactive Platonic understanding of God. This unrecognized contradiction was a key element in the development of the doctrine of sacrificial blood atonement.

As revealed in the Old Testament, the morally perfect God Almighty abhors immoral sin and desires to lead humanity into sinless ethical behavior, forgiving past sins whenever possible. (Recall that immoral sin was not a concern within the pagan pantheon. Those deities were offended only by ritual sin.) The details of punishment and forgiveness, as seen in the Old Testament, are subject to some interpretation, but in the Greek/Roman culture, discussion of the theological details were short-circuited by the imposition of platonic perfection. Plato's god could think wise thoughts, but could do almost nothing.

Could the platonic god do anything at all? In addition to thinking, god had the power of "emanation." Somehow this god of the philosophers could send out rays similar to sunshine and these rays could change things and make things happen, but only to a limited and undefined extent. If an emanation from God Almighty (i.e., the Holy Spirit) could impregnate a perfect human woman, the resulting incarnation could be the means of circumventing the platonic straitjacket. We'll look at the details soon.

**Egyptian god Ra emanating rays in the form of flowers.
Tenth or ninth century BCE. Louvre E52.**

No Christian writer in the Roman Empire ever questioned this philosophical notion of static perfection. None of the writers commented on the distinction between the Jewish understanding of God Almighty (who did show emotion) and the philosophers' understanding of god. Not only did they not question the philosophical position, but they actively sought answers to matters not addressed in Jewish writings and for their answers turned to the writings of Plato, essentially making them an unspecified part of the Bible (an uncanonical part of the canon).

Christians didn't accept everything that Plato taught about god. Timaeus spent some time talking about the mechanism of creation. After all, if god can't do anything, then god can't create. As Timaeus explained it, the perfect god created lesser gods (by emanation), which were the stars and planets, and these lesser gods created humanity. (Of course, the planets were some of the pagan deities, so there was astronomical evidence for the truth of this philosophical teaching.) This set the stage for a long-running dispute among Christians about a group of religious teachings collectively called Gnosticism. Gnostics generally took their cue from Plato and taught that God didn't directly create the world but emanated or created lesser gods, who then created still lesser gods, and the chain continued until a god was created imperfect enough to "dirty his hands" with the actual act of creation. It's an interesting part of early Christian history that we don't have time for in this book. It is worth noting that if the Christians had not presumed the Greek philosophical notion of God's "perfection," there would have been no need to explain how the "unchangeable" God could create, and Gnosticism would not have been a problem.

The concept of emanation was not exclusive property of Gnosticism. As we have said, it was the key to incarnation. When humans talk, they don't change. Similarly, God's Word (*Logos*) can go forth (or emanate) from God without changing God. Then the question is how the Word can become human. There was more than one possible answer. One answer was that God's Word can inspire a human, just as the Old Testament prophets were inspired. Perhaps God's speaking words of approval when Jesus was baptized inspired Jesus, and at that time God adopted him as a Son (Mark 1:10–11; Matt 3:16–17; Luke 3:21–22; John 1:32–33). Another answer was that the perfect Word of God (or, alternatively, the Holy Spirit) could enter a (humanly) perfect woman, who would conceive the Word in her womb (Matt 1:18–25; Luke 1:26–33, etc.). The perfect Word of God could then be born as a human being.

Notice that these are solutions to a problem that would not exist if the Christians had simply affirmed the Old Testament understanding of God Almighty and ignored the Greek philosophical notion of "perfection." However this was not an option because Christianity was moving rapidly into the Greek/Roman world where few people knew anything about the

Old Testament. Most people didn't have the conceptual tools to think of God in any way except as unchangeably perfect.

Tertullian's Attempt to Reject Philosophy

There was a great debate among early Christian writers about the role of philosophy in Christian theology, and philosophy was rejected, notably by the polemic pen of Tertullian, famous for his question, "What, indeed, has Athens to do with Jerusalem?" Philosophy, he said, is only the wisdom of the material world. He recognized that Gnosticism grew from the presuppositions of Plato (notably expressed in *Timaeus*). He trumpeted, "Away with all attempts to produce a mottled Christianity of Stoic, Platonic, and dialectic composition! We want no curious disputation after possessing Christ Jesus, no inquisition after enjoying the gospel! With our faith, we desire no further belief."[5]

Tertullian was a lawyer, and as such he was careful about words. He tried to avoid Plato's presuppositions. For example, he said that the essence of God is that God "alone is unbegotten and unmade—alone eternal, and the maker of all things."[6] Notice what is not in that statement. Tertullian avoids saying that the essence of God includes unchangeable perfection.[7]

---

5. Tertullian, *Praescr.* 7.

6. Tertullian, *Marc.* 1.7.

7. Consider this detailed statement of faith which also avoids the trap of presuming that God is unchangeable:

"Now, with regard to this rule of faith—that we may from this point acknowledge what it is which we defend—it is, you must know, that which prescribes the belief that there is one only God, and that He is none other than the Creator of the world, who produced all things out of nothing through His own Word, first of all sent forth; that this Word is called His Son, *and*, under the name of God, was seen "in diverse manners" by the patriarchs, heard at all times in the prophets, at last brought down by the Spirit and Power of the Father into the Virgin Mary, was made flesh in her womb, and, being born of her, went forth as Jesus Christ; thenceforth He preached the new law and the new promise of the kingdom of heaven, worked miracles; having been crucified, He rose again the third day; [then] having been taken away into the heavens, He sat at the right hand of the Father; sent instead of Himself the Power of the Holy Ghost to lead such as believe; will come with glory to take the saints to the enjoyment of everlasting life and of the heavenly promises, and to condemn the wicked to everlasting fire, after the resurrection of both these classes shall have happened, together with the restoration of their flesh. This rule, as it will be proved, was taught by Christ, and raises amongst ourselves no other questions than those which heresies introduce, and which make men heretics." Tertullian, *Praescr.* 13.

In spite of his efforts to set forth a pure Christian theology independent of Plato's philosophy, in the end he could not avoid Plato's understanding of the cosmos. Like every other ancient thinker, Tertullian did not have the conceptual tools necessary to think outside of Plato's notion of eternal, unchangeable perfection in God's heaven.

There was an influential pagan theologian named Varro, and no doubt people had brought to Tertullian intellectual arguments against Christianity based on Varro's teachings. Tertullian was forced to show how Varro was wrong. Of course Varro or any other defender of paganism would admit that the deities of Mount Olympus move around physically and also display emotion. Not only is this known from mythology, but also from astronomy, since some of the Olympian deities are planets. Tertullian saw this as the weakest point in Varro's theology and attacked it directly: "Varro had shown that the earth and the stars were animated. But if this be the case, they must needs be also mortal, according to the condition of animated nature; . . . And yet whence is it that the elements appear to Varro to be animated? Because, forsooth, the elements have motion. . . . he believes only such things to be animated as move of themselves, without any apparent mover or impeller from without." (In other words, nothing animated can be considered to be God.)[8]

Soon after saying this Tertullian launched into a discussion of the origin of the Greek word for god, "*Theos*." Varro asserted a folk-etymology for the word *theos*, based on a word for motion. That is why the pagan gods move. (Note that this debate was based on a theory of how words function which we no longer accept.) Tertullian objected, noting that *theos* also is used in talking about God Almighty. Although the pagan gods move, there is not "any *course* or *motion* in Him (God Almighty)." Not long after saying that God Almighty doesn't move, Tertullian said, "[God's] blessedness [*felicitas*] would disappear, if He were ever subject to change."[9]

When Tertullian expounded Christian theology he studiously avoided using words or conceptual categories related in any way to philosophy. However, when he found himself in a debate, he demonstrated that he, himself, didn't know how to talk about God Almighty without describing God the same way Plato had described god. Everyone in the Roman Empire who had not had Jewish schooling presumed that any monotheistic deity must be unchangeably perfect.

8. Tertullian, *Nat.* 2.3.
9. Tertullian, *Nat.* 2.4 and 2.6.

Tertullian had to admit that God Almighty is very limited, because if God does anything, God will no longer be perfect. God can think and God can emanate. Nothing else. The gnostics agreed that God is limited, and their various theologies were based on speculation about how emanation works. Tertullian saw the need to reclaim the concept of emanation for Christian use: "Truth must not therefore refrain from the use of such a term, and its reality and meaning, because heresy also employs it. The fact is, heresy has rather taken it from Truth, in order to mold it into its own counterfeit.... For God sent forth the Word, as the Paraclete also declares, just as the root puts forth the tree, and the fountain the river, and the sun the ray. For these are *probolai*, or *emanations*, of the substances from which they proceed."[10]

The Incarnation

The logical consequence of the truly universal assumption that God is unchangeably perfect is that God is incapable of love, in spite of what we read in the New Testament. Not only that, but God is also incapable of interacting with humanity. The early Christian writers understood the logic of their position and knew that there had to be a way to explain God's love for people. Their answer linked the love of God and God's subsequent interaction with humanity with the second person of the Trinity. They taught that God Almighty emanated Christ. But this answer doesn't solve the problem because what God emanates is the same sort of substance as God Himself. (Think of sun rays, which the ancients said are the same substance as the Sun itself.) However, in logical terms, if Christ is the same substance as God, Christ cannot be a sacrifice. Also in logical terms, how can Christ be human (with human blood in his veins, not *ichor*)?

As Christians contemplated this problem, conceptual tools from popular paganism became useful: pagan mythological religion included lots of sons (and a few daughters, notably Helen of Troy) of gods, especially sons and daughters of Zeus. These children were born of human women. (Also, a goddess, Venus, consorted with a human man, Anchises, and became the mother of a human child, Aenaeus. The Roman emperors claimed Aenaeus as their ancestor. That is why the emperors could claim to be gods.)

If the pagan deities could become parents of human children, why not God Almighty? This led to another problem: the children of pagan deities

10. Tertullian, *Prax.* 8.

were conceived as a result of lust. Zeus was noted for his lust and his wife, Hera, was noted for her attempts to thwart his lustful adventures with attractive mortal women. The sexual adventures of Zeus presented two problems for Christian theology. The early Christians were united in their moral condemnation of extra-marital sex. They knew that God Almighty cannot engage in immoral sexual activity. The second problem related to the matter of unchangeable perfection: God is devoid of emotion, so God simply cannot experience lust. How can Christ become human? (Here the logical conflict between popular paganism and platonic philosophy becomes profoundly evident.)

The answer lies both in Christ's independence (within the Trinity) and in the human perfection of the Blessed Virgin Mary. Christ (the Word of God) independently decided to become human, independent of lust, and the vehicle was human perfection: a virgin who would freely consent to being impregnated by the Holy Spirit without sexual contact.

As we saw above, if God simply emanated Christ, then Christ would be of the same substance as God and would not be human. Through the process of incarnation, Jesus/Christ had the substance of the Blessed Virgin Mary and the substance of God Almighty, something worth remembering because this theological truth provides the basis for an alternative to sacrificial blood atonement. We will consider this in chapter 8, when we turn to Irenaeus and Athanasius.

Danaë as a Pagan Alternative to Mary

The incarnation as the solution to a chain of logical problems made great sense in the world of the Roman Empire. People understood unchangeable perfection. They understood emanation. They understood that gods might become parents of humans. They understood virginal perfection. (The Vestal Virgins were an important part of Roman religious culture.) Being born of a virgin as a result of emanation from the Holy Spirit distinguished Jesus Christ from the many, many children of pagan deities. Of the very few who had been born of virgins, only one was commonly acknowledged as such.[11]

11. In the long-distant time when Rome had been a kingdom, prior to the empire and prior to the republic, the Vestal Virgins had been considered wives of Jove. Two early Vestals, both slaves, had been impregnated by Jove through the sacred fire and become mothers of kings. One of these kings was Romulus and the other was Servius Tullius. Later generations could not admit that Romulus and Remus had been born of a slave so they said that Mars had fathered them through the king's daughter. Frazer comments

SALVATION AS A MECHANICAL PROCESS

That hero was Perseus, who was subjected to trials that should have killed him. He succeeded spectacularly, even managing to kill Medusa. (Anyone who so much as looked at her face would be turned to stone.) Furthermore he rescued the princess of Ethiopia, Andromeda, married her, and fathered a significant clan. We should note that he left no teachings and was not the object of any cult or religion (although he was considered a divine patron of Tarsus, Saint Paul's hometown).[12]

The story of his birth is interesting. His grandfather (Acrisius, a king) heard an oracle that a son of his daughter, Danaë, would kill him, so he locked his daughter in a chest to keep her from having children. Zeus lusted after her and came to her in the form of a "golden shower" so that, although confined, Danaë, a virgin, conceived Perseus.

What about the "golden shower?" What is a "golden shower?" Some of the Greeks were quite cynical about this "golden shower," as these epigrams show:

> "I even think that Zeus came to Danaë, not turned to gold, but bringing a hundred gold sovereigns."
>
> "Love has thrown away his torch, bow, and arrows, and scatters Aethiopian dust instead of darts." Of course, "Love" is Eros or Cupid. "Aethiopian dust" is gold. The presumption is that the "golden shower" is money. Danaë is a woman of ill repute.
>
> Parmenion wrote a more explicit epigram addressing a prostitute he had hired: "Zeus bought Danaë for gold, and I buy you for a gold coin. I can't give more than Zeus did."
>
> Bassus had hired Corinna, and wrote: "I am never going to turn into gold, and let someone else become a bull or the melodious swan of the shore. Such tricks I leave to Zeus, and instead of becoming a bird I will give Corinna my two obols."[13]

From the story one might think that Danaë, locked away, had no choice but to accept Zeus's advances, but ancient society seems to have thought otherwise. Could she not have spurned Zeus and refused the

---

that "Such tales at least bear witness to an old belief that the early Roman kings were born of virgins and of the fire" (Frazer, *Magic Art*, 197). The notion of virginal conception had mostly been abandoned by the first centuries BCE/CE, although folklore said (with a wink) that the rivers Scamander and Meander in Asia Minor might get a maiden pregnant. The same folklore also said that the pregnancies were actually caused by young men who frequented the rivers (Frazer, *Magic Art*, 162). Thus, for practical purposes, Perseus and Jesus were the only ones for whom virginal conception was claimed.

12. Ramsay, *Cities of St. Paul*, 135–37.
13. Paton, *Greek Anthology*, #31, 1:145; #107, 5:81; #34, 1:145; #125, 1:187.

"golden shower?" We see this not only in epigrams, but in a Boeotian vase painting from the fifth century BCE displayed in the Louvre, where the shower is clearly composed of coins. In the sixteenth and seventeenth centuries this theme was picked up by several painters who did major works showing the naked Danaë welcoming coins falling from the sky.[14]

Greek interpretation of Danaë receiving the golden shower from Zeus. The "shower" is clearly money. Louvre, CA925. Image source: https://commons.wikimedia.org/wiki/File:Danae_gold_shower_Louvre_CA925.jpg.

In contrast with Danaë, daughter of a king who became independently wealthy from the largess of Zeus, the Virgin Mary was a peasant girl who received no material reward for bearing Jesus. Not surprisingly there were ancient detractors who asserted that she must have been a prostitute. According to a persistent tale, Pantera was the name of Jesus's father.[15] This

---

14. Four such paintings displayed in the United States are: Titian, 1554, Chicago Art Institute; Hendrik Goltzius, 1603, Los Angeles County Museum of Art; Artemisa(?) Gentileschi, 1612, St. Louis Art Museum; Orazio Gentileschi, 1622, Getty Museum, Los Angeles.

15. Smith, *Jesus the Magician*, 47–49.

tale, however, was never anything more than a rumor and, unlike the rumor that Jesus's body was stolen from the grave, early Christians never saw the necessity to contest it. (The rumor about the body being stolen was directly contested in Matthew 27:66—28:4, followed by 28:11–15.)

Is there a comparison to be made between the myth of Danaë and the Virgin Mary? The canonical scriptures provide nothing with which to compare them other than their common virginity, but many common people knew both stories and must have had questions. It is not surprising that we have folklore connecting the two stories.

The *Protevangelium of James* provides a possible comparison. Danaë was kept from sexual danger by being locked up. According to the apocryphal *Protevangelium*, Mary was raised in the purity of the temple. She was not locked in, but had no desire to be out in the sinful world. The isolation of both girls is in some sense comparable, but in the case of Mary, the church made a different comparison. Samuel's mother was barren and she prayed for a child, promising that such a child would be dedicated to the service of God Almighty. After Samuel was weaned, his mother took him to the temple where he was raised by the priest, Eli (1 Sam 1:22–28). Like Mary, Samuel was raised in the temple, but not locked in.

The church did accept traditions of female saints being locked away from society as girls and serving God in womanhood. The myth of Danaë was culturally important, so even though Mary and Danaë are demonstrably different, the myth of Danaë persisted in Christian legend as the story of a saint. The story of Saint Irene of Thessaloniki is a transparent borrowing of Danaë. Irene was born as the daughter of a pagan king and given the name Penelope. Even when she was a little girl her beauty attracted so much unwanted attention that her father locked her in a tower until she would be old enough for marriage. Here we ignore many details. The essence is that an angel of God visited her, gave her the new name Irene ("peace"), and convinced her that she should never marry, but serve Christ. Her story includes many events and adventures, and she was the agent through which many pagans converted to Christianity. This is likely a case of the church "baptizing" the pagan myth. The story of Saint Irene provided a way for the church to distinguish clearly between the Blessed Virgin Mary and the myth of Danaë.

We can see how legendary Irene's story is in the dispute about when she lived. As a saint in the Orthodox Church, she is said to have lived in the *fourth century*, sometime after the reign of Emperor Constantine.[16] According to all versions of the legend, she was influenced by a man named Timothy, and some versions of the story indicate that this was the Timothy who assisted Saint Paul, in which case her life would have to have been in the *first century*. In any case, second century gnostics knew the story and had their own interpretation of it, especially focusing on numbers that are part of the story. For example, when Penelope/Irene was in the tower, thirteen other girls were kept with her for company. Gnostics related this to almost anything in their teaching that had twelve, thirteen, or fourteen exemplars, such as the manifestations of Sophia (wisdom).[17]

Returning to the mother of Jesus: Mary became entangled with Plato in 1506 when Pope Julius II was convinced not to institute a feast day in memory of her sufferings. In the preceding century she had been depicted in sorrow, holding the body of Jesus after it had been removed from the cross. There was widespread identification with her sorrow, leading to a movement to institute the feast, but the Pope was advised that identifying her as a woman of sorrow might imply that she suffered some imperfection. Mary, in her perfection, could not possibly be a human being. Once again Plato won.

---

16. See "Great Martyr Irene."
17. Wirth, *Danaë*, 60. See also 16–20.

4

Blood Proves Jesus Christ Is Human

> For the life of the flesh *is* in the blood ... *it is* the life of all flesh;
> the blood of it *is* for the life thereof ...
>
> —LEV 17:11, 14 (KJV)

WHAT's the significance of Jesus?
Philosophically inclined Christians in the Roman Empire understood Jesus as the link between a far-away statue-perfect God and imperfect, sinful people who make bad decisions and live messed-up lives. Jesus was the link because he somehow incorporated God within himself. Exactly how did that work? In the last chapter we saw how "emanation" from God is the "mechanical" explanation of how the philosophically perfect God could enter a messed-up human life. Jesus had a human mother, but God Almighty was his father.

Can we dispute the humanity of Jesus? Certainly he was human, but what about Christ? Was Christ human? The matter gets confusing because some said that Jesus is the same as Christ and some said that they are different. It seems obvious that Jesus, the man from Nazareth, must have been human. If he was human, maybe Christ simply lived in (or adopted) the body of Jesus. If that's the case, then logic suggests that Jesus wasn't really the Son of God. But Jesus was (and is) the Son of God, so Jesus and Christ must be the same. Because they must be the same, it was sometimes contended that Jesus, being the same as the divine Christ, was not really human. In the first centuries the question generated a great deal of antagonism between those who said Jesus Christ was human and those who disagreed.

Docetism: The Belief that Jesus Christ Was Never Human

We can't emphasize too much how many early Christians thought about Jesus/Christ in terms of Platonic speculations about God's nature. There was an incentive to use logic to prove that Jesus was not human: If ancient Roman Christians accepted Plato and Aristotle, they could teach that Jesus wasn't human without changing their philosophical commitment. According to this teaching, Jesus looked like a human, talked like a human, and seemed to do everything humans do. However, he didn't really eat anything, because gods don't eat human food. (Of course he never had bowel movements.) He didn't really walk, but floated through the air (a low float, so it looked like he was walking). He never got dirty because getting dirty ruins godly perfection.[1]

This speculation, that Jesus was not human, was so widespread that it has its own name: "Docetism." If you think about it, you will realize that Docetism teaches that Jesus was no different from any of the pagan deities. What he taught was superior to the self-centeredness of the pagan deities, but if he wasn't human he couldn't really understand humanity and his life was not an example of the best human life.

Orthodox Christians rejected this logical temptation and Jesus has always been an example for his followers. Much of the ministry of Jesus was involved with healing, and his example has inspired thousands (or perhaps millions) of medical missionaries. Jesus provided food for people. There are six descriptions of Jesus feeding multitudes within the four Gospels, and this example has inspired Christians in every era to provide meals for the hungry. The Gospels tell us of Jesus confronting those who have power and authority whenever he found them misusing their authority, and his example has inspired others to confront the misuse of power as well as inspiring many politicians to use their power for real public service. If Jesus was not human, dealing daily with the same limitations and temptations we deal with, these examples are irrelevant to our lives.

The crucial question is how can we tell the difference between a human and a god that looks like a human? How could orthodox Christians

1. Pagels, *Gnostic Gospels*, 72–74, has conveniently collected several relevant quotations.

counter Docetism and prove that Jesus was human? The answer is "blood." A god doesn't have any blood. Instead a god has something called "*ichor*." Christians knew that Jesus was human because he bled when he was crucified.

In the second century there was an educated pagan named Celsus who wrote an extensive critique of Christianity and he used the blood-test in his anti-Christian argument. His anti-Christian book has been lost, but a generation or two after Celsus, a Christian scholar named Origen decided that the criticisms put forth by Celsus needed to be answered. In his detailed answers, Origen quotes Celsus extensively, so we know some of what Celsus wrote. Here's something Celsus said about whether Jesus was human or divine: "What is the nature of the *ichor* in the body of the crucified Jesus? Is it 'such as flows in the bodies of the immortal gods?' . . . it was no mythic and Homeric *ichor* which flowed from the body of Jesus, but that, after His death, 'one of the soldiers with a spear pierced His side, and there came thereout blood and water.'"[2] The pagan antagonist, Celsus, was convinced that Jesus was human.

If the Gospels had recorded that Jesus had bled *ichor*, rather than blood, Celsus would have given him some respect as a god. People like Celsus had more respect for some gods than others, but they did have some respect for any and every god. However, Celsus had studied the Gospels and knew that John's Gospel, in particular, says that blood flowed from the wounds of Jesus. There was no *ichor*. Therefore, according to Celsus, Jesus Christ couldn't be a god, and that's why Celsus rejected Jesus. (We'll return to Celsus at the end of this chapter.)

When Jesus died on the cross he bled, and this showed he was human, not the same as pagan gods and goddesses. Is this in any way related to sacrificial blood atonement?

First, a negative observation: If Jesus Christ had been an *ichor*-filled deity, he simply would not have died on the cross. (A well-known gnostic writing teaches that Christ abandoned Jesus before he was nailed to the cross.[3]) If Jesus Christ did not die, then obviously the crucifixion was not a sacrifice.

However, Jesus was not *ichor*-filled. The fact that he bled gave encouragement to many early Christians, especially martyrs. As we have said, if

---

2. Origen, *Cels.* 2.36; cf. Homer, *Il.* 5.340.

3. Apoc. Pet. 81.3–82.3. Note: This is not found in James, *Apocryphal New Testament*. It is a Nag Hammadi text. See Meyer, *Nag Hammadi Scriptures*, 495–96.

Jesus Christ was human then his example is powerful. Obviously most early Christians were not martyred, but martyrdom was always a possibility. We have quite a few ancient accounts of Christian martyrdom, and the martyrs often speak of the example of their Lord Jesus Christ. One such martyr is the third Christian bishop of Antioch, Saint Ignatius (d. 108). Antioch (located today in the extreme south-eastern corner of modern Turkey) was the third largest city in the Roman Empire (after Rome and Alexandria), and it was an early center of Christianity (see Acts 13:1), so the bishop in that city had a great deal of responsibility. His willingness (and even eagerness) to die for his faith came from the example of Jesus and, in turn, became an example for other Christians, especially in Antioch.

Jesus Inspired Martyrs

Persecutions in the Roman Empire were sporadic, and usually local, not empire-wide. We can never know the reason why Ignatius was arrested, but in the reign of Emperor Trajan (98–117) he was arrested, convicted, and transported through modern Turkey and Greece to Rome, where he was executed in the arena by being offered as food for beasts. During the long journey he wrote several letters, some of the earliest Christian documents after the New Testament. His letter to the church at Smyrna has a lot to say about the power of the crucifixion and the weakness of Docetism:

> You are established in immovable faith, as if nailed to the cross of the Lord Jesus Christ, both in flesh and spirit, and confirmed in love by the blood of Christ . . . and he truly suffered even as he also truly raised himself, not as some unbelievers say, that his Passion was merely in semblance [a clear reference to Docetism] . . . for if it is merely in semblance that these things were done by our Lord I am also a prisoner in semblance. And why have I given myself up to death . . . ? . . . that I may suffer with him . . . For what does anyone profit me if he praise me but blaspheme my Lord, and do not confess that he was clothed in flesh? . . . Let no one be deceived . . . there is a judgment if they do not believe on the blood of Christ. . . . They abstain from Eucharist and prayer, because they do not confess that the Eucharist is the flesh of our Savior Jesus Christ who suffered for our sins . . .[4] [We will discuss the Eucharist in chapters 5 and 6.]

---

4. Ignatius, *Smyrn.*

When we read the letters of Saint Ignatius, we find that he fully accepted the notion that the execution of Jesus was sacrificial blood atonement. The above quotation, which is a selection of phrases from throughout the letter to Smyrna, shows the power of the example that Jesus gave his followers.

Elaine Pagels is a scholar who has made a lifetime study of Gnosticism, and she reports that some gnostics were willing to be martyred for their faith, but others disparaged the idea of martyrdom. These others taught that it was foolish to give oneself up for torture and execution when it could be easily avoided by throwing incense on a pagan altar. They were ready to make an insincere sacrifice in order to live another day. What distinguished the gnostic martyrs from those who would lie to avoid martyrdom? Pagels reports that "the interpretation of Christ's death became the focus for controversy over the practical question of martyrdom. . . . one thing is clear: in every case, the attitude toward martyrdom corresponds to the interpretation of Christ's suffering and death."[5]

Pagel's study revealed that there were gnostics (who had beliefs about the cosmos and heaven quite different from any belief we are familiar with today) who believed that Christ shed his blood on the cross, and these gnostics were open to the possibility of becoming martyrs for the faith. There were other gnostics (who likewise had strange beliefs about the cosmos and heaven) who were Docetic. They did not believe that Jesus Christ was a real human. They did not believe that Christ suffered or shed blood on the cross. They disparaged the idea of martyrdom and were willing to burn incense on a pagan altar.

Ordinary People Decide between a Pagan God and Jesus Christ

Among the gods and goddesses, perhaps the most popular in the first century was Hercules (also known as Herakles). Many other gods and goddesses were also popular, but after having made many observations, including the quantity of artifacts displayed in museums and the number of casual references in ancient popular literature I am led to see Hercules as having been extremely popular.

All of this discussion of blood versus *ichor* and human vs. apotheoized deity may have been far too removed from daily life in the eyes of many ancient Christians. As they went about their daily business and interacted

5. Pagels, *Gnostic Gospels*, 82, 90.

with ordinary pagans, people devoted to the extremely popular cult of Hercules would have claimed to find no real difference between Jesus and Hercules (in spite of the fact that Jesus was a moral teacher and Hercules was definitely not).

In our day we are taught that one should avoid public discussion of religion, but this was not the case in the world of non-exclusive polytheism. Everyone believed in the immediate reality and power of deities, demons and ghosts. They had a definite role in daily life and discussion of them was common. We can imagine a conversation in the second century between a devotee of Hercules and a Christian:

> C. I worship the Son of God.
> P. Is that so? So do I. Which son of god do you worship?
> C. Jesus Christ. He is the Savior.
> P. Ah, yes. There is no point in worshiping a god who is not willing to save us. Hercules is my savior, and he has done wonderful things for me.
> C. Jesus raised people from the dead.
> P. There are lots of necromancers. Apollonius of Tyana was one. Of course Apollonius was not a son of god, but Hercules is a son of god, and he raised Alcastes.
> C. Jesus Christ also raised himself from the dead, and today he is in heaven, next to God.
> P. That's a good credential. Hercules died on the pyre because Nissus betrayed him, but Jupiter sent Mercury after him and today he is among the gods advising Jupiter himself!

This conversation could go on for a long time. What is special about Jesus? How is Jesus different from Hercules? The answer was set forth in the hymn in Philippians 2:6–11. Sometime after the year 52 Paul wrote to the congregation in Philippi and quoted this hymn (which he may have written):

> Though from the beginning he was just like [*mophē*] God,
>> he did not reckon equality with God something to be forcibly retained,
>>> but emptied himself,
>>>> becoming just like [*morphēn*] a slave when he was born in human likeness.
>>> More than this, after he had showed himself as having a human blueprint [*schēmati*],

he humbled himself in his obedience to death; yes, and death on a cross.

And for this God highly exalted him, and bestowed upon him the name which is above every name;

that at the name of Jesus every knee should bend: in heaven, on earth, and under the earth [*katachthoniōn*], and every tongue confess that "Jesus Christ is Lord," to the glory of God the Father.[6] (Phil 2:6–11, Montgomery, with significant alterations by the author)

We note three interesting aspects of the vocabulary in this hymn: (1) *Mophē*, which most translations render as "form," and which we have rendered as "just like," was the common word to describe the resemblance between parent and child. ("He's the spittin' image of his Daddy.") (2) We have rendered *schēmati* as "blueprint" in recognition of the fact that, today, an engineering design of an electronic device is presented as a "schematic" blueprint. (3) Note that if one removes the prefix, *kata*, from *katachthoniōn*, the remaining reference is to the really disreputable underworld deities, designated in modern scholarly literature as "chthonic" deities. The hymn is saying that even the most disreputable will recognize Jesus as Lord, a claim that, in the first century, might have been considered arrogant.

This hymn is the first recorded explanation of how Jesus was different from Hercules.[7] It affirms three important distinctions between Jesus Christ and Hercules: (a) Christ was already God before he was born as a human, while Hercules did not exist before he was conceived in the womb, (b) Christ made a decision to become human, and Hercules did not, and (c) Christ made a purposeful decision to die, while Hercules's death was a result of scheming and blundering. Scholars have written a library of books analyzing and explaining this hymn, but in the context of Roman culture, these are the important points.

Jesus, the eternal Son of God, made a decision to become human. An inescapable component of becoming human was humility. Jesus Christ had not only been with God, he was exactly like (*morphēn*) God. Even if Jesus

---

6. The setting of this passage as a chiasm is thanks to Gary D. Collier (in a class and personal conversation).

7. Jesus was also different from Dionysus, a point made by Origen: "But will not those narratives [the hymn in Philippians 2 and Psalm 22], especially when they are understood in their proper sense, appear far more worthy of respect than the story that Dionysus was deceived by the Titans, and expelled from the throne of Jupiter, and torn in pieces by them, and his remains being afterwards put together again, he returned as it were once more to life, and ascended to heaven?" Origen, *Cels.* 4.17.

had been born in a palace, joining the ranks of humanity would be a tremendous reduction in prestige and privilege; but Christ knew in advance what the consequences of becoming human would be: He humbled himself. Hercules was never humble (even though he was humiliated by Queen Omphale[8]).

Human birth was not the end of humility. Jesus endured one of the most humiliating forms of death imposed by the Roman judiciary. (Was it more humiliating to be crucified or to be eaten by animals in front of an audience? We can't say.) Hercules was burned to death, and that may have been equally painful, but it was not considered humiliating. To die on a pyre was sometimes seen as noble. (During the Trojan War, Onione, the spurned wife of Paris, threw herself on his pyre and was remembered for the nobility of her faithfulness to an unfaithful husband.[9])

Some people called Hercules a "savior," but the mechanism of his salvation was never specified.[10] We are never told what it would mean for Hercules to "save" a devotee. When we review the saga of his life we see that he killed more people than he ever saved. He, himself, never healed anyone. There is nothing in his death that would suggest he was a sacrifice. There are no stories of his returning to earth after his apotheosis.

Picture of Macedonian coin identifying Herakles as "soter" (savior).
Kavala Archaeological Museum, Greece.
This coin is also on display in the Art Institute of Chicago.

---

8. See, e.g., Sophocles, "Trachiniae," 255–69, along with the arrogance in the character of Hercules that Sophocles reveals later in the drama.

9. Quintus Smyrnaeus, *Fall of Troy*, ll. 289–489.

10. The word "savior" (*soter*) seems to sometimes have been simply an honorary title. See Edwards, "Archaeology Gives New Reality," 27. Even so, when a deity was called *soter*, it must have meant much more than when the word described a human.

SALVATION AS A MECHANICAL PROCESS

The great contrast between Jesus and Hercules is at the point of salvation. When a Christian and a pagan got into conversation about the "son of god," the image of the humble shepherd who became like a humble lamb and submitted to death as an atoning blood sacrifice could not be matched by Hercules or any other "son of god" or any other deity. Some have claimed that the Egyptian Osiris was similar. Some have claimed that Attis, consort of Cybele, was similar. Some have claimed that the sweet singer Orpheus was also similar. None of their stories come as close to the story of Jesus as that of Hercules, and none of these were as popular across the Empire as Hercules. (See Appendix III for a list of points of comparison between Hercules and Jesus that pagans might have made.)

In the Philippians hymn, Paul had identified the difference as preexistence, humility, and decision, but this was not sufficient for most early Christians. Most wanted an explanation of faith and salvation in mechanical terms. None of these three qualities offers a mechanical explanation or formula for achieving personal salvation.

The great difference between Hercules and Jesus was seen in the mechanical explanation of sacrificial blood atonement. Martyrs could follow the example of Jesus because he also surrendered his life. They could follow him confidently because he was savior. Ordinary people, conscious of their sin, could hope for forgiveness through the grace of God. They could be confident of that grace because, in the death of Jesus, an appropriate sacrifice had been offered. The blood of Jesus would save them.

Once again we see that the culture of the Roman Empire led the early Christians to affirm the execution of Jesus as a sacramental sacrifice that somehow pleased God and thus assured salvation. This belief allowed Christianity to conform to the notion that all religions must have blood sacrifice. It allowed Christianity to teach that Jesus Christ had been/was/is a real human with blood, not *ichor*, in his veins. It provided Christianity an explanation for the difference between Jesus Christ and other deities, such as Hercules.

Blood as Nourishment for Ghosts, Demons and Vampires

The notion of blood had its own problems. Yes, Jesus bled on the cross, but many Romans would not see his blood as having atoning power. Burriss gives us four-and-a-half pages of documented examples of Roman discomfort with blood. In general, blood was considered a spiritual pollutant that had to be ritually purified.[11] Even soldiers had to be purified after battle. Throughout the Roman Empire blood was considered to be food for ghosts, demons and vampires. Was the blood of Jesus sacrificed for the sake of ghosts, demons and vampires?

Today we consider the cosmos (or at least this world) to be inhabited by a maximum of four entities: (1) earthly creatures (including animals and people), (2) God, and maybe (3) angels and (4) devils. Of course, if we someday travel to the stars we might encounter extraterrestrial creatures, but they are of no concern to us in the present context. In contrast to our view of the world, the ancient world was inhabited by a much more complex assembly of characters: demons lived in the air and combined some of the worst qualities of gods with the worst qualities of humans; ghosts were much like demons, but while demons had been created independently, ghosts were the residue of dead people; vampires walked the earth much as they do today in television shows. The list can be extended, but that's enough for now. It's important for us to know that both ghosts and vampires had a supreme desire for blood (in which we find "life" according to Leviticus 17:11). Demons liked rich food and sexual activity, but blood would suffice in a pinch. No god or goddess needed blood, but these lower creatures did.

As we noted in chapter 2, an obvious question is why gods and goddesses wanted animal (blood) sacrifice if they didn't need blood. Probably the deities liked sacrifice because it symbolized submission. When a human offered something valuable as a sacrifice, the human was indicating loyalty to the deity and dependence on the deity.

There are stories indicating that deities needed to eat more than nectar and drink more than ambrosia. We can recall the myth about Prometheus tricking Zeus into accepting bones, gristle, and fat, leaving the meat for human consumption. This suggests that the deities needed some sort of earthly protein. In addition we have the story of the flood, both in the "Epic of Gilgamesh" and in Genesis: the deities received nourishment from the smoke of burnt offerings. Some in the Roman Empire may have believed that the deities subsisted on bones or smoke, even though the most widely accepted story was that the gods and goddesses lived exclusively on nectar and ambrosia so that sacrifices were simply a form of submission.

In any case, sacrificial blood was normally poured on the ground, and many people understood that demons in the air and ghosts in Hades

---

11. Burriss, "Nature of Taboo," 144–50.

received nourishment from this discarded blood. Demons and ghosts were extremely important in the life and culture of the Roman Empire.

If we are going to discuss demons in the ancient world we need to clarify our vocabulary. In the classical Greece of Plato and Aristotle the word "demon" (or "daimon," "daemon") was normally used to refer to a person's soul. For example, in his *Phaedo*, Plato speaks of the deceased being led to the place of judgment by their "demon," meaning their eternal essence or "soul." (113d.) The poet Pindar once praised "this man's *god-given* excellence," a phrase that could be translated as the "demonic virtues of that man."[12] No serious translator would use this translation, but we present the absurd translation possibility in order to emphasize that Pindar used the word "demon" ("*daimoniais*") to describe the man's good qualities.

Over a period of two or three hundred years the word "demon" lost its good qualities, so that by the first century it almost always referred to an evil creature.

We know that Jesus vanquished demons. Pagans battled them as well. Apollonius of Tyana, a Pythagorean philosopher who lived at the same time as Jesus, was promised by Wisdom that "you shall distinguish a god, and recognize a hero, and detect and put to shame the shadowy phantoms which disguise themselves in the form of men [in other words, demons]."[13] Philostratus wrote a long book about the life of Apollonius, and told about a number of encounters he had with demons. Once he even evicted a demon from a sixteen-year-old boy by writing a letter to the demon.[14]

Perhaps the most famous story about Apollonius involves a young student of philosophy in Corinth who was approached by a beautiful woman who expressed her love for him and invited him to her house. She provided him with good food and companionship so that he left his philosophical studies behind. His old friends were worried about him, so they appealed to Apollonius, who confronted the woman. She then admitted that she was a vampire and was fattening the young philosopher so that his abundance of blood would make a good meal.[15]

Apollonius also vanquished ghosts, and was so powerful he didn't need to use blood. Homer has told us about the time Odysseus sought the advice of the seer, Tiresias, who had died and was in Hades. In order to

12. Pindar, *Nem.* 1.9: "*keinou sun andros daimoniais aretais.*"
13. Philostratus, *Vit. Apoll.* 6.11.
14. Philostratus, *Vit. Apoll.* 3.38.
15. Philostratus, *Vit. Apoll.* 4.25, also 8.7.

attract this seer, Odysseus took some sacrificial blood down to Hades and fought off other ghosts until Tiresias came along. After having consumed the blood, Tiresias was willing to talk. This story of Odysseus demonstrates the importance of blood for ghosts, but Apollonius boasted of not needing blood to commune with ghosts. When he was in the vicinity of the tomb of Achilles he decided to sleep there so as to be able to converse with the hero of the Trojan War. His friends feared the ghost of Achilles would kill him since he had no present for the hero and the hero's ghost needed blood. Apollonius refused to take blood with him to the tomb, saying, "I shall talk to him more pleasantly than his former companions; and if he slays me, as you say he will, why then I shall repose with Memnon and Cycnus, and perhaps Troy will bury me 'in a hollow sepulcher' as they did Hector."[16]

Our point in detailing these events from the epic of Apollonius is to highlight the fact that, in the days of the Roman Empire, people took ghosts, demons, and vampires very seriously, and that such creatures desired blood.

In the fourth century the Christian historian, Eusebius of Caesarea, turned to a pagan philosopher, Porphyry, for expert advice on how to expel or at least propitiate demons. Eusebius apparently took Porphyry at face value, and that matter-of-fact attitude demonstrates that the cultural acceptance of demons was a part of normal life: First, purify yourself. Otherwise the demon may attack while a blood sacrifice is being offered. (Of course this might also apply to the Eucharist if it is seen as a blood sacrifice.) Then you can get rid of the demon by going into the place (pagan temple or Christian sanctuary) and (a) cracking a whip and (b) dashing animals on the ground so as to kill them, then spreading their blood around the place. Alternatively, propitiate the malevolent demon by a multi-step process involving libations, the entrails of sacrificed animals, incense, and prayers to the demon.[17]

None of these instructions is compatible with Christian faith and practice, so Christians had to depend on other powers to ward off demons. Basic was the power of the risen Christ, but they augmented that power with amulets and ceremonies that didn't violate Christian principles.

---

16. Philostratus, *Vit. Apoll.* 4.11, citing Homer, *Il.* 24.707.
17. Summarized from Eusebius, *Praep. Ev.* 4.20–23.

Taking a Bath in Bull's Blood: Not for the Sake of Salvation

We are saying that blood, the guarantee that Jesus Christ was human, was not widely considered a sign of atonement or an agent of salvation.

Some readers of this book will have heard of the ceremony called "*taurobolium*" in which a person bathes in a shower of bull's blood. If blood is nourishment for undesirable creatures, why would anyone bathe in blood? This is precisely the question raised by Prudentius, an early Christian writer of hymns.[18] The answer is that the ceremony had nothing to do with sacrificial blood atonement. It was a ceremony in the religion of Cybele whose priests had to be eunuchs.[19] There was a law against Roman citizens making themselves eunuchs, and the *taurobolium* was a substitution. As part of the ritual's liturgy, the one who had received the bloody shower would say, "It is my blood that you see, not that of an ox."[20]

Other Instances of Bathing in Blood

King Ahab (husband of the infamous Jezebel) was killed in battle, leaving his armor and chariot a bloody mess. The conclusion of this story, 1 Kings 22:38, tells us, "They washed the chariot by the pool of Samaria; the dogs licked up his blood, and the prostitutes washed themselves in it, according to the word of the Lord." No one has ever been sure how to understand this reference to prostitutes. Martin Luther put the reference in parentheses and the King James translators refrained from referring to the women.

It is surprising that advocates of sacrificial blood atonement have not widely preached on the irony that is evident when the death of King Ahab (an evil king) is compared to the death of the righteous Jesus: unrighteous prostitutes bathing in the evil king's blood, versus righteous followers of the way bathing in Jesus's blood. Perhaps the reason is that there are problems with the comparison. 1 Kings 22:38 presents translation problems, and, in spite of songs such as "Are You Washed in the Blood of the Lamb?,"[21] the

---

18. Turcan, *Cults of the Roman Empire*, 49. Prudentius, *Hymns* X, 1028–40.

19. This ceremony has also been related in the minds of some students with Mithraism, a religion that featured bull sacrifice. The reason for this is some confusion in the memoirs of Roman Emperor Hadrian. Turcan, *Cults of the Roman Empire*, 8.

20. Turcan, *Cults of the Roman Empire*, 51, quoting Prudentius, *Hymns*, X, 1007.

21. Words and music by Elisha A. Hoffman, 1839–1929. The words of the refrain are: "Are you washed in the blood, in the soul-cleansing blood of the Lamb? Are your garments spotless? Are they white as snow? Are you washed in the blood of the Lamb?"

Bible does not discuss bathing in Jesus's blood. Instead Revelation 7:13–14 makes reference to the saints having washed their *robes* in the blood of the lamb.

Beyond these problems, bathing in blood remained, at best, an ambiguous symbol. The *Historia Augusta* tells us about Faustina, wife of Marcus Aurelius, being attracted to a gladiator. She confessed this attraction to her husband, and he sought the advice of magicians who gave him the cure: he should have the gladiator killed; his wife should bathe in the gladiator's blood; and while she was still sticky with gore, the emperor and his wife should have intercourse. We are told that this strange prescription did cure her lust for the man, although her son and future emperor, Commodus, was widely believed to have been fathered by the gladiator, not by the emperor.[22] How could early Christians who were aware of this story encourage the symbol of bathing in blood?

Might Pagan Deities Have Occasionally Had Blood?

Celsus's assertion that *ichor* is the only evidence of divinity is questionable, because some who were considered divine did have blood instead of *ichor*.

We have spoken at length about Jesus Christ as a human with blood in his veins. Now we need to return briefly to the matter of Jesus Christ as God. If he were really God, wouldn't he have *ichor* in his veins? We have said, "Not necessarily." For one thing, sons of Zeus were human, even though their identity was confusing. We are told of a Greek town that was divided over the worship of Herakles (Hercules), because there were two sacrificial liturgies, one suitable for heroes and another for gods. Herakles was both, so which liturgy should the townspeople employ? They finally compromised, dividing the sacrificial animal in half and observing both liturgies.[23] The myth tells us that Herakles (with blood in his veins) was "promoted" to divinity after he died. He then drank nectar and his blood changed to *ichor*. People felt that there was a sense in which he was divine while he was still human, a divinity with blood.

---

22. Magie, *Historia Augusta* 19.3-4. In addition to the website given in the bibliography, this part of the *Life of Marcus Aurelius* can be found at: http://penelope.uchicago.edu/Thayer/E/Roman/Texts/Historia_Augusta/Marcus_Aurelius/2*.html.

23. Pausanias, *Descr. (Corinth)* 2.10.1. According to Garland, *Greek Way of Death*, 112, the difference between the two rituals had to do with what was done with the food. In a ritual for a god, worshipers shared in the repast. When the ritual was for a hero (who was a human), no one was allowed to eat from the sacrifice.

More to the point is the "cult of the Emperor." Beginning with Julius Caesar almost every Roman emperor was declared to be a god, temples were built in the emperor's honor, they were staffed with priests and other functionaries (salaries paid by the government), and sacrifices (animal, grain, and incense) were offered. When Christians were arrested and threatened with execution, they were most often accused of being (in modern language) unpatriotic. They could escape punishment by throwing a handful of incense on an altar fire in front of a statue of the emperor along with reciting some patriotic words.

At first emperors were declared gods only after they died, but Emperor Gaius Caligula (37–41 CE) had himself declared a god while he was still alive, and after that there were few restrictions.[24] The emperor was a god who had blood, not *ichor*, in his veins.

Summary

What we see in the present chapter is that the challenge of Docetism led Christians to emphasize that when Jesus Christ was executed on the cross he bled real, human blood. This demonstration of his humanity confirmed his suffering, and he thus became a model or example for future martyrs. Not only for martyrs, but for all Christians in every age who surrender their own ego-driven self-centeredness to serve those whom Christ served, in life as well as in death.

Saint Paul, in his letter to the Philippians, had taught about the distinction between Christ, the humble son of God Almighty, and the pagan hero/god, Hercules. Maybe salvation is to be found in emulating Christ's humility. This was not sufficient for popular imagination. People wanted a mechanical explanation of Christ's salvation, not a moral explanation.

---

24. Caligula erected two temples to himself as "god" in Rome and attempted to erect his statue in the Jewish temple in Jerusalem. Cassius Dio offers many specifics about Caligula's pretensions to godhood, and makes him sound like an unmitigated mad man. We see this throughout book 59 of Dio's *Roman History*, and particularly *Rom.* 59.28.1–7. Philo of Alexandria tells us of the attempt to erect a statue of Caligula in the Jerusalem Temple and the ensuing riots (*Flacc.* 6.43). The next emperor to claim the title "Lord and God" was Domitian (81–96 CE, another madman), who awarded Ephesus the title of "temple warden" in conjunction with their erection of a temple near "city hall." It harbored a colossal seated statue of the emperor (five meters high). After Domitian's assassination his statue was destroyed and the city rededicated the temple to his father, Vespasian. The massive head and right forearm from Domitian's statue are on display in the Selçuk Museum.

Blood atonement satisfied the need for mechanical explanation, and satisfied the presumption that all religion involved sacrifice, but the blood was not without problems.

We looked at a number of issues related to rites involving blood.

Our habits have led us to think that every time we come across a reference to the blood of Christ it must be a reference to sacrificial blood atonement. This is not necessarily the case. We must look carefully at what is said, because the point is often not blood atonement but Christ as a real human being who can serve as a model or example.[25]

---

25. Origen, *Cels.* 1.31: "for certain mysterious reasons which are difficult to be understood by the multitude, such a virtue that one just man, dying a voluntary death for the common good, might be the means of removing wicked spirits, which are the cause of plagues, or barrenness, or tempests, or similar calamities. Let those, therefore, who would disbelieve the statement that Jesus died on the cross on behalf of men, say whether they also refuse to accept the many accounts current both among Greeks and Barbarians, of persons who have laid down their lives for the public advantage, in order to remove those evils which had fallen upon cities and countries?"

5

Eucharist as Sacrifice and Participation

> Come together, break bread and hold Eucharist, after confessing your transgressions that your offering [*thysia*] may be pure; but let none that has a quarrel with his fellow join your meeting until they be reconciled, that your sacrifice [*thysia*] be not defiled.
>
> —DIDACHE[1]

WHEN Saint Paul wrote to the Corinthian church, he let us know clearly that the Eucharist was one of the earliest aspects of corporate Christian worship. Mark, Matthew, and Luke were written a generation after Paul wrote to Corinth and make it clear that Jesus had initiated the Eucharistic celebration and instructed his followers to continue it. Luke also tells us about the risen Jesus sharing a meal with two disciples in the town of Emmaus. At the instant when he broke the bread they recognized him, and then he vanished (Luke 24:30–31). The Emmaus experience seems to have been similar to the Eucharist, almost equivalent to an instruction.

Our question now is whether, how, and to what degree this essential Christian observance should be seen as a sacrifice. In particular, does it represent the crucifixion of Jesus as an atoning blood sacrifice? What else might the Eucharist mean?

---

1. *Did.* 14.1–2.

Let's look at the texts. We present them in chronological order based on current scholarly consensus. Paul wrote in the mid-50s (20–25 years after the first Easter). Mark was published shortly after the destruction of the Jerusalem temple in 70 CE (15–20 years after Paul's letters). Matthew and Luke were both written around 80 CE (10–15 years after Mark). John was published sometime prior to 100 CE (10–15 years after Matthew and Luke). Each was written for a different readership in a different part of the Roman Empire. Probably both Matthew and Luke had access to a copy of Mark when they wrote. What other written sources any of them may have had is a topic of considerable scholarly discussion and debate.

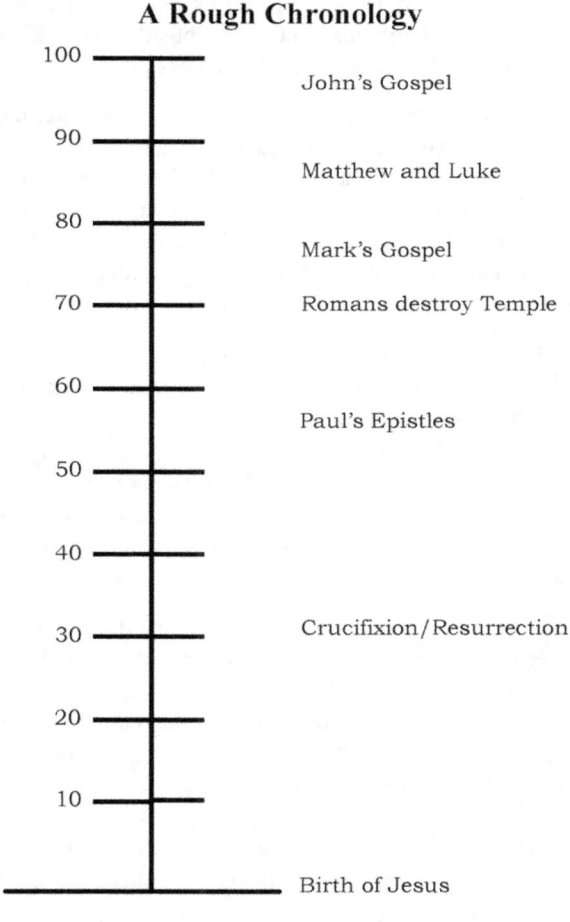

Timeline of Gospel composition.

> The cup of blessing that we bless, is it not a sharing [*koinonia*] in the blood of Christ? The bread that we break, is it not a sharing [*koinonia*] in the body of Christ? Because there is one bread, we who are many are one body, for we all partake of the one bread. Consider the people of Israel; are not those who eat the sacrifices partners [*koinonoi*] in the altar? (1 Cor 10:16–18)

> For I received from the Lord what I also handed on to you, that the Lord Jesus on the night when he was betrayed took a loaf of bread, and when he had given thanks, he broke it and said, "This is my body that is for you. Do this in remembrance of me." In the same way he took the cup also, after supper, saying, "This cup is the new covenant in my blood. Do this, as often as you drink it, in remembrance of me." For as often as you eat this bread and drink the cup, you proclaim the Lord's death until he comes." (1 Cor 11:23–26)

> While they were eating, he took a loaf of bread, and after blessing it he broke it, gave it to them, and said, "Take; this is my body." Then he took a cup, and after giving thanks he gave it to them, and all of them drank from it. He said to them, "This is my blood of the covenant, which is poured out for many. Truly I tell you, I will never again drink of the fruit of the vine until that day when I drink it new in the kingdom of God.'" (Mark 14:22–25)

> While they were eating, Jesus took a loaf of bread, and after blessing it he broke it, gave it to the disciples, and said, "Take, eat; this is my body." Then he took a cup, and after giving thanks he gave it to them, saying, "Drink from it, all of you; for this is my blood of the [new] covenant, which is poured out for many for the forgiveness of sins. I tell you, I will never again drink of this fruit of the vine until that day when I drink it new with you in my Father's kingdom." (Matt 26:26–29)

> He said to them, "I have eagerly desired to eat this Passover with you before I suffer; for I tell you, I will not eat it until it is fulfilled in the kingdom of God." Then he took a cup, and after giving thanks he said, "Take this and divide it among yourselves; for I tell you that from now on I will not drink of the fruit of the vine until the kingdom of God comes." Then he took a loaf of bread, and when he had given thanks, he broke it and gave it to them, saying, "This is my body, which is given for you. Do this in remembrance of me." And he did the same with the cup after supper, saying, "This cup that is poured out for you is the new covenant in my blood." (Luke 22:15–20)

Jesus said to them, "I am the bread of life. Whoever comes to me will never be hungry, and whoever believes in me will never be thirsty." . . . "I am the bread of life. Your ancestors ate the manna in the wilderness, and they died. This is the bread that comes down from heaven, so that one may eat of it and not die. I am the living bread that came down from heaven. Whoever eats of this bread will live forever; and the bread that I will give for the life of the world is my flesh."

The Jews then disputed among themselves, saying, "How can this man give us his flesh to eat?" So Jesus said to them, "Very truly, I tell you, unless you eat the flesh of the Son of Man and drink his blood, you have no life in you. Those who eat my flesh and drink my blood have eternal life, and I will raise them up on the last day; for my flesh is true food and my blood is true drink. Those who eat my flesh and drink my blood abide in me, and I in them. Just as the living Father sent me, and I live because of the Father, so whoever eats me will live because of me. This is the bread that came down from heaven, not like that which your ancestors ate, and they died. But the one who eats this bread will live forever." . . .

Jesus, being aware that his disciples were complaining about it, said to them, "Does this offend you? Then what if you were to see the Son of Man ascending to where he was before? It is the spirit that gives life; the flesh is useless. The words that I have spoken to you are spirit and life." (John 6:35, 48–58, 61–63)

The New Covenant

If we read these carefully, we notice several things. One is that Paul, Mark, Matthew and Luke all agree that Jesus referred to his blood as being (or providing) a "new covenant." Covenants are a rich part of the biblical saga. Genesis and Exodus tell us about God establishing covenants with Noah, Abraham, and Moses, not for their individual sakes, but for the sake of the people they represent. The Ten Commandments constituted an important covenant summary, and a copy was placed in the Ark of the Covenant, which was an important symbol for the people at least until the time of Jeremiah.[2] There were other covenants mentioned in the Old Testament, but the testimony of the prophets was that the people failed to keep their

---

2. There is a tradition that at the time of the destruction of Jerusalem by the Babylonian army the prophet Jeremiah hid the Ark in a mountain cave. It has not been seen since. Jeremiah prophesied that the Ark would be forgotten (Jer 3:16).

SALVATION AS A MECHANICAL PROCESS

part of the bargain. In response, God commended Jeremiah to proclaim a new covenant:

> Behold, the days come, says the LORD, that I will make a new covenant with the house of Israel, and with the house of Judah: Not like the covenant that I made with their fathers in the day that I took them by the hand to bring them out of the land of Egypt; my covenant which they broke, although I was a master to them, says the LORD: But this shall be the covenant that I will make with the house of Israel: After those days, says the LORD, I will put my law inside them, and write it on their hearts; and I will be their God, and they shall be my people. (Jer 31:31–33, KJV, alt.)

Isaiah also proclaimed:

> As for me, this is my covenant with them, says the LORD: My spirit that is upon you, and my words which I have put in your mouth, shall not depart out of your mouth, nor out of the mouth of your children, nor out of the mouth of your grandchildren, says the LORD, from henceforth and forever. (Isa 59:21, KJV, alt.)

The new covenant resides and endures within us, but what is it? It seems worthwhile to point out that "covenant" (*diathḗkē*) is not a material thing. The "covenant" is in the mind of God, and any physical thing related to it is a sign or symbol.

The New Testament book of Hebrews (8:8–10; 10:16; 12:24) teaches that Christians considered the covenant symbolized by Jesus's blood as proclaimed at the Last Supper to be the covenant of which Jeremiah spoke, and presumably also the covenant of which Isaiah spoke. In this book we are claiming (contrary to Hebrews) that the Eucharistic celebration can be a symbol of Jeremiah's testimony, and (as we shall see) can be considered some sort of sacrifice, but it need not be seen as related to blood sacrifice.

Covenants are contracts, and in all ages there has been a need that contracts be guaranteed somehow. In the book of Ruth (4:7) we are told of an interesting guarantee which had become obsolete by the time that Ruth was written: a sandal was exchanged. The guarantee is always a sign or symbol.[3] In the United States today, if you contract to purchase a house you will

---

3. "Semiotics," the study of signs and symbols, is a field in which there is little agreement about technical terms. Different authors use the words "sign" and "symbol" in different ways. For our purposes we can consider the two words synonyms. Incidentally, the word "symbol" is sometimes used as a synonym for "Eucharist," but we are using the word "symbol" in the more general sense of something that represents something else.

be asked for a payment of "earnest money." Even "earnest money," although it is real money, is a relatively small symbolic payment. Once a contract is offered along with a suitable symbolic guarantee, the other party must accept it. Acceptance involves some activity such as endorsing an "earnest money" check, or, if the contract is informal, shaking hands. So it has been in every civilization for thousands of years.

In the Old Testament, God initiates covenants with people. Humans do things to indicate acceptance of the contract. Note that even though there is human activity, which may symbolize acceptance of the contract/covenant, it is God who provides and guarantees the contract. What does God offer to guarantee a covenant? Simply God's own good word. Pagan deities were duplicitous. One could never trust them.[4] In contrast, God Almighty is trustworthy and faithful to his word.[5]

What symbol indicates acceptance of a covenant with God? The ancient tradition was that blood was the covenantal symbol. At one point in Abraham's long relationship with God we read about Abraham asking God for a guarantee that the covenant was valid, and in response God told Abraham to make a blood sacrifice (Gen 15:7–21). The ceremony described in this passage strikes us as being very strange, but the important point for our discussion is that even though Abraham kills the animals, God is the initiator and guarantor of the covenant. Abraham understands the guarantee when, during the ritual, a theophany appears to him as a dream or vision (Gen 15:17). When Abraham carries out the ritual he accepts God's contract (an act of faith). The ritual is Abraham's "handshake" with God. (The ritual over which Abraham presided, strange as it sounds to us, was apparently common in all cultures several thousand years ago.[6])

Circumcision is a symbolic acceptance of God's contract/covenant (Gen 17:1–14). Even though Genesis 17:10 indicates that circumcision

---

4. A good example of how untrustworthy pagan deities were is found in Homer's *Iliad*, 22.232–303. During the Trojan War, Hector avoided battle with Achilles until his brother, Deiphobus, vowed to stand and fight beside him. As it turned out, the vow was actually made by the goddess, Athena, who was impersonating Hector's friend so as to work on behalf of Achilles and engineer Hector's death. (One might wonder if the apparent etymology of the name, "deiphobus," is ironic. Should one be afraid of the ancient pagan deities?)

5. In Hebrews the Word of God is the incarnate Christ, so the guarantee is Jesus's blood. This is much less clear in Saint Paul's writing. We will discuss the matter below and in chapters 7 and 9. As we have said, we dispute the necessity of a literal interpretation of Hebrews. For background see Behm, *diathḗkē*, 160–61.

6. Day, "Dog Burials," 27–28, n28.

really is the covenant, that is obviously a shorthand figure of speech of a sort we find in other places.[7] It is people who symbolically indicate that they accept the covenant and its guarantee by performing circumcision.

Luke informs us that it became a custom to make a blood offering in addition to circumcision, apparently for purification or as a recognition of paternity[8] (Luke 2:22–24). We get the sense that this additional offering was not about ratification of the covenant but was an offering of the people to God Almighty. We have seen how ambiguous the motivation for offerings from people to God might be.[9] Some people probably saw the offering as thanksgiving for a safe and healthy birth. Some probably saw it as petition that the child might survive and become a strong, productive man who would care for his aging parents. Still others might have seen it as a ritual that was simply a social requirement. (Of course, we don't know how Mary and Joseph understood it. We also don't know what prayers were said at the time of this sacrifice. As we have seen, in making the offering Joseph may have been accepting the baby as his true son.) Our point is that the additional blood sacrifice was beyond or outside of the covenant ratified (accepted) by circumcision.

Since circumcision ratifies the covenant, and since the covenant comes from God, not from the people, we should not be surprised that God later attempted to help the people see that the covenant relates to attitude, not to blood (the external symbol of acceptance). Thus God commanded circumcision of the heart.[10] Not only that, but God asserted God's own authority to personally perform that circumcision (Deut 30:6). The requirement that God's people change their attitude then shows up elsewhere without reference to "circumcision" (e.g., Joel 2:12–13). The conclusion we draw from all of this is that, from the perspective of Moses and the prophets, the new covenant is not ratified by the shedding of blood, animal or human.

---

7. E.g., 1 Corinthians 8:4 with respect to the existence/nonexistence of idols, in addition to shorthand Eucharistic words of institution.

8. See chapter 2 along with our discussion of Eisenbaum, "Remedy for Having Been Born," in chapter 7.

9. Consider what Burriss, "Nature of Taboo," 144–50, has to say about general uneasiness with blood in the Roman Empire. See chapter 4.

10. Deut 10:16; Jer 4:4; 9:26, where it is contrasted with physical circumcision; Ezek 44:7, where it is paired with physical circumcision. See also the Dead Sea Scroll, Commentary on Habakkuk, 1QpHab 11.13. St. Paul understands the distinction between physical and spiritual circumcision: Rom 2:29.

Abraham lived a long time ago, and God is free to change the way a covenant is guaranteed and accepted. The acceptance of the new covenant was in living a righteous life and was bloodless.[11] The new covenant involved a focus on God's *initial* words to Abraham in Genesis 17:1–2, "be blameless and I will make my covenant."

In spite of the bloodless nature of the new covenant, early Christians understood Jesus to be talking about his own blood in relation to the new covenant. Since our two earliest authorities, Paul and Mark, tell about this, it seems likely that there was no mistake or misunderstanding. Jesus said it. Why? We can propose all sorts of tangential reasons (metaphor, hyperbole, etc.) but the easiest reason is that Jesus meant what he said. Even so, it might be most appropriate to look past the notion of blood sacrifice when thinking about the Eucharist. Why?

Those to whom Jesus was speaking, as well as Jesus himself, were part of a culture in which the tradition of blood sacrifice was firmly fixed. Furthermore, "righteousness" is a difficult concept to grasp while "blood" is concrete. Jesus had a talent for communicating by using concepts that people understood well. Conceptual communication is not the same as literal communication. Jesus was not speaking in metaphor when he said "my body" and "my blood," but he was speaking in terms of a culturally bounded set of concepts.

Cultural/conceptual understanding is different from metaphor, but it is also different from universal reality. Matthew and Mark both record that Jesus spoke of the cup as "blood of the covenant," and they both may have meant it without further reflection. Alternatively they may have intended what Luke said explicitly: the cup is the "new covenant," including all that that term implies. (As we saw above, some early manuscripts of Matthew 26:28 say "new covenant" rather than simply "covenant.") If we assert that the Eucharist is blood sacrifice but at the same time are willfully unrighteous, then participating in the Eucharist does not symbolize acceptance of God's covenant. We accept the new covenant when we willfully attempt to lead a righteous life.[12]

---

11. To see the confusion around the issue of "blood" see Eisenbaum, "Remedy for Having Been Born," 678–80, and 698–99. (It is not Eisenbaum who is confused here: she is only reporting.) Traditionally the "new covenant" is ignored and the blood that pollutes is also seen as expiating pollution, a clear contradiction.

12. The synoptic Gospels speak of Jesus's blood in only one more place, Mark 10:45 = Matt 20:28 (which speak of "ransom," and which we will discuss in chapter 7). At best the synoptic Gospels offer only equivocal support for the notion of blood atonement.

All Worship, Whether Jewish, Pagan, or Christian, Involves Participation

When we consider Saint Paul, it appears that the first thing to understand is that the Eucharist is a meal (or the memorial of a meal). It is a sacred meal. He showed that he understood how the profundity of a sacred meal was part of all cultures when he used a form of the word, *koinonia*, and talked about Jews "participating" in the altar when they ate the meat following a Jerusalem temple sacrifice and then jumped immediately into discussion of a similar pagan practice (1 Cor 10:14–22). He says that Christians should participate in the Eucharist instead of participating in pagan sacrificial meals, and somehow inserts the Jerusalem temple sacrifices in the midst of the discussion. This somewhat confusing shift of topics has to do with a basic point being made in this book: in ancient times all religion was focused on sacrifice and all deities (for most sacrifices) returned the edible portions of the meat to the people so they could eat it. This is the source of sacred meals.

If Christianity was to be considered a legitimate religion, Christians needed a sacrifice and a sacrificial meal. In all ancient cultures a sacrificial meal was a *koinonia* (community or fellowship or participatory) meal. Since he lived in a sacrificial culture, Eucharist-as-sacrifice made sense to him even though, as we shall see in chapter 7, he did not have a firm doctrine of crucifixion-as-sacrifice.

Can Eucharist Be Anything Other than Blood Sacrifice?

Although we say that Paul did not have a *firm* doctrine of crucifixion as blood sacrifice, Lietzmann cites 1 Corinthians 10:14–22 as evidence that Saint Paul saw the Eucharist as "sacrifice."[13] Then Lietzmann notes that Eucharist soon came to be seen in all Christian communities as the Christian act of sacrificial worship. If this is the case, we must ask in what sense the Eucharist is a sacrifice. Lietzmann offers three points to help us understand in what way the Eucharist was seen as a sacrificial meal:

1. It was a service of thanksgiving to God: "thanksgiving" is the meaning of the Greek word, *eucharistia*. Prayers of thanksgiving were offered, and Christians did consider prayer a form of sacrifice: "prayers and

---

13. Lietzmann, *History of the Early Church*, 2.129n4.

giving of thanks, when offered by worthy men, are the only perfect and well-pleasing sacrifices to God."[14]

2. In addition to bread and wine, the people brought other gifts to the altar, such as money to be used to help the poor. Such gifts were considered sacrifices.[15]

3. God accepted the gift of bread and wine along with the prayers that accompanied them. The bread and wine became "miracle-working, sacrificial food for the church."[16]

In chapter 7 we shall suggest that "spiritual sacrifice" is an appropriate way to speak of what Lietzmann describes.

Lietzmann's observations about the Eucharist as sacrifice are enlightening both for what he says and what he doesn't say. None of his observations require that the Eucharist be seen as blood sacrifice. After two thousand years we still accept the teaching of the early Christian writers that sacrifice includes prayers, praise, thanksgiving, and gifts of money to assist the poor. Regarding Lietzmann's third point, talk about miracles is not in style in our time, but the Eucharist can still be a source of miracles without any reference to blood sacrifice.

Liturgical reference to the Eucharist as a blood sacrifice makes little sense in the world of the twenty-first century. When, in a new era, the concepts are no longer part of society's mental structure, there is a need to translate them.[17] For translation we can turn to Saint Paul. In addition to his identification of the Eucharist with traditional sacrifices (both Jewish

---

14. Justin, *Dial.* 117.2.

15. The Greek word *"thysia"* referred to "offerings" as well as "sacrifices." Consider the unfortunate story of Ananias and Sapphira testifying falsely as they tried to compete with Barnabas, Acts 4:34—5:11. The word "offering" is not used in the Acts account, but it is clear that the concept is involved. It is also clear that Christians shared with the poor.

16. Lietzmann, *History of the Early Church*, 1.129.

17. For example, consider the ancient symbol of the caduceus, known today as a symbol of medicine. Our point has to do with what this symbol meant in the ancient Greek and Roman world. In those days a man carrying the caduceus on the battlefield was understood by everyone to be a messenger, and was allowed safe passage across battle lines. This man was known as a *"caduceator."* (The reader can intuit why this symbol was used to identify medical personnel in World War I.) The Roman historian Livy (*Ab Urbe Condita* 31.38.9—10) tells us about the *caduceator* having safe passage, and the question is how we should translate it. The closest today's society comes to the concept of *caduceator* is "one who carries a flag of truce," even though there is no similarity between a white flag and two snakes wrapped around a pole.

and pagan), as we have just seen, he also offers us the notion of *koinonia* as an additional approach to understanding this sacrament. We need to say more about this.

In 1 Corinthians 10:16 he speaks of the Eucharist as a "sharing" or "participation," using the evocative Greek word *koinonia*. This word requires a multitude of English translations, including "sharing," "participation" and "fellowship." It expresses a complex and profound concept that is rooted deep in the human psyche: we need to affiliate, to associate, to join with others. We need one another, not just for survival, but to be fully human. Common meals are a universal feature of human culture, and when the meal is seen as sacred it binds people together in sacred fellowship.[18]

Is this primal human need for *koinonia* what Paul is talking about in 1 Corinthians 10? Probably so, because he notes that while Christians have *koinonia* with Christ, others have *koinonia* with demons (1 Cor 10:20). The sense seems to be that everyone has *koinonia* with some transhuman entity, either divine or demonic. The Eucharist is the Christian *koinonia* with the divine.

Lietzmann says, "The Lord's Supper appeared as the Christian sacrificial meal and effected a mystic fellowship with Jesus analogous to the fellowship which the pagan theologians deduced from table-fellowship with their gods; for the idea of the sacredness of a sacrificial meal, and its power of making the participants into brethren, derives from the prehistoric roots of nature religion."[19] Lietzmann is not saying that Eucharist is prehistoric nature religion, but that there has been a universal need to join with other people in order to participate in the sacred. This need is primal. We were created to share fellowship with one another and with God.

Ignatius understood this: "Seek, then, to come together more frequently to give thanks [probably speaking of celebrating the Eucharist] and glory to God. For when you gather together frequently the powers of Satan are destroyed, and his mischief is brought to nothing by the concord of your faith."[20]

---

18. Willis, "Koinonia of Christians—and Others," presents a somewhat detailed study of "koinonia" in the Pauline understanding of the Eucharist. There is not complete correspondence between the argument of this book and Willis's argument, but the level of correspondence is very high. The reader with a particular interest in Paul's discussion of the Eucharist in 1 Corinthians 10:14–22 is encouraged to read Willis.

19. Lietzmann, *History of the Early Church*, 1.63, 140.

20. Ignatius, *Eph.* 13:1.

When the first followers of Jesus gathered, they remembered their master, Jesus Christ, and one way of remembering was to join in the Eucharist. They recalled that Jesus, himself, had said, "Do this in remembrance of me" (Luke 22:19). Eucharistic *koinonia* is both a participation with Christ and also a memorial to Jesus, remembering his birth, his life, his teaching and ministry, his betrayal and execution, his resurrection. This is much more than a memorial to his suffering and death.

Once again we point out that even though *koinonia* was crucial to the Eucharist, the fact remains that blood sacrifice made sense to everyone gathered at the Last Supper. Blood sacrifice also made sense to Ignatius. It made sense to everyone in ancient culture: everyone lived daily with temple sacrifices. Gladiator games, featuring human death in the arena, were also held regularly in every major city, and the gladiators were also regularly dedicated to the gods. It was a culture that we struggle to comprehend.

Traditions die hard, and it was from a culture and tradition saturated with blood sacrifice that the anonymous author of Hebrews reached back to the Torah to specify that a sprinkling of blood was necessary to ratify the new covenant (Heb 12:24), in spite of the biblical witness that the new covenant was to be bloodless.

Conceptual Tension: Ambivalence about Blood

The ancients lived with a conceptual tension which carries over into our theology today. In chapter 4 we cited Burriss's study demonstrating that people in the Roman Empire were not comfortable with blood, even though they engaged regularly in blood sacrifice and attended bloody gladiator exhibitions. As a matter of fact, a pagan priest was considered impure after making a sacrifice until he changed into a clean garment. When Emperor Caligula performed a sacrifice and spattered blood on himself, it was not considered a purification but a sign of his impending death. There were certain festival days on which all blood sacrifice was forbidden. Blood was useful in ("black") magic because it was the seat of the soul. Thus a man's blood could be used to command the power of his soul. Because of this power, the blood of foreigners was dangerous: Roman soldiers had to be ritually purified after battle. The worry about and even fear of blood was sometimes carried to extremes. Grapes were considered to contain a sort of "blood," so the "chief priest" of Rome, the *Flamen Dialis*, was not only forbidden to touch or even talk about raw meat, but was also prohibited from walking under a grape vine on a trellis.

How could gentile Christians in the Roman Empire relate to the notion that the (bloodless) new covenant involved the blood sacrifice of the messiah? This became part of the universal conceptual tension. The culture proclaimed that relief from the tension required proper liturgy. With proper liturgy the new covenant could be ratified and the atoning blood sacrifice could be affirmed.

Pagan sacrifice had to be administered by a priest who knew the correct words and gestures, and who was willing to assume personal liability if the sacrifice went wrong and the deity became angry. Here we see a key reason for the development of the Christian priesthood. Ancient culture adopted the notion that liturgy had to be perfect. The sacrifice of Eucharist had to be a function of priests who knew how to do it and assumed liability in case Jesus got angry.[21] The pagan assumption that the deity would get angry unless a sacrifice was done according to an exact formula no doubt influenced the way Christians understood Paul's caution against participating in the Eucharist "in an unworthy manner" (1 Cor 11:27). (Through the centuries there has been much discussion of "unworthy manner." I suggest that "unworthy" should be interpreted in light of *all* that Paul says about Eucharist and common meals, e.g., "to the glory of God" [1 Cor 10:32] and "wait for one another" [1 Cor 11:33].)

Fellowship Meals

Of course the Christian priesthood didn't develop immediately. As we know from 1 Corinthians, Eucharist began as a fellowship (*koinonia*) meal. This might have sometimes been what we know as a "church supper" (1 Cor 11:20–22). In the experience of Justin Martyr (writing about a century after Paul was in Corinth) the Eucharist seems to have been such an informal time of worship during which the people were taught how to live the life of faith. In this worship, bread, wine and water were shared.[22] In

---

21. On the assumption that liturgy must be flawless, see Pliny the Elder, *Nat.* 28.3.2, and Livy, *Hist.* 25.1.11–12.

22. In the ancient world wine and water were normally consumed together. The wine purified possibly contaminated water, so water was not served without wine mixed in. Wine was consumed without water only for "recreational" purposes, such as at meetings of Dionysiac associations.

conjunction with the sharing of the elements the congregation leader offered "prayers and thanksgivings according to his ability." (As we shall see below, this seems to be consistent with the *Didache*, written about the same time.) Translation of this last phrase is subject to dispute, but it strongly suggests that there was no fixed liturgy, no verbal formula that would guarantee divine benediction.[23] As we shall see, Justin firmly taught that the Eucharist was blood sacrifice, but without a priesthood and fixed liturgy it was certainly a strange sacrifice by ancient standards. Perhaps Justin, a trained philosopher, wished there were fixed prayers.

There were probably other ways that the fellowship meal was celebrated. In the Roman Empire there was an established custom of eating meals at the tomb of the deceased (the custom went back to their Greek heritage), and this custom was observed by some Christians. (We even have sarcophagus lids with small holes. Clearly the family would actually share wine with the deceased by pouring it into the casket.[24]) The Eucharist was not a meal with the deceased, but as time went on, just as pagans came to the tomb on the anniversary of a person's death to offer sacrifices, Christians came to celebrate Eucharist at a person's tomb on the anniversary.[25] Even when the meal with the deceased was not Eucharist, it may have had some of the same affective resonance: *koinonia* with the deceased and remembering that the deceased family member was now with Christ in heaven.

---

23. Justin Martyr, *1 Apol.* 67. On the disputed phrase, see Roberts and Donaldson, *ANF*, 1:286n1914. Justin used the same phrase in *1 Apol.* 13, when he was pointing out that the Christian God doesn't need blood sacrifice (or even incense sacrifice), so Christians simply praise God and offer thanksgiving "to the best of their ability" or "the utmost of their power."

24. Snyder, *Ante Pacem*, 88–91. Seligmann, *Mirror of Magic*, 88, tells us that such feeding of the deceased was also practiced among Greek/Roman pagans. Garland, *Greek Way of Death*, 114, speaking of classical Greece, reports that "feeding-tubes made of clay-piping" inserted into the ground sometimes were used to permit drink to be given directly to the dead. We are left to imagine how this practice might have developed over the next several centuries.

25. Lietzmann, *History of the Early Church*, 3.137.

Bringing gifts to a deceased person. As we see here, eggs or cakes were a common gift (see Garland, *Greek Way of Death*, 113), and one must wonder if some were consumed at the tomb. Fourth century BCE. British Museum GR1849.5-18.4 (Vase F283).

The Gospel According to John: Beyond Fellowship

John's Gospel gives us a different way of looking at the Eucharist. In contrast to Paul, John makes no mention of a memorial meal. But he also does not compare the Eucharist to Jewish and pagan sacrificial meals. John teaches us that the meal is mystical.[26] John seems to have recalled Jesus as "playing" with his antagonists in Capernaum when he talked about eating flesh and drinking blood. (We have reviewed Jewish law regarding blood and blood sacrifice in chapter 2.) According to Jewish law, eating flesh was all right

---

26. Bernard, *St. John*, clxvii, comments: "John's doctrine of 'feeding' on Christ is, indeed, a spiritual and mystical doctrine; but it is not doubtful that he means, in John 6:51b–58, to suggest that at any rate one mode of thus 'feeding' on Christ is through the sacrament of the Holy Communion." Lefebure, *Toward a Contemporary Wisdom*, 44n158, refers us to a scholarly debate as to whether verses 51–58 were an original part of John's Gospel or were a later addition. For the sake of argument we will presume that they are original with John.

as long as it wasn't an unclean animal such as a pig (Deut 14:3–20). Eating human flesh was not all right (Deut 28:53–57 describes this as the greatest curse). Drinking blood of any kind was never all right (Lev 17:10–14; 19:26; Deut 12:16, 23–24). John tells us that after his opponents had left, Jesus explained to his followers that he was speaking about the eternal, nonmaterial Son of Man. He said, "The flesh is nothing." This suggests that John, the Gospel writer, did not think that the Eucharist is a blood sacrifice.

Any discussion of John 6:51–58 needs to take into account the long exposition of Jesus as the "bread that came down from heaven" in John 6:25–51. This exposition is a development of the poem that began John's Gospel: "In the beginning was the Word . . . the Word became flesh and dwelt among us," that is, the Word = bread, came down from heaven. The sixth chapter of John emphasizes the cosmic existence of Christ almost to the exclusion of his human existence. If John's Gospel had been lost and archaeologists discovered a mere scrap (as they have with other lost ancient documents) with no more than John 6, scholars would probably declare it to be Docetic Gnosticism. The flesh and blood reality of Jesus is strong in other parts of John's Gospel (such as weeping for Lazarus [11:35] and dying [19:30]). In John 6, Jesus is clearly not talking about his earthly flesh and blood. "The bread that came down from heaven" is the same as the "Word (that) dwelt among us," and it is spiritual bread, not literal bread. This is similar to Jesus offering the woman of Samaria "living water" (John 4:7–15; see also John 7:37–38).

In spite of the explanation, many of those who had been following Jesus considered the imagery of eating flesh and drinking blood to be too repugnant. John tells us that a large number of those who had been following Jesus departed (John 6:66).[27]

It does seem that John understood the Eucharist in terms of mystical experience, not in terms of flesh and blood, or even of bread and wine. The importance of Eucharist for John seems to be *koinonia* with God Almighty.

In the twentieth century, W. T. Conner, a conservative Protestant theologian (Southern Baptist) seemed to consider John 6 as defining the nature

---

27. There is dispute as to whether John understood Jesus to be interpreting his coming execution as a blood sacrifice. Bernard, *St. John*, clxvi, says that John understood Jesus to be the Passover lamb. This is a different issue from interpreting the Eucharist as a blood sacrifice. The Passover lamb was, and still is, food for the people (substance for a journey), not a sacrifice to please God. When Revelation presents Jesus as a "lamb," the metaphor is about meekness (with intended irony: the "lamb" exercises authority), not about sacrifice.

of the Eucharist, saying, "Paul and John, in the good sense of the word, are mystics. They emphasize the immediate contact of the soul with the living Christ." It is interesting that a conservative, who espouses belief in Anselm's notion of (objective) blood atonement would simultaneously espouse belief that the Eucharistic elements are simply mystical (subjective). (Certainly part of the background of his teaching is the Protestant/Catholic disagreement about the "real presence.") We emphasize that Conner was a sophisticated professor of theology. It does seem odd that one would objectify the necessity of the crucifixion for salvation while holding that the memorial of the crucifixion has only subjective meaning.[28] We will return to this in chapter 9.

If we are under the influence of the present common understanding of atonement, as we look retrospectively at church history we would expect St. Paul and the Gospels to be unequivocal in their view of the Lord's Supper/Eucharist as a blood sacrifice. As we have stressed, because blood sacrifice was considered the essence of religion, there was pressure on Christians to have some sort of blood sacrifice. It is surprising that there is any alternative way to interpret the Eucharist.[29]

What Happened Next

It is well known that Christians ultimately taught that the Eucharist is a sacrifice of blood. This became a crucial issue at the end of the Middle Ages when modern scientific thinking was emerging. Those who advocated a "common sense" view of the world were called "Nominalists" and were rejected and even persecuted by the "Realists." The "Realists" (following Plato's teaching about essential Ideas) taught that the Eucharistic wine really turned to blood (its real heavenly essence), while the "Nominalists" believed that whatever we see, touch, hear, smell, or taste doesn't change.

---

28. Conner, *Christian Doctrine*, 215. The section is titled, "Paul and John as Mystics." See also page 194 on the Eucharist as mystical. His assertion of blood atonement is page 175, following a discussion of the meaning of Christ's death that begins on page 169. The reader will see that he does not make a logical connection between his discussion of Christ's death and blood atonement, but simply asserts blood atonement at the end of his discussion. It should be noted that his textbook, first published in 1935, is still in print almost a century later.

29. For more on the development of the Eucharist see: Metzger, "Considerations of Methodology." In note 77 he gives a long list of studies of the "formation and transmission of the words of institution of the Lord's Supper."

Bread is simply bread and wine is simply wine. This "Realist/Nominalist" conflict came a thousand years or more after the era we are discussing. It did have an impact on our theological teaching in the twenty-first century, so we will touch on it again, but it has little or nothing to do with how the Christians of the first three centuries understood the Eucharist.

6

The Eucharist in the Early Centuries

If therefore He for our sakes renounced His repose, was not ashamed of the cross, and did not esteem death inglorious, why do not we imitate His sufferings, and renounce on His account even our own life, with that patience which He gives us?

—CONSTITUTIONS OF THE HOLY APOSTLES[1]

Various Second-Century Interpretations of the Eucharist

BASED on our tacit assumptions about the Bible we would anticipate that Christians of these first centuries would affirm both the crucifixion as sacrificial blood atonement and the Eucharist as an expression of sacrificial blood atonement. We assume that no one questioned the death of Jesus as a sacrifice. Everyone at least "paid lip service" to that notion. Our assumption is incorrect. The notion was really important to only a few of these early Christians, and fewer still taught that the Eucharist is an expression of atonement. We will look at a small number of examples as a demonstration that some accepted the blood sacrifice understanding of Eucharist and some ignored or rejected it.

First, an anonymous document called "*The Didache*" or "*The Teaching of the Twelve Apostles*" was a book of instruction for Christians which was

---

1. See "Constitutions of the Holy Apostles," 5.1.5, in Roberts and Donaldson, *ANF*, 7:438–39.

probably published sometime between 100 and 200. Much of it is moral instruction, but there is also instruction about baptism and the Eucharist. The instructions for the Eucharist consist almost entirely of prayers.

The prayer over the wine was, "We give thanks to Thee, our Father, for the Holy Vine of David thy child, which thou did make known to us through Jesus thy child; to Thee be glory forever." The prayer over the broken bread: "We give Thee thanks, our Father, for the life and knowledge which Thou did make known to us through Jesus, Thy child. To Thee be glory forever. As this broken bread was scattered upon the mountains, but was brought together and became one, so let thy Church be gathered together from the ends of the earth into Thy kingdom, for Thine is the glory and the power through Jesus Christ forever."[2]

After the service (which was apparently a full meal) there was to be a prayer of thanks:

> We give thanks to Thee, O Holy Father, for thy Holy Name which thou set in our hearts as in a holy meeting place,[3] and for the knowledge and faith and immortality[4] which Thou made known to us through Jesus Thy child. To Thee be glory forever. Thou, Lord Almighty, created all things for Thy Name's sake, and gave food and drink to humanity for their enjoyment, that they might give thanks to Thee, and you have blessed us with spiritual food and drink and eternal light through Thy Child. Above all we give thanks to Thee because you are mighty. To Thee be glory forever. Remember, Lord, Thy Church, to deliver it from all evil and to make it perfect in Thy love, and gather it together from the four winds, in holiness, into thy kingdom which is prepared. For Thine is the power and the glory forever. Let grace come and let this world pass away. Hosanna to the God of David. If any person be

---

2. *Did.* 9.

3. "Camp" or "campground" is the best translation from modern Greek to English. The traditional translation is "tabernacle," a word which may not mean today what it meant in the first century. Ancient people did have ("holy") campgrounds where they would go for a holiday combined with worship. We can see this today at the ancient (pagan) site of Dion, Greece, at the base of Mount Olympus, a place with many temples along with space for camping and recreation. We can imagine ancient families taking the two-day trip from Thessaloniki to this holy site and truly enjoying a week there. Thus it is appropriate to hear the ancient Christians praying about God's "campground." In this prayer, "campground" may distract modern readers and "tabernacle" may not communicate clearly. That is why we have chosen to use "holy meeting place."

4. Ignatius, *Eph.* 20.2, called the bread of the Eucharist "medicine of immortality."

holy, let that one come! If any person be not, let that one repent. Maranatha. Amen.[5]

These prayers suggest that the focus of the Eucharist was on thanksgiving and fellowship, the *koinonia*, just as Justin Martyr (writing about the same time) implied. There is no indication that these prayers constitute fixed, formal liturgy. Instead they represent prayer according to the leader's "ability."

The *Didache's* Eucharist was a service of Communion. There is no mention of blood or body or sacrifice. The people give thanks for Jesus revealing Christ ("the vine of David") to us. The reference to the bread having been scattered on the mountains is outside of our concern, except that the focus is on the bread being brought back together, just as, in the closing prayer, the petition is that the church be gathered from the "four winds." We can ask if the concern is apocalyptic: the church is to be gathered together in heaven. Perhaps the concern was present-day: that everyone would be able to return to the place of worship on another day. In this service God is asked to keep the church from evil, perfect it in love, and bring it together, whether now or through eternity.

This instruction manual makes one more reference to the Eucharist. The very brief chapter 14 specifies that the Eucharist is to be celebrated (at least) weekly. The service of bread and wine is to be preceded by confession of sins. No one is to participate who is involved in an unreconciled quarrel. This is buttressed by a quotation from the first chapter of the Old Testament prophetic book, Malachi, to the effect that sacrifices should be pure. Thus there is an acknowledgement that the Eucharist is a sacrifice, but the nature of the sacrifice seems to be the prophetic "pure heart" ("Rend your hearts and not your clothing" [Joel 2:12–13]; "The sacrifice acceptable to God is a broken spirit" [Ps 51:17]). The concern seems to echo the concern of Jesus: "So when you are offering your gift at the altar, if you remember that your brother or sister has something against you, leave your gift there before the altar and go; first be reconciled to your brother or sister, and then come and offer your gift" (Matt 5:23–24). Again the concern in the *Didache* is for communion/*koinonia*, not blood sacrifice.

We next turn to a couple of early church leaders who did understand the Eucharist to be blood sacrifice. Saint Ignatius, Bishop of Antioch, was executed for his faith in the Roman arena under Emperor Trajan (98–117) and Saint Justin Martyr was also executed in Rome a couple of generations

---

5. *Did.* 10, revised from Lake by the author.

after Ignatius. Both unequivocally advocated that the Eucharist is really Christ's body and blood, and in both cases the reason had to do with affirming the humanity of Jesus Christ in opposition to the Docetic notion that Christ was never human. Patterson argues persuasively that physical resurrection of the body was important within the Roman Empire where martyrdom was a realistic possibility, while a spiritual resurrection was acknowledged among Christians outside of the empire, where martyrdom was far less likely.[6] Pagels has found a similar disjunction between orthodox Christians and gnostics.[7] Similarly we could anticipate that among those who anticipated martyrdom, the presence of the body and blood of Jesus in the Eucharist would be more important than it might be among those who did not anticipate martyrdom.

We have already quoted Ignatius as encouraging Christians to participate in the Eucharist as often as possible so as to destroy the powers of Satan. In chapter 4 we have seen that he taught firmly that the execution of Jesus was a blood sacrifice, and he was equally firm in his belief that the Eucharist is a blood sacrifice. He said, "I desire the 'bread of God,' which is the flesh of Jesus Christ, who was 'of the seed of David,' and for drink I desire his blood, which is incorruptible love."[8] We can safely assume that his use of the word "love" is a reference to Eucharist, which was often called a "love feast." He also taught that the Eucharist unites true Christians: "Be careful therefore to use one Eucharist (for there is one flesh of our Lord Jesus Christ, and one cup for union with his blood, one altar, as there is one bishop with the presbytery and the deacons my fellow servants), in order that whatever you do you may do it according unto God."[9]

As we have said, belief that the Eucharist was the literal body and blood of Christ gave Ignatius confidence to face martyrdom. There was another practical reason to teach that the Eucharist is sacrificial blood atonement. Docetists rejected the notion of the Eucharist as sacrificial blood atonement. Ignatius says that where there is division regarding the blood of the Eucharist there are false Christians, especially the Docetists. Docetists avoid the Eucharist because they don't "believe on the blood of Christ."

For the Docetists, the bread cannot be flesh because they think Christ was not incarnate, but was some kind of ghost. Of course, if Christ was not

---

6. Patterson, "Platonism and the Apocryphal Origins."
7. Pagels, *Gnostic Gospels*, 82–83, etc.
8. Ignatius, *Rom.* 7.3.
9. Ignatius, *Phld.* 4.1.

incarnate then he was not raised from the dead, and if he was not raised from the dead then there is no hope for us when we die (and when Ignatius wrote this he was on his way to Rome where he knew he would be killed).[10] All of this is very clear. Ignatius was firm in his belief that the Eucharist was the presence of the sacrificial blood atonement. There is an amazing difference between his exposition of the Eucharist and that of the *Didache*.

Saint Justin was a bit younger than Saint Ignatius, having been born around the year 100 and executed around 165. His writings probably come from sometime after 150. Like Ignatius, Justin thought that the Eucharist is a blood sacrifice: "For not as common bread and common drink do we receive these; but in like manner as Jesus Christ our Savior, having been made flesh by the Word of God, had both flesh and blood for our salvation, so likewise have we been taught that the food which is blessed by the prayer of His word, and from which our blood and flesh by transmutation are nourished, is the flesh and blood of that Jesus who was made flesh."[11] He based this understanding on the words of institution in Mark, Matthew, and Luke, but he was also concerned about Docetism.

In addition, like Paul, Justin emphasized that the Eucharist is in memory of Jesus, again basing this on the Gospel record of Jesus's teaching. He explains the memorial with a theological sophistication clearly reflecting the century of discussion that had taken place among Christians since Paul wrote his letters. Justin said,

> the Eucharist, the celebration of which our Lord Jesus Christ prescribed, in remembrance of the suffering which He endured on behalf of those who are purified in soul from all iniquity, in order that we may at the same time thank God for having created the world, with all things therein, for the sake of man, and for delivering us from the evil in which we were, and for utterly overthrowing principalities and powers by Him who suffered according to His will.[12]

He follows this with the quotation from Malachi that we found in the *Didache*. It is very possible that Justin would have studied the *Didache*, and perhaps had its prayers in mind when he wrote his *First Apology*. (At that time he might have felt them inadequate.) Justin also related Isaiah 33:13–19 to the Eucharist (seldom, if ever, referenced by other early Christian

---

10. Ignatius, *Smyrn.* 6–7.
11. Justin, *1 Apol.* 66.
12. Justin, *Dial.* 41.

writers), saying, "Now it is evident, that in this prophecy [allusion is made] to the bread which our Christ gave us to eat, in remembrance of His being made flesh for the sake of His believers, for whom also He suffered; and to the cup which He gave us to drink, in remembrance of His own blood, with giving of thanks."[13]

Among those who did not teach that the Eucharist is sacrifice was Irenaeus. He thought that Eucharist was too important for it to be called "sacrifice." Instead, he saw Eucharist as having ontological significance. When we drink Christ's blood and eat Christ's body, that food becomes part of our body so that we become part of Christ's body. Thus, the Eucharist is not a sacrificial propitiation. It is an ontological transformation.[14] As we shall see in chapter 8, this sort of analysis prefigures Athanasius, a couple of centuries later, and we will see that it could provide us with an option to sacrificial blood atonement.

One note of caution: we must not take Irenaeus literally at this point, even if he intended to speak literally about our transformation into Christ's body. If we take Irenaeus literally, we inevitably revert to a mechanical understanding of salvation: the Eucharist becomes the tool that God uses to save us. Certainly God's gracious salvation needs no tool or instrument.

Everyday Christians: Magic or Morality?

What is the significance of the Eucharist for daily life? It is a memorial, a time of *koinonia* and a time of instruction. What else? Was the crucifixion of Jesus and its memorial considered by some to be magic? This may have been a real issue. Stephen Benko notes that Ignatius referred to the Eucharist as "medicine of immortality." In Greek this is *pharmakon athanasias*, and *pharmakon* was often used in reference to a magic potion. Benko asks if magic could have been very far from the thoughts of early Christians when they contemplated the Eucharist.[15]

It is worthwhile to ask if the pagan purpose of "sacrifice" relates at all to the Christian understanding of "Eucharist." As we have said, the most popular understanding of "sacrifice" was *quid pro quo*: God will do something for me if I sacrifice. In Christian terms, God will forgive my sins if I participate in the Eucharist. (And of course, as a descendant of Adam and Eve, I

---

13. Justin, *Dial.* 70.
14. Irenaeus, *Haer.* 5.2.
15. Benko, *Pagan Rome and the Early Christians*, 123.

have sinned.) No doubt there were (and still are) Christians who reasoned about the Eucharist in this fashion. This would be the magic "medicine of immortality." The word *"eucharist"* refers explicitly to "thanksgiving" and such thanksgiving could either be simple gratitude or else fear that unless one says "thank-you," God will withhold blessings. In other words, participation in the Eucharist might be mature worship or might be a reversion to pagan-like thinking.

We have already seen that Clement of Alexandria saw no need for Christian sacrifice, and he didn't understand Eucharist as sacrifice. However he took Eucharist seriously as the primary expression of the *koinonia* of Christ. The word "Communion" (*koinonia*) does not sound special, but it was so closely identified with this essential Christian ritual that Clement of Alexandria was scandalized to hear that a heretical leader was using the word to refer to the sexual orgies of the group that leader had organized. Clement says, "Communion is good when the word refers to sharing of money and food and clothing." In other words, "communion" could refer to life within the congregation beyond the rite, but whatever was included under that heading had to be moral.[16]

Morality, whether enforced by the threat of eternal punishment, or a free response of gratitude to God, was seen by all of the early Christian writers as the essence of Christianity. For them, even though the notion of religion may imply sacrifice, the sacrifice was secondary to morality.

We see that the earliest understandings of the Eucharist were diverse. We have suggested that one strong reason for Christian understanding of Jesus as a sacrifice was cultural pressure. We have also noted existential pressure. It is significant that both Ignatius and Justin were martyrs for the faith and that their thoroughgoing acceptance of the blood atonement strengthened them when they faced execution.

Literal belief in the body and blood could be profoundly misunderstood. The pagan philosopher and antagonist against Christianity, Porphyry, argued that Jesus was simply human; therefore if Eucharistic bread and wine were really transformed into body and blood, the transformation must be the work of an evil demon. In other words, the Eucharist must be magic, and Porphyry considered all magic to be evil. As it happened, Porphyry was close to Emperor Diocletian (reigned 284–305), and his arguments may

---

16. Clement of Alexandria, *Strom.* 3.4 (On Marriage).

have directly supported the emperor's decision to launch his devastating persecution of Christians.[17]

Gradually the crucifixion of Jesus as the ultimate sacrifice became an important part of Christian theology, and was clearly included in the Eucharistic ritual in the fourth century.[18] Perhaps Christians would have been better off if they had simply seen the Eucharist as a memorial ritual, an occasion of participation and fellowship. Even so, today we are able to see that there were ancient alternative understandings, and we should feel free to adopt such an alternative.

---

17. Digeser, *Threat to Public Policy*, 164–65. See also 98–99 on ritual and magic.
18. Lietzmann, *History of the Early Church*, 3.288–94.

7

Searching the Bible

It will be incumbent on him who treats the declarations of the Gospels philosophically, to establish these doctrines by arguments of all kinds, not only derived directly from the sacred Scriptures, but also by inferences deducible from them.

—ORIGEN[1]

CERTAINLY there is a history to the doctrine of blood atonement, but many Christians will ask a simple question: Is the blood atonement biblical? If so, it must be theologically true. History, for many people, is irrelevant to the question.

Yes, the notion of sacrificial blood atonement is set forth by New Testament authors. The notion was not strange to them because it fit into the cultural presuppositions of the ancient world. We have seen how the ancient notion of "religion" entailed "sacrifice." How blood was the distinguishing mark of a creature in contrast with a deity. How difficult it seemed for a perfect god to care about a human. How most people thought it unlikely that a god would forgive human "sin," no matter how "sin" might be defined. How even more unlikely it was that a deity would take the form of a human with real blood in his veins. All of these ancient presuppositions,

---

1. Origen, *Cels.* 4.9.

among others, related to the way the death of Jesus on the cross could be seen as the key to the forgiveness of sin.

As we read and ponder the message of the New Testament, the question is not whether we can find the notion of sacrificial blood atonement there. The question is whether that notion is essential to Christianity. Certainly the death of Jesus on the cross is historical and significant. The literary structure of the Gospels emphasizes the significance of the crucifixion by presenting the ministry of Jesus as fomenting an escalating conflict with the authorities leading inevitably to his death. What, however, is the significance of the crucifixion? Is the notion of sacrificial blood atonement the only legitimate way to interpret the crucifixion? Does the Bible endorse other ways of understanding the crucifixion? While the thrust of this book is to look at sacrificial blood atonement in relation to ancient culture, not in terms of biblical theology, in this chapter we will take a brief look at how the notion is expounded in the Bible. It will necessarily be brief because a full consideration would require an extensive book of its own.

If Jesus had not been raised from the dead, the Gospel accounts of escalating conflict would have the structure of classical tragedy, and would lead us to ponder the story in far different terms than we do. The interpretation of a tragedy seeks an answer to the question, "Why?" Why did people die? Who was responsible? How could it have been prevented? Pondering any tragedy can lead to several interpretations. For example, the classic Greek drama, "Hippolytus" by Euripides, was rewritten in New Testament times by the Roman stoic philosopher, Seneca (with a new title, "Phaedra"), showing a quite different interpretation of the death of the hero.

Throughout Christian history there has been a secondary response to the execution of Jesus in terms of classical tragedy, asking questions such as: "Who was responsible for the trial, conviction and execution?" "Was the trial legal under Roman law?" "Why was Barabbas released?" "What might have prevented Jesus's execution?" Saint Paul even makes himself a party to this discussion when he says of the authorities, "None of the rulers of this age understood this; for if they had, they would not have crucified the Lord of glory" (1 Cor 2:8). All such questions are subject to various answers and none have cosmic implications. These are simply the questions we ask about tragedy. None relate to the matter of execution as atonement. The fact that we often chose to debate such questions demonstrates our general discomfort with the notion of sacrificial blood atonement.

The New Testament avoids the view of the execution of Jesus as tragedy. The resurrection of Christ changes the nature of the questions. If the resurrection was necessary, then death was necessary. If death was necessary then perhaps death was, in some sense, "good." If so, in what way was it "good?" This question is a basic theme of the New Testament.

As we have seen, the church has answered the question in terms of the Eucharist (Holy Communion, the Lord's Supper). It is mentioned in all four Gospels and 1 Corinthians (all of which we quoted in chapter 5. Within those quotations, these are the references to the blood: Matt 26:28; Mark 14:24; Luke 22:20; John 6:53–56; 1 Cor 10:16; 11:25). The cup was considered to be, in some sense, the blood of Christ, following the teaching in the six New Testament references. It was the concrete ratification (or symbol of acceptance) of a new covenant, and those who drank from the cup "participated" in this ratification. For many Christians, these facts are sufficient warrant for saying that the notion of sacrificial blood atonement is an essential part of the Christian faith, although we pointed out in chapter 5 that there are other ways to interpret it: if blood is "life," those receiving the cup participate in Christ's entire life, his birth, teaching, ministry, betrayal, execution and resurrection.

The Epistle to the Hebrews

If we want to find the notion of sacrificial blood atonement in the New Testament, our best source is the anonymous book of Hebrews. This book's unequivocal support for the notion is made plain in the first verses: "He [Christ] is the reflection of God's glory and the exact imprint of God's very being, and he sustains all things by his powerful word. When he [Christ] had made purification for sins, he sat down at the right hand of the Majesty on high" (Heb 1:3). In this one verse we find orthodox (or standard) theological views of the Trinity's second person, creation by the Word, and sacrificial atonement for sins. Traditional conservative theology rests in Hebrews. Sacrificial blood atonement is expressed in some detail in Hebrews 9: "For if the blood of goats and bulls . . . sanctifies . . . How much more will the blood of Christ, who through the eternal Spirit offered himself without blemish to God, purify our conscience from dead works" (Heb 9:13–14). The letter ends with a soaring benediction which says, in part: "May the God of peace, who brought back from the dead our Lord Jesus, the great shepherd of the sheep, by the blood of the eternal covenant, make you complete" (Heb 13:20). The blood is apparently the means by which we can be made "complete."

There is wide recognition that the role of sacrificial blood in Hebrews is different from the role of sacrificial blood in the Torah, in spite of the apparent relationship between Hebrews and Jewish religion. In particular, Hebrews teaches that the sacrificial blood of Jesus will purify sinners, while the Torah (as we have seen) teaches that sacrificial blood is not an agent of purification. This is a distinctive feature of Hebrews. There have been a number of suggestions to explain this discrepancy.[2]

Apparently there are two ways to understand the notion of blood atonement in Hebrews: (a) extremely literal and (b) poetic. A key word here is 'hilaskesthai and cognates, most frequently translated as "expiation" or "propitiation," but sometimes as "forgiveness," "ransom," etc. Literalists debate at length about whether each suggested translation really represents the attitude or mindset of God. Poets suggest that no word, by itself, can represent God's attitude, but taking several near synonyms together is the best we can do.

Kidner, a scholar of Hebrew and Greek, seems to be a poet. In a long and complex word-study of 'hilaskesthai and cognates he reviews the debate regarding "expiation" versus "propitiation," along with reviewing other suggestions. He presumes that God desires blood sacrifice, and reviews the various sacrifices described in Leviticus, concluding that the Old Testament sacrificial system could not atone for sin as well as the one sacrifice described in Hebrews. Consequently none of the single-word descriptions of the consequences of various sacrifices is satisfactory. Given the different denotations and connotations of "expiation" and "propitiation," both must be used together (and we presume must be understood poetically).[3]

A good friend of mine, who defends the notion of blood atonement, points out that 'hilaskesthai and cognates "have to do with the Mercy Seat on the Ark of the Covenant, the place where God and man met, the place where revelation happened, the place where grace and mercy took away sin and guilt."[4] The poetic approach is obvious. As Arnobius said, "nothing can be revealed in human language concerning God."[5]

2. Reasoner, "Divine Sons," 160–61, 164.
3. Kidner, "Sacrifice."
4. Personal correspondence.
5. Arnobius, *Apology* (or *Against the Heathen*) 3.19, in Roberts and Donaldson, *ANF*, 6:469.

Thomas Breidenthal also has a poetic view of Hebrews. We will see in the final chapter that he finds the theme of Hebrews to be "the reconciliation of neighbor with neighbor as the heart of Jesus's work" within an atonement context.[6] He contends that, in Hebrews, atonement is not for any individual's sake.

We cannot say whether the author of Hebrews was a poet or a literalist. In any case, as Kidner made clear, this anonymous author's point of reference was the catalog of sacrifices in Leviticus (no matter whether the reference correctly reflects the Torah). According to Hebrews, the best way to understand the crucifixion of Jesus is as a Levitical sacrifice that does not require repetition.

After the establishment of the New Testament canon, many subsequent literalists have taken Hebrews as their guiding text through which to interpret the rest of the New Testament. If one is so inclined the position is unassailable. Hebrews is the clearest New Testament statement about the judicial execution of Jesus being an atoning (expiating, propitiating, etc.) sacrifice.

Everyone can find much that is truly inspirational in Hebrews, especially its discussion of faith in chapters 11 and 12. For those who think the notion of sacrificial blood atonement makes sense, the entire letter is inspirational. For those who question sacrificial blood atonement, the obscure rabbinical logic undergirding the argument in Hebrews doesn't convince.

The First Epistle of John

The focus of this brief epistle is love undergirded by faith (or belief). These connect with atonement because "love comes from God" (1 John 4:7, NIV). God's love is manifested in atonement.

In terms of blood atonement the First Epistle of John contrasts significantly with John's Gospel: "if we walk in the light . . . the blood of Jesus cleanses us from all sin. . . . If we confess our sins, he who is faithful and just will forgive our sins and cleanse us from all unrighteousness . . . if anyone does sin we have an advocate . . . he is the atoning sacrifice for our sins and . . . for the sins of the whole world" (1 John 1:7—2:2). "In this is love, not that we loved God but that he loved us and sent his Son to be the atoning sacrifice for our sins" (1 John 4:10). "This is the one who came by water and blood, Jesus Christ, not with water only but with the water and the blood

---

6. Breidenthal, "Blood of Abel," 115.

... There are three that testify: the Spirit and the water and the blood, and these three agree" (1 John 5:6–8).

In this Epistle, Jesus is clearly a sacrifice, and blood is more than a symbol. In this sense, 1 John is similar to Hebrews. Blood has objective power (and so does the water of baptism). Did John, the author of John's Gospel, write this? If so, why didn't he write these sentiments in his Gospel? There has been much scholarly study of the question of whether or not the Gospel and Epistle have the same author. Such studies begin with a detailed study of vocabulary and syntax and proceed to the substance of the writing. In the end there is no definite consensus. 100 years ago, both Bernard and Brooke wrote influential commentaries arguing that these two works were written by one person. Today the general feeling is that different hands were at work in the two. It seems likely that the Epistle was written by someone from John's "school," because it follows closely John's style of writing and thinking, but on an issue such as sacrificial blood atonement there is a great difference. If the Epistle was written by someone else, that person was clearly more influenced by the ancient notion of sacrifice than was John.[7]

Saint Paul, Sacrifice, and the Cross

Outside of Hebrews and 1 John, we must turn to Saint Paul, the one who is most often cited by those advocating the sacrificial blood atonement. His "theology of the cross" is said to have influenced all subsequent Christian writers. Paul's Epistles are the earliest Christian writings we have, some of them perhaps a mere seventeen or eighteen years after the first Easter. Several years after his first visit to Corinth he wrote letters back to the church he had organized in that city focusing on organizational issues and the individual life of faith, but he also spoke specifically about the significance of the cross: "For Christ did not send me to baptize, but to proclaim the gospel, and not with eloquent wisdom, so that the cross of Christ might not be emptied of its power. For the message about the cross is foolishness to those who are perishing, but to us who are being saved it is the power of God" (1 Cor 1:17–18). He also said, "Christ died for our sins according to the scriptures" (1 Cor 15:3). See also Romans 8:3, where Christ is identified as a sin offering. Ephesians may or may not have been written by Saint Paul, but it also affirms the death of Jesus as a sacrifice: Ephesians 1:7; 2:13–16 (see below), etc.

7. Brooke, *Johannine Epistles*. Bernard, *St. John*.

We suggest that Paul was involved in a profound existential struggle that involved his personal experience of sin, his cross-cultural experience as a child in Tarsus, his background as a student in Jerusalem, his understanding of both rabbinic argument and Aristotelian logic, his admiration for Jesus Christ (especially Jesus's humility), and his tacit assumptions about family life. Out of his complicated life experience he came to understand the death of Jesus as a sacrifice for human sin, but he also understood other sacrifices someone might offer, including "faith," as atoning sacrifices.

Bringing Gentiles into Abraham's Family

There is no question that Paul envisioned the death of Jesus as atoning for our sins, but we should take a closer look at his teaching, because he may not have understood it in the same way that the author of Hebrews did. Although there are connections between the letters of Paul and the letter to the Hebrews in terms of their discussion of sacrifice, there is also divergence. Not only does Paul advocate for the effectiveness of various kinds of sacrifice, he also sees the purpose of sacrifice somewhat differently than Hebrews. We will look at a perceptive study by Eisenbaum.

Eisenbaum notes that Paul never explicitly explains how gentiles are brought into God's promises. She asks, "Why is it necessary that Jesus's death be a sacrificial one in order to accomplish this task?"[8] She answers the question by combining the science of anthropology with biblical exegesis:

1. She reviews ancient cultural practice in Israel, Greece, and Rome, and observes that children in these cultures were considered part of the family only after the father had recognized them as such. This recognition involved a sacrificial ritual which could mean more than recognition, but certainly signified recognition. Although Eisenbaum doesn't mention it, the temple sacrifice in Luke 2:22–24 could have meant that Joseph accepted Jesus as his legitimate son. There is no basis for this notion in Torah, but Eisenbaum makes a good case. The only Torah basis for Luke 2:22–24 is Leviticus 12:6, purification of Mary, the mother, and that is not relevant to our discussion. As Eisenbaum says, a sacrifice can serve multiple purposes.

2. Paul presumes the cultural notion of sacrifice as filial recognition without making it explicit, and by analogy presumes that, on a cosmic

---

8. Eisenbaum, "Remedy for Having Been Born," 676.

level, sacrifice is necessary to bring a gentile into God's family, that is, the family of Abraham.

3. Sacrifices of filial recognition are offered by the father. The child cannot initiate them. In the case of bringing gentiles into God's family, the one making the sacrifice has to be God Almighty.

4. Male circumcision (recall what we said earlier about circumcision as a symbol of acceptance of the covenant) is sometimes seen as the sacrifice that brings a child into the family of God Almighty, but Paul rejected circumcision for two reasons:

    a. God made the covenant with Abraham prior to circumcision.

    b. Jewish (and Christian) descent from Abraham is through Isaac, not Ishmael. The Genesis account gives great emphasis to the circumcision of Ishmael, but gives only brief mention to the circumcision of Isaac. Most important about Isaac is that he is the child of promise, the child who represents Abraham's faith. (When thinking about gentile circumcision, we must not ignore the practical problems Saint Paul faced in evangelizing the strongly anti-circumcision Roman society.[9])

5. One must be cleansed before coming into God's family. For Jews this cleansing is circumcision. If circumcision is not the sacrifice that brings gentiles into the family of Abraham (or God's family), and if God, as Father, must initiate the sacrifice, Paul concludes that the only possible sacrifice is God's offering of Jesus Christ.

6. Jesus Christ as a sacrifice fulfills two functions:

    a. It removes the pollution of gentile sin, just as circumcision removes the pollution of Jewish sin. The sacrifice is a sin offering (Lev 16).

    b. It incorporates the one who is "in Christ" into the family of Abraham, just as sacrifice on behalf of a newborn recognizes the baby as a member of the father's family.[10]

Eisenbaum's analysis goes beyond the Torah when she interprets Paul as understanding the death of Jesus as the sacrifice that accompanies God's filial recognition of gentiles. A good example, even though the authorship

---

9. Davies, *St. Paul in Macedonia*, 227–36.
10. Eisenbaum, "Remedy for Having Been Born," 698.

is in dispute, is Ephesians 2:11–19. (Eisembaum does not cite this passage.) There is no explicit Torah ritual for accepting a child into a family. Even so, Eisenbaum makes a good case that Paul would have tacitly had such filial recognition in mind. According to this analysis, Paul had in mind two sacrificial purposes for the death of Jesus: a sin offering and gentile incorporation into Abraham's family. Is Eisenbaum (and others whom she cites, especially Stowers[11]) correct with regard to what Paul actually intended to say? It seems likely that Eisenbaum's analysis reflects tacit cultural assumptions from which Paul was working, but that he intended to say more. That is the reason for his struggle with logic, which we will discuss below.

If we think carefully about Paul's teaching and the teaching in the letter to the Hebrews, of course we find similarities, but we also find that there are important, though subtle, differences. We note that Hebrews departs from Paul when interpreting the crucifixion as a propitiation/expiation. Hebrews does not consider propitiation/expiation to be filial recognition. What about the sin from which the blood is said to free us? In contrast with Hebrews, Paul's understanding of sin was not Levitical. Paul's understanding of sin had to do with the human body (*sarx*).

Paul's Quest for Righteousness in the Face of Human Sinfulness

Why was the sin offering an important part of Paul's thought? The answer has to do with the "stuff" of humanity, what Paul calls "flesh." Paul uses the word "flesh" (*sarx*) in various ways, but the most general reference is to the fact of being alive in a body, moving around on the earth.[12]

In 2 Corinthians 5:16–21 Paul wrote a great and soaring statement about how we can be reconciled to God through Christ. Verse 21 concludes: "For our sake he made him to be sin who knew no sin, so that in him we might become the righteousness of God." (Compare this with Galatians 3:13 and Romans 8:3–4. Ephesians 2:5 speaks of God redeeming us while we were still sinners, without the thought that Christ became identified

---

11. Stowers, *Rereading of Romans*.

12. This is certainly a simplified view of what Paul says. Ancient culture featured elaborate parsings of human existence using words such as "body," "flesh," "mind," "spirit," and "soul." All of these words are also in our current vocabulary, but the connotations, if not the denotations, have changed over the centuries. Likewise the presumed relationships among these human elements have changed. Thus, serious and nuanced study of what Paul meant by "flesh" is appropriate. However, for our purposes, the simplified statement about "human existence" serves us well.

with sin.) Paul's assumption is that every human is sinful because every human is flesh. When Christ became human, Christ, because of the flesh, must have become sinful. Paul's question: how can sin be transformed into righteousness?

As we read this we should have in mind a related statement, Romans 4:24–25: "[Faith] will be reckoned [as righteousness] to us who believe in him who raised Jesus our Lord from the dead, who was handed over to death for our trespasses and raised for our justification." This statement follows a discussion of the faith in God that characterized Abraham. (Eisenbaum said that Christians have overemphasized Paul's concern with Abraham's faith and undervalued Paul's concern with Abraham's family. We can accept her analysis and also point out that Abraham's faith is important to Paul's discussion.)

Saint Paul is saying that if we have faith in God equivalent to that of Abraham, we will be justified before God. Into this he has inserted an identification of God (an important point in a polytheistic pagan world): God is the one who raised Jesus, and Jesus is the one "who was put to death for our trespasses and raised for our justification." This identification of Jesus as dying for our trespasses and then justifying us is usually understood as the essence of Paul's so-called "theology of the cross." In Paul's mind it may have been the necessary identification of God Almighty and Christ when speaking to a pagan and pagan-influenced audience.

The notion of "righteousness" is what links 2 Corinthians 5:21 and Romans 4:24–25. "Righteousness" (think of "doing what is right") is obviously opposed to sin or trespasses. Saint Paul was acutely aware of his own sinfulness, and pondered how he might become righteous (Rom 7:7–25). Abraham became righteous simply by faith (obedience to God). Paul sensed that his own sin was too great to be forgiven as a result of obedience. Paul's reasoning was logical (syllogistic):

> Humanity in the flesh is sinful.
> Christ became a human.
> Christ became sinful. (2 Cor 5:21)
> Even though he was in the flesh (i.e., was sinful), Christ committed no sin.
> A person who commits no sin is a morally perfect person.
> Christ was a morally perfect person.
> A sacrificial victim imputes its quality to the worshiper.
> The perfect Christ was a sacrificial victim.

The perfect Christ imputes perfection to the (faithful) worshiper. (Rom 5:8–9, 16, 18, etc.)

In other words, when we worship in faith, we participate in the perfection of Christ, thus becoming righteous in God's eyes so that we are justified.[13] "Righteousness" is an ethical/moral concept while "justification" is a legal concept. We seek justification in God's metaphorical "law court" where God is our judge. We can walk out of the court having been justified (declared not guilty) if we are righteous (good or perfect). However, we are not righteous. How else can we be justified? In a law court we can be justified by paying a fine or other penalty, such as a term in jail. (We speak of this in a business metaphor as "paying a debt to society." We seem not able to speak of these cosmic concerns without getting tangled in a confusing array of metaphors.) The metaphor of heavenly justification is that God asks us how we plead. Guilty or not guilty? Before we can answer, Christ, our attorney, says, "Your honor, my client is guilty, but I have paid the fine."

This metaphor of a heavenly law court fits with everything we know about ordinary legal proceedings and it also fits with everything that was presumed in ancient times about the purpose of animal sacrifice. Both Saint Paul and those to whom he wrote understood law and understood religious sacrifice. Not every pagan religious sacrifice was tied to a legal metaphor, but everyone had the conceptual background required to understand Paul's law-court metaphor.

It is a fact that Saint Paul was raised in a culture that presumed any deity wanted animal sacrifice, and he was educated in a Jewish culture that had both a strong legal code and a strong sense of God's requirement that we be ethical and moral. He saw himself as subject to God's judgment for his own great sins, especially the sin of persecuting followers of Christ. It makes sense that he would see his only hope in the great sacrifice that was Christ's voluntary submission to crucifixion. Thus his "theology of the cross."

Romans is Paul's best exposition of sacrificial blood atonement. The theme of sacrifice/righteousness/justification is explicitly raised in Romans 5: "Christ died for the ungodly . . . While we were still sinners Christ died for us . . . we have been justified by his blood . . . we were reconciled to God by the death of his Son." Starting in 5:12, Paul engages in what is likely a rabbinic argument saying that the perfection of Christ negates the sin of

---

13. We will see in chapter 8 how Athanasius used this understanding to formulate an understanding of Christian salvation that does not require sacrificial blood atonement.

Adam. The summary of this argument is Romans 5:18, "Therefore, just as one man's trespass (the sin of Adam) led to condemnation for all, so one man's act of righteousness (Jesus submitting to crucifixion) leads to justification and life for all."

One can wonder if what Saint Paul presented starting in verse 12 was a standard explanation of temple sacrifice among the rabbinical leaders.[14] During Paul's life, daily sacrifices were offered to God Almighty in the Jerusalem temple. (Sacrifice ceased when the temple was destroyed by the Roman Army in the year 70, fifteen or more years after Paul's execution.) Paul had witnessed temple sacrifices when he was a student in Jerusalem. We suggest that Paul's explanation, beginning in Romans 5:12, is based on sacrifice in the Jerusalem temple.

A Path to Righteousness that Does Not Involve Blood Sacrifice

Maybe Paul's temple experience gave him a way of seeing how his own deep sinfulness could be transformed into righteousness. If so, then maybe his memory of temple sacrifice formed for him a particular analogy rather than a universal truth. We can check this by asking if he ever indicates that the crucifixion might have a significance other than sacrificial blood atonement. Let's look again at some things he wrote. First, a statement that is very popular among today's Christians:

> We know that all things work together for good for those who love God, who are called according to his purpose. For those whom he foreknew he also predestined to be conformed to the image of his Son, in order that he might be the first-born within a large family. And those whom he predestined he also called; and those whom he called he also justified; and those whom he justified he also glorified. (Rom 8:28–30)

The emphasis here is not on justification as a result of the crucifixion, but justification as a result of God's call. Many followers of God Almighty have had a sense that they have been called by God for a particular purpose (for example, see Jeremiah 1:4–10), and Paul shared that sense of call

---

14. A cynic might ask if the sacrificial bull in Leviticus 16 was righteous. A cynical scholar might point out that in pagan sacrifices, the sacrificial victim (such as a bull) had to agree that it was surrendering its life for the greater good. When the animal came to the altar of sacrifice, someone would sprinkle water on its head, causing it to shake its head up and down. This was assumed to be a signal of agreement.

(Acts 9:1–19). The matter of "predestination" is raised in this passage, and a discussion of that would lead us away from our topic. Certainly there is no indication in Acts or Paul's Epistles that Paul considered his call to be a result of predestination. His call was a result of the gracious love that God Almighty has for sinners. Maybe response to God's call is the universal key to righteousness.

The discussion of the call of the Jewish people continues through Romans 9 and into Romans 10. In Romans 10 we read: "if you confess with your lips that Jesus is Lord and believe in your heart that God raised him from the dead, you will be saved. . . . For, 'Everyone who calls on the name of the Lord shall be saved'" (Rom 10:9–13, quoting Joel 2:32).

Crucifixion as sacrifice doesn't have anything to do with the discussion in Romans 10. Chapter 10 involves heavy use of the Prophets and Psalms. Faithful prayer, moral life, and confession of sin are requirements for eternal salvation. This is in the spirit of Old Testament prophetic writing such as:

> I hate, I despise your festivals,
> and I take no delight in your solemn assemblies.
> Even though you offer me your burnt offerings and grain offerings,
> I will not accept them,
> and the offerings of well-being of your fatted beasts
> I will not look upon.
> Take away from me the noise of your songs;
> I will not listen to the melody of your harps.
> But let justice roll down like waters,
> and righteousness like an ever-flowing stream." (Amos 5:21–24)

It seems that Romans 8–10 gets away from the "theology of the cross" and considers eternal salvation in terms of a dialogue between each human person and God Almighty. God calls the person to obedience, but the person is not strong enough and petitions God for help. If such a dialogue is sufficient for eternal salvation, what sense do we make of the crucifixion?

There is a Roman concept with which Paul would have been acquainted that is relevant here. The concept is not the total answer, but it provides a start. Let's think about this:

> While we were still weak, at the right time Christ died for the ungodly. Indeed, rarely will anyone die for a righteous person— though perhaps for a good person someone might actually dare

to die. But God proves his love for us in that while we still were sinners Christ died for us. (Rom 5:6–8.)

It is fairly common for a person to give up his or her life for another, often a family member or a fellow soldier in battle. This can call to mind the Roman battle practice of "*devotio*," a commander allowing himself to be killed in battle. We will discuss this practice at length in the next chapter, as well as giving it a brief mention below when we discuss John's Gospel. Strictly speaking, in *devotio*, the commander was sacrificing himself to a pagan god in expectation that the god would grant battlefield success to his army. In the twenty-first century we would not see it as sacrifice to some god, but consider it to be an example of self-sacrificing heroism to other soldiers. Either way, the commander was dying for others. Is this why Christ submitted to the cross? We have many accounts of martyrdom in which the martyr surrendered his or her life as an example, or witness, to others based on the example that Christ left. (The word "martyr" means "witness.")

Paul continues in verse 9: "Much more surely then, now that we have been justified by his blood, will we be saved through him from the wrath of God" (Rom 5:9). This is usually considered to be a statement about blood atonement, but it could equally be a statement about *devotio*. Christ dies in the battle with evil, so that his followers can conquer evil and thus be justified in God's eyes. Christ definitely doesn't sacrifice himself to an evil deity, but Christ does offer himself as an example for others, the modern understanding of ancient *devotio*.

Paul certainly had a sense that crucifixion was more than an example for us to follow in our daily life. The temporal death of Jesus has eternal consequences in terms of justification when we face God's judgement. Even so we see elsewhere that Christ's example of humility was very important for Paul (e.g., Phil 2). Humility is a major criterion describing those who seek justification.

Spiritual Sacrifice

Apart from all of this, we can turn the question around and ask how Paul understood "sacrifice" in a Christian context. Was there a way for Christians to offer a sacrifice independent of what Christ, himself, had offered on the cross? Can there be a "spiritual sacrifice?" Yes. Consider Philippians

2:17: "Even if I am being poured out as a libation over the sacrifice and the offering of your faith, I am glad and rejoice with all of you."

"Libation" is metaphorical. Likewise, the word "sacrifice" seems to be metaphorical, but maybe not. In this sentence, clearly "sacrifice" is identical with "offering of faith." Is "the offering of your faith" metaphorical? Certainly not. The Philippian congregation had sent hard money as an act of faith. Maybe Paul is really saying that a person's faith can be their sacrifice. Saint Paul, who was the "libation," could legitimately consider himself a blood sacrifice, as we see both in 2 Corinthians 11:23–29 and in the firm tradition that he was executed as a martyr.

Symbols and metaphors can change from occasion to occasion. Philippians 2:17 is not about blood sacrifice. When Paul speaks of himself as a "libation," he is not the sacrifice. We see in ancient pictures that libations were often poured onto the altar during the burning of a sacrifice or offering (both "sacrifice" and "offering" are denoted with the word *thysia*). The reference in Philippians 2:17 is to the offering made by the Philippian congregation, an offering representing faith, so faith is the sacrifice over which Saint Paul is "poured out." Furthermore, this is clearly a reference back to Philippians 2:7, about Christ being "poured out" when he was born as a human being. Paul was referencing his own imitation of his Master.

Lar pouring a libation and a pan specifically intended for libations. Both first or second century CE. Both British Museum. Lar: GR1772.3-2.18, Pan: GR1772.3-4.8.

Paul picks up this theme again at the end of the letter, Philippians 4:18–19: "I have received from Epaphroditus the gifts you sent, a fragrant offering, a sacrifice acceptable and pleasing to God." At first glance this is nothing more than saying, "Thank you for the financial support you have sent to me." Surely "fragrant offering," which normally refers to burning frankincense on a sacrificial altar, is a metaphor. But Paul says that their financial offering is really given to God and God is pleased with it. This is not entirely metaphorical, not even the "fragrant" part, because the frankincense was intended to please the deity. Paul is saying that the money they have sent to him is literally a Christian sacrifice. Again, we emphasize the earlier reference to "faith" in Philippians 2:17, which is also a reference to the money they have sent to him. The money was sent as an act of faith, and, as such, it is a "sacrifice" that can be compared to any ritual sacrifice on an altar. In other words, Paul is literally saying that there are Christian sacrifices that do not involve blood or altars. There are spiritual sacrifices.

Saint Paul didn't have to invent the notion of spiritual sacrifices, because it already existed in the Psalms. Keel notes that, "The official sacrificial cultus with its immolations is hardly mentioned in the Psalms.... Yahweh, who could be identified with no earthly entity, was seen early on to be independent of any earthly means of sustenance.... Animal sacrifices may have continued to be presented (because they allowed even the poor to celebrate by eating their fill), but the *hymn of thanksgiving superseded the sacrifice*" (italics added).[15]

This notion of spiritual sacrifice was accepted by later Christians. When we look at the *Didache* we see that one Greek word, *thysia*, was used both for "sacrifice" and "offering." Any offering to God is a sacrifice.[16]

Paul also apparently believed and taught that a money offering is acceptable to God only if the one making the offering is truly faithful (Phil 2:17, 2 Cor 8:1–7, etc.). That is, hypocritical offerings are not accepted by God. We see in Rom 3:25 that this understanding has implications for his teaching about salvation through the cross. Paul says that we participate in the sacrifice of Christ by faith, and God offers the sacrifice in the spirit of divine forgiveness. On our side, faith is real, not hypocritical. On God's side, forgiveness is likewise real.

The brief text in Romans 3:25 is seen as Paul's most unequivocal statement in support of blood atonement. There is a scholarly debate about the possibility that Paul copied Romans 3:24–25 from an earlier document. If so, these verses represent a very early form of belief in blood atonement in relation to the faith of the believer.[17] We will see that this text is a strong statement about blood atonement, but it is subject to various interpretations. In chapter 8 we will look again at Romans 3:24–25 in light of Abelard's theology.

---

15. Keel, *Symbolism of the Biblical World*, 323-335..
16. *Did.* 14.1–2.
17. See Shoberg, *Perspectives of Jesus*, 97n176.

A Couple of Other Interpretations of Paul's "Theology of the Cross"

Hartman makes a different observation about Paul's references to the crucifixion, and Hartman's interpretation does not involve seeing the crucifixion as a sacrifice. Paul says to the Corinthians and also to the Galatians that recognition that Christ endured degrading crucifixion should inspire them to be humble. (As we said, humility is one of Paul's themes.) Everyone to whom Paul wrote knew that crucifixion was the most degrading form of execution used by the Romans. Hartman understands the underlying issue addressed in 1 Corinthians as correcting the members of that congregation because "the Corinthians [had indicated that they] detest the shameful death on the cross through their veneration of men."[18] If the key to understanding the cross is that it calls us to humility, it does so by calling us to emulate Christ.

Libraries have been written about Saint Paul's theology, but we will move on after noting one more interpretation of the crucifixion found in his epistles: "The sufferings of Christ flow over into our lives" (2 Cor 1:5). This seems to be another aspect of the crucifixion as an example for people. Paul certainly suffered in his travels, he suffered in jail, and he suffered in many other ways (2 Cor 11:23-29). Luke records that suffering was part of Paul's call (Acts 9:16). Saint Paul is saying that when we suffer while doing Christ's work, we imitate Christ.

More on "Spiritual Sacrifice"

We also find the notion of "spiritual sacrifice" in 1 Peter 2:5. We are all called to be a "holy priesthood" offering "spiritual sacrifices."

Moving to another source, as we speak of "spiritual sacrifices," Tertullian is interesting:

> Every institution is excellent which, for the extolling and honoring of God, aims unitedly to bring Him enriched prayer as a choice victim. For this is the spiritual victim which has abolished the pristine sacrifices. "To what purpose," saith He, "[bring ye] me the multitude of your sacrifices? I am full of holocausts of rams, and I

---

18. Hartman, "Is a Crucified Christ the Center," 180-81. Also found in *Approaching New Testament Texts and Contexts: Collected Essays II*. Mohr Seibeck, 57-67 (p. 61.). Also at: http://web.comhem.se/~u18344626/centrent.htm

desire not the fat of rams, and the blood of bulls and of goats. For who hath required these from your hands?" [Isa 1:11, LXX.] What, then, God *has* required the Gospel teaches. "An hour will come," saith He, "when the true adorers shall adore the Father in spirit and truth. For God is a Spirit, and accordingly requires His adorers to be such." [John 4:23–24.] We are the true adorers and the true priests, who, praying in spirit, sacrifice, in spirit, prayer,—a victim proper and acceptable to God, which assuredly He has required, which He has looked forward to for Himself! This *victim*, devoted from the whole heart, fed on faith, tended by truth, entire in innocence, pure in chastity, garlanded with love, we ought to escort with the procession of good works, amid psalms and hymns, unto God's altar, to obtain for us all things from God.[19]

While this paragraph is both compact and prolix, if we take time to understand what Tertullian is saying we find an ambiguity. If we read it with the preconception that Christ must be a sacrifice rather than an example, we will understand the paragraph as speaking of Christ as the victim. However, if we set aside our preconceptions, Tertullian seems to be saying that the real sacrifice is our earnest and spiritually pure prayers: "prayer—a victim proper and acceptable to God." In the pagan world, a "victim" was a sacrificial animal. It was draped with flower garlands and brought to the altar in a ritual procession with appropriate prayers. Tertullian is saying that, for the Christian, heartfelt prayer is an appropriate "victim" to offer as sacrifice to God.

The Crucifixion in the Gospels

We also need to take seriously the traditions of Jesus recorded in the Gospels. Although the Gospels were not written until 20 or 30 years after Paul's writings, when they quote Jesus the burden of proof is on those who believe that Jesus never said the quoted words.

---

19. Tertullian, *Or.* 27–28.

John's Gospel

John 3:13–18

One of the most important texts for those who advocate the theological necessity of sacrificial blood atonement is John 3:13–18. We need to consider it carefully. Translators have determined that verse 10 through verse 15 is a statement by Jesus. Starting in verse 16 we have John's comment.

Verses 13–15: [Jesus said,] "No one has ascended into heaven but he who descended from heaven, the Son of Man. And as Moses lifted up the serpent in the wilderness, so must the Son of Man be lifted up, that whoever believes in him may have eternal life."

Verses 16–18: [John commented,] "For God so loved the world that he gave his only Son, so that everyone who believes in him may not perish but may have eternal life. Indeed God did not send the Son into the world to condemn the world, but in order that the world might be saved through him. Those who believe in him are not condemned, but those who do not believe are condemned already, because they have not believed in the name of the only Son of God."

Many people can quote John 3:16, and can even extend their quotation to verse 17. The preceding two verses in which Jesus teaches about Moses and a serpent are less familiar and even puzzling, but they are crucial to the argument. Verses 14–15 refer back to an event recorded in Numbers 21. During the Exodus the children of Israel were beset by poisonous snakes and many were dying. Moses sought God's help and was directed to manufacture a bronze snake. Anyone who was bitten would gain relief by looking at the bronze snake. (The bronze snake was subsequently destroyed to keep it from being worshiped as an idol [2 Kgs 18:4].)

SALVATION AS A MECHANICAL PROCESS

Lamp cover featuring entwined snakes (notice the wick hole between the snake heads). Snakes were a common sculptural feature in the millennia before Christ. This lamp cover is from the Sumerian city of Girsu, third or fourth millennium BCE. Louvre, AO12843.

John's point in quoting Jesus's citation of this 1,300-year-old precedent is that there is a parallel between the bronze snake and Jesus. Jesus was saying that his followers can look to the Son of Man for healing/salvation. (The Greek word *soter* means both "healing" and "salvation.") Some authors oversimplify this comparison by saying that Jesus, *lifted up on the cross*, is compared with the bronze snake, *lifted up on a pole*. Conner, for example, says that John 3:14 makes our eternal life dependent on the "lifting up" of Jesus on the cross.[20] However this contention misses a large part of what Jesus said.

The seemingly simple question is, "What did Moses do with the bronze snake?" The simple answer is that he set it up on a pole (as almost all Bible translations tell us); however, the simple answer is not correct. The word "pole" is an interpretation. God told Moses that the bronze snake was to be a "sign" or "ensign" (*nes*), like a battle flag that, in ancient times, showed soldiers where their unit was moving. (If you join a tour group today the guide may carry some sort of flag or marker to help you keep up

---

20. Conner, *Christian Doctrine*, 171. He says, " Moses lifting up the serpent in the wilderness, makes our obtaining eternal life dependent on the *lifting up* of the Son of man."

with your group.) Since an ensign is displayed on a pole, the usual translation can help the modern reader understand what happened. However, when the Hebrew Bible was translated into Greek for Greek-speaking Jews throughout the Roman Empire (a translation called the Septuagint and usually abbreviated as LXX), Numbers 21:8–9 said clearly that God told Moses to make the bronze serpent as a "sign" (*semeiou*), and when Saint Jerome translated the Bible into Latin (known as the *Vulgate*) he retained the word "sign" (*signum*). Moses may or may not have set the bronze snake on a pole so all could see it. To say it was "lifted up" on a pole is an interpretation. Moses might have as effectively put the snake-sign on a display table in the market.

Jesus makes reference to the account of the bronze snake (John 3:14), which would have been familiar to Jesus's audience, and Jesus takes the idea of a "sign" and expounds it. Jesus says that the bronze snake was "exalted" (*hupsoō*) and the Son of Man (the Messiah) must be similarly exalted. Even though many translations of John 3:14 translate *hupsoō* as "lifted up," this translation is too prosaic to really capture Jesus's meaning. Jesus is not simply referring to his coming execution, but to his resurrection and ascension, and when we understand *hupsoō* to simply mean "lifted up," we miss the full extent of what Jesus is saying.[21]

The exaltation of Jesus is one of the themes of John's Gospel. John affirms that Jesus was a human, like any of us, but John is greatly concerned that we understand the cosmic significance of the "Word" coming and dwelling with us. (See John 1:1–2. The "Word" is Christ.) John wants us to understand that, if Caesar was an exalted person, Jesus was more exalted. Roman intellectuals who criticized Christianity wrote that Jesus Christ could not possibly be a Son of God because he was not highly exalted. A Son of God must be a royal person, not a Galilean peasant, and certainly no God would permit a Son to be executed on a cross, the most degrading execution possible.[22] When John quotes Jesus's use of "exalted," he is countering these elite Roman writers. John has a strong sense of the irony inherent in human life, and when crucifixion becomes exaltation it is the ultimate irony. Jesus, as quoted by John, comes back to this: "When you have *exalted* the Son of Man, then you will realize that I am he." This

---

21. This is a subtle point, and even competent New Testament scholars miss it. For example, see Hartman, "Is a Crucified Christ the Center of New Testament Theology?" 184–185.

22. Origin, *Cels.* 1.28–30, etc.

anticipates a question asked later by the crowd: "How can you say that the Son of Man must be *exalted*? Who is this Son of Man?" (John 8:28; 12:34). Again, "exalted" is a form of *hupsoō*, and is usually (mis-)translated "lifted up," a gratuitous translation based on assumptions about what Moses must have done with the bronze snake.

However, it doesn't stop there. John knows that exaltation is more than crucifixion. The exaltation of Jesus is a chain of authenticating events. Crucifixion leads to resurrection, which then leads to ascension, returning to the cosmic home. The call to belief and salvation in John 3:14–17 is not focused on blood sacrifice, but on the total event of exaltation. When Saint Ignatius (martyred ca. 112) quoted this passage and related it to resurrection, what he looked forward to was the culmination of exaltation.[23]

One more thing: the key word in verse 14 is "must" (in Greek, *dei*): "so *must* the Son of man be exalted, that whoever believes in him may have eternal life." Although *dei* means "must," we may ask what the nature of the compulsion is. The standard New Testament Greek-English dictionary listing for *dei* gives several ways a person might be compelled: (a) fate or divine destiny, (b) duty, (c) law or custom, (d) situational need, (e) requirement to achieve a result, and (f) that which is fitting and proper.[24] Most who advocate sacrificial blood atonement see the execution as (a) divine destiny. Their only other option is to see it as (e) a requirement to achieve a result.

Are there other appropriate meanings for "must" in this verse? Why would it not mean (d) a situational need? That is, can we ask what would have happened if Jesus had decided to leave town after the Last Supper? He might have gone into self-exile rather than going to the Mount of Olives, where he could be arrested. But if he had done that, his movement would not have taken root. The situation required that he open himself to arrest, trial, and execution. He couldn't go into self-exile without destroying his mission.

As we said above, there was a contemporary Roman model of self-sacrifice through which people could have understood Jesus's steadfast journey to crucifixion: "*devotio*." We have no way of knowing whether Jesus ever had *devotio* in mind, but it seems to apply to the notion of "situational need" or even to "requirement to achieve a result." It also seems to apply to Jesus's reference to a good shepherd laying down his life for his sheep (John

---

23. Ignatius, *Smyrn*. 1.
24. Bauer et al., *Greek-English Lexicon*, 171.

10:11–17). It is a concept that was available to early Christians, especially to those who themselves faced martyrdom. Christian martyrs in the Roman Empire saw themselves as imitating Jesus. We will look carefully at *devotio* in the next chapter, but it would have been possible to reinterpret it beyond of its pagan origins and see it as self-sacrifice for a higher cause.

Recall that John 3:16 is the beginning of John's comment about Jesus's teaching. If we read John 3:16 along with the verses that precede it, John is commenting that God's love for humanity is shown in the exaltation/resurrection of Christ. "Whoever believes in him" believes in his resurrection and will thus share "eternal life" with him. "Sacrifice" and "atonement" are not implied unless one assumes a definition of "believe in him" that entails these concepts.

Jesus's Trial in John's Gospel in Light of John 3:16

There is one more reference to the crucifixion in John's Gospel that is worth mentioning. We are told that, as that fateful Passover drew near, Caiaphas said, "It is better for you to have one man die for the people than to have the whole nation destroyed" (John 11:50; referenced again in 18:14). Caiaphas was making a pragmatic (or economic) judgment, but in John's account it becomes ironic. John, as a literary artist, had prepared his reader for this question when he wrote, "God so loved the world that he gave his only son" (John 3:16), telling us that Christ was made available through the decision of God (Father, Son and Holy Spirit), not through the cynical pragmatic decisions of political leaders.

Incidentally, to say that "Christ was made available through the decision of God" is not the same as saying that "divine destiny" compelled Jesus to be executed. "Made available" and "compelled" are not equivalent.

The vocabulary Caiaphas uses betrays his cynicism. When Caiaphas makes reference to "people" and "nation" he apparently refers to them as synonyms. In contrast, John and his readers are aware of a difference between these two terms. Throughout the LXX and the New Testament, the word "nation" (*ethnos* in Greek) refers to the gentile (pagan) nations, while the word "people" (*laos* in Greek) makes reference to the people of God (who are not pagan). John 3:16 continues, "that whoever believes in him should not perish but have eternal life." John is telling his readers that the *"laos"* (people) are now those "who believe in Him," no matter what "nation" they come from. The "people" and "nation" of Jesus is larger than anything Caiaphas ever imagined.[25]

Atonement as Accepting Jesus's Gifts

Except for the reference to the Eucharist in John 6:53–56, we find no doctrine of sacrificial blood atonement in John's Gospel, and we have seen in the chapter on the Eucharist that even this is not about blood atonement.

In the fourth gospel, the "goodness" of the death of Jesus has to do with his "exaltation," "glorification," revealing his status as the Son of God. Jesus is the revelation of God, the one who came from God and who returns to God. He is the "bread from heaven" (John 6:31–40) and the 'living water" (John 4:7–15; 7:37–38). He is exalted like Elijah, especially in the way he leaves earth (2 Kgs 3:16–18; John 7:33; 8:21; 14:19; 16:5–7, 16). He is also the "good shepherd" who lays down his life for the sheep (John 10:11–17; 17:12ff) in response to the prophecy of Ezekiel 34. Ezekiel does not speak of the shepherd giving his life for the sheep, but such self-sacrifice is implied there and it does arise in Zechariah 13:7. Sometimes the forces against the shepherd are overwhelmingly strong. Jesus, the shepherd, is killed because the world hates him, and the world will similarly hate and kill his followers (John 15:18–21, etc.), but in the cosmic conclusion Jesus and those who believe in him will be exalted in triumph and have eternal life.

In John's Gospel, atonement with God is the result of accepting the bread from heaven, the living water, the miraculous wine of Cana, the roasted fish on the beach, the food provided to the crowds of four thousand and five thousand... that is, accepting the gift of life in Christ. The ultimate gift of life is eternal life. There is no threat of hell in this gift as John recalls Jesus's message. There is no blood sacrifice in John's gospel, not even the sacrifice of the Eucharist. When we read John's Gospel we often import our presuppositions from other New Testament teachings.

Matthew, Mark, and Luke

Let's turn briefly to Matthew, Mark and Luke, the "Synoptic Gospels." In summary, the thrust of Jesus's teaching in these Gospels is the establishment of a kingdom of righteousness, justice, morality and good ethics, both private and public.

25. Duke, *Irony in the Fourth Gospel*, 88.

In Matthew's Gospel (where we find the Sermon on the Mount, fount of ethics and morality) there is a hint of sacrificial blood atonement in Matthew 27, where we find, in the description of the trial of Jesus, a string of references to "blood" not paralleled in the other Gospels. Many think, with good reason, that Matthew's Gospel was written for a strongly Jewish audience (possibly in Jerusalem), and such readers would interpret these references to "blood" in terms of Levitical instructions about sacrifice, especially Leviticus 17:11-14, in which blood is identified with life. As we have seen, Roman judicial execution satisfied none of the requirements for sacrifice, but a person can make the identification as long as one doesn't reflect too carefully on the matter.

In addition, Matthew (along with Mark 10:45 = Matt 20:28) quotes Jesus as saying, "the Son of Man came not to be served but to serve and to give his life as a ransom [*lýtron*] for many." This statement was echoed in 1 Timothy 2:6, "Jesus Christ who gave himself as a ransom [*antílytron*] for all" (*lýtron* and *antílytron* mean the same thing). In addition, the idea was echoed, without using the same word, in Titus 2:14, "Jesus Christ, who gave himself for us to redeem [*lytrōsētai*] us from all iniquity and to purify for himself a people of his own who are zealous for good deeds." The word, *lýtron*, has a long and complicated history, and one could argue that Jesus meant something other than his impending death being a sacrifice, but the traditional interpretation of the statement seems most likely: Jesus said that his death would be a sacrifice. This is the only time he is quoted as saying such a thing. Such a statement was meaningful to a first-century audience, but makes little sense for a twenty-first-century audience. We quote what we said above in chapter 5: "Jesus had a talent for communicating by using concepts that people understood well . . . he was speaking in terms of a culturally bounded set of concepts."[26]

Beyond Matthew's account of the trial and Jesus's statement in Matthew 20:28 and Mark 10:45, the major hint of blood atonement in these three Gospels is in the establishment of the Eucharist in Matthew and Mark. We looked at these passages in the chapter on the Eucharist. It is interesting that the most ancient manuscripts we have on the Last Supper, Luke 22:17-23, do not mention sacrifice or blood. Also, Luke 24:30-31, the account of the meal at Emmaus, gives us a Eucharistic-like occasion

---

26. *Lýtron* in the New Testament occurs only in Matthew 20:28 and Mark 10:45. On *Lýtron* see Büchsel, "lýō," 543-47. We should note that Büchsel's discussion of this word anachronistically imports Anselm's interpretation of blood atonement in extensive detail.

that is revelatory but not sacrificial. If the support for blood atonement in Matthew and Mark is equivocal, support in Luke is even less certain.

Take Up Your Cross

These Gospels record that Jesus repeatedly instructed his followers to "take up their cross" and follow him (Matt 16:24 = Mark 8:34 = Luke 9:23; also Matt 10:38, similar to Luke 14:27). This clearly could not have been intended as a literal statement because not every follower of Jesus could be crucified. More likely it was a call to self-sacrificing service, a call to humility. However it also denies any notion that crucifixion is automatically an atoning sacrifice. When Jesus says that anyone who wants to follow him must take up a cross, he is saying that their self-sacrifice is in some way similar to his own self-sacrifice. Their self-sacrifice may not be of the same magnitude as his, but there is a similar quality. If the only way to understand his death is as blood sacrifice, how can the self-sacrifice of his followers be qualitatively similar? On the other hand, if his death carries some aspect of *devotio*, the self-sacrifice of his followers can also carry some aspect of *devotio*.

In the final chapter we will look at examples of extreme self-sacrifice that, in twenty-first-century terms, can be seen as taking up a cross in the sense of *devotio*.

Conclusions about Blood Atonement in the New Testament

Our brief review of the New Testament ends with some simple conclusions:

1. Hebrews and Saint Paul are the major New Testament sources for the notion of sacrificial blood atonement, although there are crucial differences. We find some of the minor epistles attributed to Saint Paul as definitely advocating blood atonement.

2. The major epistles of Saint Paul indicate that he was not of "one mind" about blood atonement.

3. The institution of the Eucharist is also a source, but it is also a complex source which we have examined separately.

4. Hebrews and 1 John are the only unequivocal sources.

5. The Gospels do not provide unequivocal support for blood atonement.

8

Alternatives to Sacrificial Blood Atonement

> He who was the Son of God became the Son of man, that man, having been taken into the Word, and receiving the adoption, might become the son of God.
>
> —IRENAEUS[1]

WE have seen how assumptions, logic, and culture "forced" Christians into teaching that the execution of Jesus was a sacrifice to atone for the world's sins. Were they really "forced"? Might they have come to a different understanding of the earthly mission of Christ and of his execution? As we ask this question we will ask whether we, ourselves, might come to a different understanding. Is there any need to teach the sacrificial blood atonement to Christians in the twenty-first century?

In chapter 7 we saw that one of the New Testament proponents of sacrificial blood atonement, Saint Paul, did not exclusively interpret the execution of Jesus as a sacrifice and did not consider eternal salvation to be exclusively tied to the notion of sacrifice. We saw that in Romans 10, Paul ties salvation to faithful prayer, moral life, and confession of sin. We also cited Hartman's interpretation of the references to crucifixion in 1 Corinthians as calling the Corinthians to humility: If Christ is willing to endure the degradation of crucifixion, the members of the Corinthian congregation shouldn't exalt themselves. So we find a variety of ways to

---

1. Irenaeus, *Haer.* 3.19.1.

understand the significance of Christ's execution. There are things to be said about alternatives to sacrificial blood atonement.

We start with the assumption that Christ had a purpose in becoming human. Might that purpose have been something other than serving as a human sacrifice? We have suggested several times that the purpose might have been to set an example for human life at its best. This is not a strange suggestion. It is biblical, and many Christians have taught it.

John's Gospel tells us about what Jesus did at the last supper: When the disciples had gathered, he washed their feet, a clear example of humility and service. When he had finished he said, "I have set you an example, that you also should do as I have done to you" (John 13:15). A little bit later he said, "I give you a new commandment, that you love one another. Just as I have loved you, you also should love one another" (John 13:34). The explicit instruction to follow Jesus as an example was the culmination of the example he had been setting for them during their time of discipleship (and maybe even earlier, if some had known him prior to their formal call). The thrust of all four canonical Gospels is Jesus-as-example.

Some may object that much of Jesus's activity was not as example but was intended to glorify God. Such people will point to the instances of Jesus raising the dead, saying that such activity could not possibly be an example for ordinary behavior. There are two responses: (a) it remains that much of Jesus's activity was exemplary, and (b) even raising the dead could be an example. Consider Jesus's raising of the daughter of Jairus (Mark 5:40–42) and compare it with Peter raising Tabitha (Acts 9:40–41). It seems clear that Peter, confronted with this monumental task, imitated his master, first sending extraneous people out of the room, then speaking words that echo the words of Jesus. Jesus said, "*Talitha cum*" and Peter said, "Tabitha *cum*." One can see this as Peter being overwhelmed, then (as one who had remained in the room with the girl) remembering what Jesus did.

We have called attention to the hymn in Philippians (2:6–11) which, in addition to being a statement about Christ's origin and destiny, is surely a call for those who follow him to be humble as he was. In fact, humility is a major theme in Paul's epistles.

Later in this chapter we will call attention to 1 Peter 2:21, a graphic statement about Jesus as example. This short epistle says, "as he who called you is holy, be holy yourselves in all your conduct," thus emphasizing Jesus Christ's behavioral model simultaneously with suggesting that Jesus was a sacrifice on our behalf (1 Peter 1:15–19). We can accept the "behavioral model" notion even if we do not accept the "sacrifice" notion.

We will also call attention to Romans 3:25, a statement that clearly affirms blood atonement, but find it interesting that Gregory of Nyssa was able to look at Paul's statement and find a call to follow Jesus's example. He said that everyone who thinks about Jesus's crucifixion should "become himself a propitiation, sanctifying his soul by the mortification of his members."[2] We become good (sanctified) through humility (mortification). In other words, every Christian learns ethical behavior from Jesus.

Few will object to what we have said, but the adherents to sacrificial blood atonement will say that "inspirational example" is not enough. It does not explain the crucifixion. Why was the Son of God subject to judicial execution? Of course they ignore the teaching of Jesus that everyone should "take up your cross and follow me" (Matt 16:24; Mark 8:34; Luke 9:23; as well as Matt 10:38 and Luke 14:27. Interestingly, Mark 10:21, an instruction from Jesus to give up everything and follow him, can be seen as related to the "take up your cross" theme). Perhaps Jesus's willingness to give up his human life was intended to show us that neither earthly possessions nor earthly life are supremely important. Perhaps Jesus really meant that we should be prepared to give it all up and even face crucifixion. At the very least, we should be willing to surrender our earthly treasures. Certainly our life is limited. Of course our death will not have cosmic significance. In contrast, the death of Jesus, as Son of God, has cosmic significance, but that significance may be that Jesus Christ is a moral example for everyone on earth, present and future.

Early Christian Writers for Whom Blood Sacrifice Was Not Important

Let's look at some historical "snapshots."

Second-century writers, except for Justin's *Dialogue with Trypho*, had little or nothing to say about the crucifixion. Their concern was redemption from the sin of Adam (which was uniformly considered to be sexual sin), and this redemption comes through grace and obedience. The notion of Christ's death as a sacrifice developed slowly in spite of the logic from which it came and in spite of the possibility that some believed it before

2. Bray, *Ancient Christian Commentary*, 102, citing Gregory of Nyssa, "On Perfection," FC 58:105.

Saint Paul wrote anything, as well as in spite of the fact that it was also attested in several of the writings (following Saint Paul) that were later canonized as the New Testament.

A serious and influential, although controversial, Christian from the end of the second century was Clement of Alexandria (150–215). His teaching was officially condemned 1,400 years later by Pope Sixtus V. Clement apparently found no need for an atoning sacrifice because God's grace is available to all who have faith. He never said that he rejected the notion of sacrificial blood atonement, so it's difficult to make a conclusive argument that he rejected it, but at least he ignored some good opportunities to speak about the matter.[3]

In the first chapter we briefly mentioned Clement's long chapter about the cruelty of pagan deities who demand human sacrifice. In that passage he does not mention the death of Jesus as a sacrifice even though it would be natural in this context. Later in the same book he wrote a long exhortation urging his readers to accept Christian salvation. He quotes several New Testament passages and emphasizes faith and wisdom, but never mentions sacrifice.[4] It appears that Clement (and by implication, those whom he taught) had no concern either for sacrifice in general or for a cosmic understanding of the death of Jesus. His exhortation is based on an underlying concern for sin, but in his theology saving grace does not require an atoning sacrifice. For example: "O the prodigious folly of being ashamed of the Lord! He offers freedom, you flee into bondage; He bestows salvation, you sink down into destruction; He confers everlasting life, you wait for punishment, and prefer the fire which the Lord 'has prepared for the devil and his angels.'"[5] This brief exhortation (which is typical) is focused on reforming one's life and accepting Christ as savior, an evangelical message familiar in our own day. The blood of Jesus is not part of the message.

Arnobius (225–330) was a Christian writer who lived late in the early period. Much of the Christian system of belief had been articulated during the two centuries before he was born, but he struggled to understand the divine/human combination that lived in Jesus Christ. (Arnobius died more than a century before the Council of Chalcedon would establish the official

---

3. We have pointed out in chapter 1 that Ensor, "Clement and Atonement," disagrees with the position taken in this book. This is not the place to engage in debate with Ensor, but examination of his article should reveal its weakness.

4. Clement of Alexandria, *Protr.* 3, 9.

5. Clement of Alexandria, *Protr.* 9, with reference to Matt 25:41, 46.

answer to the question of how Jesus and Christ are related.) He thought about pagan religion and concluded that Jesus died but Christ didn't die. Strictly speaking, this is heresy, but Arnobius was not a heretic. He was simply trying to understand who Jesus was. He reasoned about it through an analogy with pagan religion.[6]

Arnobius noted that at the well-known temple of Apollo at Delphi, a priestess inspired by the pagan god, would speak oracles about the future. The words spoken were thought not to be the words of the priestess, but the direct words of the god. Both Arnobius and Origen said that if someone were to kill the priestess, only her body would die. The god would not die. The case of Jesus and the Christ (Logos) must be similar because Jesus was human while Christ is God.[7]

Arnobius was not arguing for Docetism or for its inverse, adoptionism. We know this because he offers his argument as a tentative answer to the question. He finally says the crucifixion is a mystery that he doesn't understand. This is a true case of what Augustine and Anselm would later call *fides quarens Intellectum* (faith seeking understanding). It is possible for us in the twenty-first century to look back at Arnobius's intellectual struggle and say that he was on the right track. He may not have had a full or satisfactory answer to the question of the meaning of Jesus's crucifixion, but his line of thinking was more satisfactory than the thinking that led to understanding the crucifixion as sacrificial blood atonement.

Athanasius was a powerful figure in church politics in the years after Emperor Constantine made Christianity legal, and his leadership eventually led to the Nicene Creed, a statement of faith recited weekly by many

---

6. Arnobius, *Apology* (or *Against the Heathen*) 1.38, in Roberts and Donaldson, ANF, 6:423, talked about the benefits given by Christ: "he to be honored by us, who, by instilling his truth into our hearts, has freed us from great errors; who, when we were straying everywhere, as if blind and without a guide, withdrew us from precipitous and devious paths, and set our feet on more smooth places; who has pointed out what is especially profitable and salutary for the human race; who has shown us what God is, who he is, how great and how good; who has permitted and taught us to conceive and to understand, as far as our limited capacity can, his profound and inexpressible depths; who, in his great kindness, has caused it to be known by what founder, by what creator this world was established and made; who has explained the nature of its origin and essential substance, never before imagined in the conceptions of any; whence generative warmth is added to the rays of the sun; why the moon, always uninjured in her motions, is believed to alternate her light and her obscurity from intelligent causes"; etc. Note that sacrificial blood atonement is not mentioned.

7. Arnobius, *Apology* (or *Against the Heathen*) 1.62, in Roberts and Donaldson, ANF, 6:431; Origen, *Cels.* 2.9.

Christians today. That creed says that Jesus is "of one substance with the Father," and this statement represents Athanasius's signature issue. The Son of God is also God, not a separate being. If we ask why this was important to Athanasius, we find that it has to do with redemption from sin.

We will follow historian Has Lietzmann at this point because, as Lietzmann says, Athanasius's writings are "immeasurably prolix and tautologous."[8] Lietzmann's reconstruction of Athanasius's argument demonstrates that Athanasius never summarized or set forth his argument in one writing, but if one is willing to comb through the writings, the argument becomes evident.[9]

We might start with the American folk saying, "One rotten apple spoils the barrel," because Athanasius seems to turn this saying on its head. The folk saying means that a bad apple causes its adjacent apples to go bad, and by analogy, the folk wisdom says that a bad person will corrupt those within his/her circle. According to Athanasius, when God became human, all humans could become good, as if a barrel of rotten apples could become fresh and crisp by having a good apple placed among them. (Paul said something like this in Romans 5, his discussion of the "bad apple," Adam, corrupting all humanity, and the "good apple," Christ, making humanity good again. Later Irenaeus affirmed this approach.[10]) In physical terms this is the reversal of entropy.

We need to look at this more closely. Athanasius understood that Adam's sin had led to eternal death for every one of Adam's descendants. The Logos had created these people, grieved for them, and found their eternal condemnation unacceptable. However, because God is perfect, God couldn't change God's decision to condemn Adam for sin. Any change would demonstrate that God is imperfect. (Again we see the consequences of adopting the Platonic/Aristotelian understanding of God and its definition of perfection.)

Something had to be done to correct this state of affairs. After all, the Logos had created humanity in God's very image. How could God's image be eternally in the hands of the devil? (We can see that Athanasius creatively extended Paul's exposition in Romans 5.)

---

8. Lietzmann, *History of the Early Church*, 3:247.

9. Lietzmann, *History of the Early Church*, 3:247–52. See also Hiestand, "Not 'Just Forgiven.'"

10. Case, "Will the Real Athanasius Please Stand Up?," 289–93, presents an extensive argument that Athanasius was dependent on Irenaeus.

The solution was for the Logos to become human, fully human, including flesh, reason, and soul. As a human, the Logos worked miracles as a way of teaching and convincing people that the teachings were from God. Notice the importance of this. Athanasius was saying that miracles of compassion were not for the sake of loving compassion, nor were they intended to teach compassion by example. The miracles of compassion were simply intended to attract attention. Shall we agree with this? No, but we will see that, at least, this line of reasoning provides an alternative to blood atonement, and if through the centuries theologians had taken it seriously it could have led to a reasonable theological explanation for the significance of Christ's life and death.

Next comes a difficult logical juncture in Athanasius's reasoning. When the Logos died, because it was human flesh (human substance) that died, the death of the Logos was death for all humans. It was for all humans the eternal death that had been the penalty for Adam's sin. As a result of Christ's death, humans no longer needed to die eternally.

Now there is another juncture in the chain of reasoning. The Logos was not only human substance, but also the substance of God, and just as the death of the Logos was death for all humans (all human substance), likewise resurrection of the substance of God imparted the substance of God to all humanity. "Our own flesh was sanctified, cleansed from evil qualities, and awakened to a new life in which we should no longer be led astray by the seductive arts of the Devil, but guided by the Logos."[11] (It is interesting to compare this purported cosmic process to the pagan notion of apotheosis of a hero, such as Hercules. Culture provides for everyone the mental models with which they think about the world.) Humans can claim this redemption through baptism, and presumably through participation in the Eucharist. (Recall from chapter 6 that Irenaeus had taught that when we eat the bread and drink the wine of the Eucharist, our body is transformed into the substance of Christ's body.)

We can see how this line of argument made the Nicene Creed a crucial part of Christianity. The argument made by Athanasius depended on the Logos, or Christ, having the same substance as humanity as well as being the substance of God.

For our purposes the interesting thing about Athanasius's explanation of redemption is that it does not depend on a sacrifice or any kind of payment. The historical fact that Jesus was executed by the Romans is not

---

11. Lietzmann, *History of the Early Church*, 3:249.

crucial. The unstated logic argues that, for Athanasius, redemption would have been the same if Jesus had died by any means, including death from old age. (In his essay "On the Incarnation," Athanasius recognized this and addressed it unconvincingly, asserting that such a death would make Christ look weak.[12])The death of Jesus simply initiated the reversal of entropy. Hiestand observes in the writings of Athanasius what we have just summarized and then quotes him in support of blood atonement.[13] His verbal support for blood atonement is not surprising, but the logical consequence of his "reversal of entropy" theology simply demands that Christ-as-human die in order to eliminate death. (Hiestand notes that Athanasius's emphasis is ontological, not legal.) The death of Christ could have been from old age. This is logically true regardless of any quotation someone might cite from the writings of Athanasius.

Certainly Athanasius doesn't think that Jesus-as-example is important. He has a metaphysical explanation that is strange to twenty-first-century ears. His position that Christ's resurrection imparted Christ's (God's) substance into humanity led people to speculate about the mechanics of this process, and the normative answer to the mechanical question is that the Eucharist is the instrument that transfers God's substance to us.[14] In this way, Irenaeus's statement about the Eucharist has been taken literally, even today. In this book we are arguing that no mechanical explanation of salvation is satisfactory. Even so we can wonder what theologians would have done with this over the next 1500 or 1600 years if the explanation of Athanasius had become the normative explanation and had been considered apart from mechanical curiosity.

If Athanasius (as we have understood him) is correct, what is the significance of the crucifixion, a judicial execution? We revert to our own answer. As we have said, Jesus was forced into it by circumstances. If he had avoided crucifixion by going into self-imposed exile, his movement would have had no effect. No lives would have been changed. The world would not have been a better place.

---

12. Athanasius, "On the Incarnation," 4.21.
13. Hiestand, "Will the Real Athanasius Please Stand Up?," 57–58.
14. Nutt, *General Principles of Sacramental Theology*, 111–18.

Later Options to Blood Sacrifice

Interest in the notion of sacrificial blood atonement seems to have been more important at some times than at others. Interest heated up in the twelfth to fourteenth centuries, a time when blood sacrifice had not been practiced for several hundred years (except in very isolated places where paganism persisted). Even though sacrifice was no longer part of the culture, sacrificial blood atonement was part of Christian teaching, and the standard explanation for it was embarrassing.

Crucifixion (detail) by Lippo Memmi, 1340. Louvre R.F.1984-31.

The embarrassing question was, "If Jesus was a sacrifice that released souls from hell, and thus was a payment of ransom, to whom was the payment made?" The standard answer was twofold: (a) payment was made to the devil, because he "owned" the souls, and (b) it was a sham payment because the devil couldn't keep the soul of Christ. In other words, God had tricked the devil with a bogus payment. We can go back to the fourth century to see this in an ancient Christian sermon by a bishop: Gregory of Nyssa (335–394) said that God Almighty offered Jesus Christ as a ransom for Adam and Eve, and their descendants. Satan accepted the offer, not realizing that Christ could not be held in Satan's kingdom. The atonement was a trick played by God against Satan. Did Gregory tell this story with a wink? Three cheers to God for fooling the devil![15]

By the twelfth century this explanation about tricking the devil had become embarrassing because it suggests that God is not always faithful—sometimes God pays bills with counterfeit money.[16] In the twelfth century, Anselm of Canterbury found a solution to this embarrassment that retained the sacrificial blood atonement while affirming God's integrity.[17] His solution is a bit complicated and requires the mind of a business lawyer: (a) God cannot disobey God's own laws. (b) God's laws require payment for sin, that is, require that sinners go to hell. (c) Although God has no use for sacrifice, the ignominious death of Christ satisfies the legal requirement of payment for sin. According to this scheme, no payment is made to the devil and God doesn't require payment either, so we can't say that God is "bloodthirsty" or cruel. The payment is simply a legal requirement.[18] Anselm's understanding of the sacrificial blood atonement has become the standard understanding to this day.[19]

---

15. Gregory of Nyssa, *Great Catechism* 25. See also 26 (Schaff and Wace, *NPNF2*, 5:493).

16. The great poet W. B. Yeats has preserved for us a legend about Kathleen O'Shea who sold her soul to the devil in order to save the people of her town. In the end, according to the legend, the agents of Satan were not able to deliver the soul of this virtuous lady to Satan. Satan's agents had made a bad bargain, and Satan was very upset with them. In this story there was no duplicity. O'Shea sold her soul honestly, yielding her life and soul for others, but the agents of Satan were not able to comprehend such purity. This folktale could provide another way to think about the death of Jesus. Yeats, *Fairy and Folk Tales*, 211–14.

17. In this general (relatively brief) time, graphic artists emphasized blood in their depictions of the crucifixion of Jesus. See illustration on p. 121. For similar depictions, see Francesco di Vannuccio, 1385, Louvre R.F.2006-2; Giotto, 1320, Alte Pinakothek, Munich; and a mosaic from the 1200s in Church of the Dormition, Daphne, Greece. A full-page reproduction of the Greek mosaic has been published in Leith, "Creating Woman," 60. Leith asserts that blood is emphasized in Byzantine representations of the Crucifixion, but the fact remains that graphic emphasis on Christ's bleeding is restricted in time.

18. Anselm, *Cur Deus Homo* 2.5ff.

19. As we saw in chapters 1 and 6, the word "ransom" is in the New Testament (Mark 10:45; Matt 20:28; 1 Tim 2:6) and was set forth in the early "Epistle to Diognetus" (*Diogn.* 9.2–3), so it is not surprising that it has survived in spite of the embarrassment it causes. In 1875 Henry W. Baker wrote a hymn ("I am not worthy, holy Lord") that includes the stanza:

> I am not worthy; yet my God,
> How can I say Thee nay;

Anselm's contemporary, Abelard, was also engaged in an intellectual wrestling match with the notion of sacrificial blood atonement, and developed a different perspective on the matter that has not been so well-received. Essential to his explanation is that when people know that the eternal Christ lived among us as a human being and voluntarily submitted to crucifixion on our behalf, people with this knowledge will be filled with love for God. Our appreciation for the gift Christ has given us will be unbounded.[20]

Abelard retained the notion that something metaphysical and cosmic happened when Jesus was executed. Salvation is in God's control. But it seems that, for Abelard, the mechanism of salvation is based inside on the human response, not in some sort of sacrificial payment. Apart from Abelard we can find this sort of subjective, human-response understanding of salvation in Romans 3:24–25, "[Believers] are justified by his [God's] grace as a gift, through the redemption that is in Christ Jesus, whom God put forward as a sacrifice of atonement by his blood, *effective through faith*."

The Greek in this text is difficult, not because the grammar is difficult, but because the conceptual presuppositions from which Paul speaks don't match our conceptual framework. What Paul says is that the sacrifice of atonement must be accessed (or made effective) through our faith in Christ's blood. In other words, it appears that Paul is saying that atonement is subjective, within the believer. It is not an objective result of the historical execution of Jesus. This is not the only way to interpret Romans 3:25, but it is a legitimate way. Abelard may have considered Romans 3:25 and understood from it that salvation depends on human response, not sacrificial payment.

The notion that salvation might be based on the subjectivity of faith was, at some junctures, a live option to the mechanistic view. For example, Origen said, "[God] has by innumerable proofs established the claims of Jesus . . . who, as the Word, did, for the salvation of our race, show Himself before all the world in such a form *as each was able to receive Him*."[21] This implies that God reaches out to each person in terms of what that person

---

Thee, Who didst give Thy Flesh and Blood

My *ransom* price to pay?

This hymn was widely reprinted in the late twentieth century.

20. Marenbon, *Pagans and Philosophers*, 94.

21. Origin, *Cels.* 8.11.

can comprehend. It implies that redemption/salvation is not an objective function of the death of Jesus.[22]

Thus, in the twelfth century, the Christian world was offered two interpretations of the execution of Jesus, each of them related to salvation. We can imagine that, over the next thousand years, Abelard's interpretation could have led to an understanding of the execution that would retain the notion of atonement without depending on blood sacrifice. The same is true regarding the teaching of Athanasius, the teaching of Arnobius, and the teaching of Clement. None of these teachers is a satisfactory guide for us in the twenty-first century, but if any of their teachings had become the basis of Christian theological discussion and debate over the next thousand or more years, in our day we might have a more adequate explanation for the execution of Jesus.

As we know, Anselm's interpretation was accepted, and the notion of sacrificial blood atonement is still with us. Here's a "preacher story" from about 150 years ago that demonstrates how Anselm's solution is still accepted. A century and a half may seem like a long time, but in the realm of theological development it is only yesterday.

> It is said that an ancient king once had a law passed, the penalty of which was that the eyes of the transgressor should be put out. His own son was the first to break the law. If he allows him to go unpunished, then the law becomes a dead letter; no one will regard it. But he loved his son. What can he do to vindicate the law, and at the same time be merciful to his son? He did this: He had one of his own eyes put out and one of his son's, and thus the demands of the law were met, and his love and mercy manifested to that son. This is what God has done in the atonement of the Lord Jesus

---

22. Theologian Karl Barth was not willing to see the reference to "faith" in Romans 3:25 as subjective, so he provided an idiosyncratic translation of the verse saying that "faith" in this verse references the faithfulness of God, not the faith of the believer. I know of no translation of the Bible that interprets the verse the way Barth interprets it. Martin Luther's translation, which Barth would have known well, clearly speaks of the faith of the believer: "through faith in his blood" (*"durch den Glauben in seinem Blut"*). Barth, *Romans*, 104–7. Barth was Swiss, and an earlier Swiss theologian who was very careful about his use of biblical texts, John Calvin, said, "God is reconciled to us as soon as we put our trust in the blood of Christ, because by faith we come to the possession of this benefit." Calvin, *Romans and Thessalonians*, 76. Once again, we are clear that the primary focus of this text is the sacrificial blood atonement, but our point here is about faith versus magic or faith versus mechanics.

Christ, only he has borne all the penalty, and allows the sinner, by accepting the Lord Jesus Christ as his substitute, to go free.[23]

Of course, to make sense of this analogical story we need to understand the Christian teaching that Jesus Christ is identical to God Almighty. If one doesn't understand this, then one will wonder about the Son of God being punished. The son in the story apparently deserved punishment, but the Son of God was innocent. You, dear reader, surely understand this complexity, but Sunday school students, for whom Rev. Ritchie was writing, might not have understood it. The sacrificial blood atonement was easy to understand in ancient times and even in the middle ages when the ancient mindset was widely current even though blood sacrifices were no longer officially offered. By the nineteenth century, sacrificial blood atonement made no sense except in terms of some sort of religious nostalgia. The notion had to be reinforced by stories such as this and students had to be persuaded not to search too carefully for alternatives.

Was the Crucifixion Simply an Instance of Roman Brutality?

Perhaps the crucifixion could (should) be understood within the context of a repressive Roman government. In other words, perhaps the crucifixion of Jesus had nothing to do with his purpose. We know that the Roman government executed many people without cause (in spite of their advanced understanding of justice).[24] Society was brutal and life was cheap. For example it was even the case that no testimony was acceptable from slaves unless the testimony came from torture victims. In the eyes of the Roman authorities Jesus was both a dangerous leader of rebellion and a worthless nonentity. Eliminating him couldn't be bad for the empire and might be good for governmental stability.

There is a reasonable objection to the assertion that Jesus's execution was nothing more than a fairly ordinary part of the brutal Roman society. The Gospels show us a picture of Jesus making a positive decision to open himself to the possibility of execution. (His prayer in the Garden suggests

23. Ritchie, *Matter and Manner for Christian Workers*, 182.

24. Arnobius notes that "Pythagoras of Samos was burned to death in a temple, under an unjust suspicion of aiming at sovereign power." *Apology* (or *Against the Heathen*) 1.40, in Roberts and Donaldson, *ANF*, 6:424. His point is that leaders other than Jesus were killed unjustly by tyrannical governments, but their teachings endured in spite of their deaths.

that he didn't think the execution was inevitable, even though it was highly likely: Matthew 26:39, 42, 44; Mark 14:35–36, 39; Luke 22:42.) As we have already said, Jesus could have avoided going to Jerusalem for the Passover or could have run away after he had been betrayed.

Why would he have opened himself to the possibility of execution? Could he have been demonstrating by example that nothing on earth is supremely important, not even our own lives? We can be sure that self-exile would have destroyed the movement he was preparing. We know this for certain because immediately after Jesus's death the disciples were ready to forget his teaching and leadership and go back to their fishing business. They changed their mind only when the risen Christ appeared to them and talked with them (John 21). Certainly Jesus made the decision that the movement was more important than his own life on earth, even if his death had cosmic consequences.

Once again we suggest that the purpose and power of the crucifixion has to do with its being an "inspirational example." As Jesus said, "Greater love has no one than this: to lay down one's life for a friend" (John 15:13, NIV, see KJV). This idea was powerful before Jesus and has continued to be powerful. When we realize that it is a quotation from Jesus we automatically think that he must have been referring to his inevitable execution in terms of sacrificial blood atonement. We think that "lay down for" must mean "sacrifice to God for." Maybe not. Maybe he had his own execution in mind, but not necessarily in terms of an atoning sacrifice to God. After all, there has always been a notion that one could sacrifice oneself for the sake of others even it if wasn't a sacrifice to a deity.

In mythological times the Greek city of Thebes had been under attack and Tiresias (a seer/soothsayer who appears as a supporting character in many mythological stories) advised that the city would be saved if a descendant of the Sparti (who had founded the city) died. Menoeceus was such a descendant, so he threw himself off the city walls and died. The city was saved.[25]

Saint Augustine, in an effort to keep the Christian martyrs humble, tells us of several such pagan instances.[26] One of them was Curtius. The Romans had been under attack and were told by the gods that they could be saved only if they threw the best thing they had into the gulf waters. They

---

25. Hyginus, *Fabulae* 68.
26. Augustine, *Civ.* 5.18. Also relevant is Origen, *Cels.* 1.31, also cited (and quoted) above, 59n25.

decided that their best would be an excellent soldier, so Curtius voluntarily donned his armor, mounted his horse, and rode off a cliff into the rocks and water below. Augustine noted that Christians have a better "country" and a better Lord who said, "Do not fear those who kill the body, but cannot kill the soul" (Matt 10:28).

Roman Devotio

Within Roman culture there was a specific highly influential legend about a Roman military battle involving the practice called "*devotio.*" It might have been possible for Christians to interpret this legend as an explanation of Jesus's willingness to be executed. We looked briefly at *devotio* in the previous chapter, but now we look at it more carefully. We must stress that this is strongly hypothetical. Christians could not cite *devotio* directly in its pagan form. Even so it is worth mentioning in spite of the fact that it would have required interpretation. In fact this was one of the Roman self-sacrifices with which Saint Augustine was familiar and mentioned in the *City of God*.

Decius was a general who consecrated himself and the enemy to the infernal deities (who were really reprehensible) and then made a suicide attack on the enemy army. The elaborated legend says that it was not only Decius but three generations of men who did this. The story was best told by Livy in his *History of Rome*. Decius took a religious vow: "I devote the legions and auxiliaries of the enemy, together with myself, to the divine Manes and to Earth."[27] He then mounted his horse and plunged into the ranks of the enemy. After he was killed, the enemy troops were stricken with fear and the Roman troops rallied and defeated them.

What is this about, and how might it have helped early Christians understand the crucifixion? In 1976, H. S. Versnel made a careful study of the Roman concept of "*devotio,*" and explained that originally "*devotio*" was an offering of the enemy forces as well as their lands and people and everything else to the "infernal" or "chilothnic" or underworld deities, in hope that these deities would grant victory.[28]

We can even find this sort of offering in the Bible, although in the Bible the "devotion" is to God Almighty, not to an underworld deity. After the conquest of Jericho, the Israelites "devoted to destruction" everyone and everything in the city and they burned the city except for objects of silver,

27. Livy, *Hist.* 8.9.8. For the full story read all of 8.9.
28. Versnel, "Two Types of Roman *Devotio.*"

gold, bronze and iron. These metal things were placed in the treasury of the Lord. However two men took some of these devoted objects. Consequently the Lord withdrew the military assistance the Israelites had been receiving. Joshua petitioned the Lord for an explanation, and was told, "Israel has sinned . . . they have taken some of the devoted things; they have stolen." The culprits were executed, "then the Lord turned from his burning anger" (Josh 7:11; for the full story see 6:21—7:26).

Sometimes it seemed good to sweeten the deal by offering more immediate sacrifices, since the deity would not get the enemy persons and goods until the battle was over. These immediate sacrifices might be sacrificial animals, but in the case of Decius (or the three Decii), the general who led the army offered himself as the additional sacrifice.

Is there a meaningful analogy between the Decii and the execution of Jesus? If there is such an analogy, it would speak to the Roman gentiles who were well-acquainted with the tradition of the Decii. The first problem with the analogy is that the *devotio* contract was with disreputable underworld deities, but if Joshua could make a *devoto* contract with God Almighty, perhaps the additional offering of the Messiah would fit the Decii model. The next problem is identifying the analogical enemy. The strict parallel would be the Roman and Jewish officials who arrested, condemned and executed Jesus. Jesus had gone purposefully into their midst.

If the enemy is the Roman Empire, then for the death of Jesus to be seen as an analog of military *devotio*, the Roman Empire should have been overthrown and the kingdom of God established on earth. This did not happen immediately, but Eusebius (and others) would argue that the conversion of Emperor Constantine (almost three hundred years later) destroyed the enemy. A battle against an army can be won in a day, a week, or some other relatively short span of time. A battle against an empire will take much longer.

Devotio could also have explained the cosmic significance of the death of Jesus if the enemy were seen as metaphysical entities such as the demons of the air and their prince, Satan. These were certainly enemies of Jesus, and one might say that Jesus's descent into Hades (Eph 4:9–10; 1 Pet 3:18–20; 4:6) is analogous to the general plunging into the midst of the enemy forces. If the enemy is outside of everyday earthly life, then the resulting victory or salvation could be outside of everyday earthly life. If the analogy holds thus far, we need to ask to whom the immediate sacrifice is made. Decius sacrificed himself to the demons, but if the demons are the enemy, sacrifice of the Son of God must be made to someone else. If we follow the book of Joshua, the sacrifice is made to God Almighty. This doesn't work because it returns us to the image of God Almighty as a bloodthirsty deity. No analogy can be stretched without limit. There comes a point when the strict analogy with Decius is no longer appropriate. The death of Jesus is an act of *agape* and an inspirational example. Strictly speaking it is not a sacrifice.

When we, in the twenty-first century, read Livy's report of Decius being killed in battle, and he says the enemy

> abandoned the field in flight. At the same time the Romans—their spirits relieved of religious fears—pressed on as though the signal had just then for the first time been given, and delivered a fresh attack,[29]

we think, "Of course, the enemy was psychologically devastated by the general's unbelievable show of bravery, and that same demonstration of bravery inspired the Roman troops to similar bravery." Livy's intention was to tell us that the underworld deities frightened the enemy and gave hope to the Roman troops because these deities liked the sacrifice. This pagan theology makes little sense to us in the twenty-first century, but we easily interpret it in terms we understand.

We see that the ancient tradition of *devotio* is worth recalling because it can be construed as an analogy that makes sense in our time, more sense than the analogy of sacrifice. In the twenty-first century we see the commander who charges into the enemy ranks on a suicide mission as inspiring his followers rather than as propitiating some underworld demons. If we think about Jesus's trial and execution as *devotio*, we, in the twenty-first century, don't need to ask to whom the dedication or sacrifice was made. We understand that God honors self-sacrifice, and the test or proof of that honor is seen in the resurrection of Jesus.

When we turn to the accounts of martyrdom among early Christians, we see (in twenty-first century terms) this sort of inspirational example at work. The bravery of Jesus inspires the bravery of the martyrs. On this basis we can accept the analogy between the execution of Jesus and Roman *devotio*. Having accepted a twenty-first-century understanding of *devotio* we are free from the notion of blood sacrifice in relation to Jesus's execution.

If Satan and his demons constitute the enemy, they have not yet been destroyed (Eph 2:1–7), but victory has come to certain individuals and will

---

29. Livy, *Hist.* 8.9.12–13.

continue to come to others. Ultimately victory over Satan will be accomplished, as taught in the book of Revelation.

Furthermore, we should keep in mind that Jesus didn't succumb to the devil and his demons when he went to Hades. Instead he led out those trapped in Hades who would follow him. Even though many Christians today are not familiar with this notion, the tradition is strong. In the New Testament, in addition to citations from Ephesians and 1 Peter, we can appeal to John 5:25, 28–29. The early Christian writers did not cite Revelation 1:18, a reference to Christ having the keys to the kingdom of Hades, but if they had it would have made sense. Clement of Alexandria seems to have referenced Matthew 27:52–53, even though, at best, Matthew's description of the dead rising from their tombs is tangential to the issue. Clement wrote a long essay defending the notion of Christ going to the kingdom of Hades, saying, "If, then, He preached the Gospel to those in the flesh that they might not be condemned unjustly, how is it conceivable that He did not for the same cause preach the Gospel to those who had departed this life before His advent?" Clement reasoned that Christ would not only free righteous pagans from Hades, but also disreputable pagans who, after death, regretted their sinful life on earth. Clement said it was the flesh that had led them into sin, and after death the pure soul was left behind to repent.[30] Beyond all of this, it has been argued that a strange-sounding story in the non-biblical Gospel of Peter tells of Christ leading a large number of people out of Hades.[31]

---

30. Clement of Alexandria, *Strom.* 6.6.
31. Crossan, *Birth of Christianity*, 488–89.

Schematic of the *Anastasis* icon.

Among Eastern Orthodox icons, probably the most familiar is the *Anastasis*, or the Resurrection icon, a depiction of the risen Christ standing on the broken doors of hell while pulling Adam, or Adam and Eve, out of their sarcophagi. The iconography comes from the early fourteenth century or earlier.[32] By implication the depiction represents the salvation of the descendants of Adam and Eve. As one contemplates this icon, it becomes clear that Christ is in charge. Christ has not been taken to hell as an impotent sacrificial animal. Christ has purposely come to hell with the mission of destroying it. This interpretation is consistent with a modern interpretation of the legend of the Decii.

Why did theologians of the early middle ages opt for "sacrifice" instead of "*devotio*"? Recall that, in the first three centuries, there seems to

32. Srejović, *Museums of Yugoslavia*, 82.

have been little need for an explanation of Jesus's crucifixion. Later, when the doctrine of blood atonement was being thought through and codified, there were two realities supporting the notion that Jesus's death was a sacrifice: (a) The Old Testament described temple sacrifice, and theologians felt a need to assert that temple sacrifice had been replaced by the single sacrifice of Jesus. (b) These later theologians were not intimately familiar with sacrifice. Jerusalem temple sacrifice had not been practiced for several centuries, having been eliminated in the year 70 when the temple was destroyed. Pagan sacrifice had not been openly practiced since the time of Emperor Theodosius (390s, two generations after Constantine). By the time that the notion of sacrificial blood atonement became doctrine, theologians had not experienced the reality of sacrifice, so didn't realize the ways in which crucifixion was not sacrifice. Of course it took several centuries to decide to whom the sacrifice of Jesus was made.

An extension of *devotio* may lose its sacrificial denotation while retaining a connotation of "inspirational example," something that is congenial to our twenty-first-century way of thinking. In the next chapter we will look at a couple of examples of this sort of self-sacrifice.

Devotio and What It Might Mean to Say, "Christ Became Sin"

Now we need to look again at the strange notion that Christ became sin for our sakes and we will see that this notion relates to *devotio*, as interpreted for the twenty-first-century mind.

We return to 2 Corinthians 5:21 (which we discussed in the last chapter), "For our sake he made him to be sin who knew no sin, so that in him we might become the righteousness of God." We noted in the last chapter that this is the conclusion of a rich passage expounding the role of Christ in reconciling us to God and thus to one another. We cannot begin to exegete or interpret the richness of this entire passage, but will restrict ourselves to one more brief comment on verse 21. We note that this sentence is an exercise in proportional analogy. We are sinful. Christ is righteous. If Christ, in some sense, becomes sinful, then we, in some sense, become righteous. It is a somewhat mathematical relationship. It can also be read as the reversal of entropy, as we mentioned in our discussion of Athanasius.

The question for our larger discussion of *devotio* is how (or in what sense) Christ becomes sinful.

We have noted that Paul's basic explanation has to do with "flesh" (*sarx*). Paul thinks of "flesh" as inherently sinful, so when Christ was born in the flesh he was born into sin. The cosmic Son of God had been living in celestial purity and he abandoned purity to become a human in the flesh, therefore "sinful."

Another traditional explanation has to do with the crucifixion. In his letter to the Galatians Paul says something quite similar to what he wrote in 2 Corinthians: "Christ redeemed us from the curse of the law by becoming a curse for us—for it is written, 'Cursed is everyone who hangs on a tree'" (Gal 3:13). Again we have the proportional analogy or the reversal of entropy: Christ is righteous, we are cursed. Christ redeemed us by becoming cursed. Paul's reference is to the Torah, Deuteronomy 21:22–23. According to Deuteronomy the curse was an immediate consequence of being crucified.

Let's think again about *devotio*. The early Christians could possibly have invoked a third explanation of Christ becoming sin based on *devotio*. The general who sacrificed himself (along with the entire enemy army) to the underworld deities took on a personal curse in order to relieve the curse of national defeat. The two curses are not identical. The curse of national defeat is not caused by the underworld deities, but the general hopes the underworld deities can prevent the curse of national defeat. To gain this benefit he will allow the underworld deities to curse him. When the early Christians read in Paul's letters that Jesus accepted the curse, it would be possible according to a readjustment of the *devotio* analogy to understand that when Jesus went to Golgotha he did so to destroy evil. (Think again about the *Anastasis* icon. Also consider Luther's hymn: "Though this world with devils filled should threaten to undo us . . . one little Word shall fell them.")

Once the cosmic enemy has been conquered, we are still responsible for works of righteousness. As Zechariah sang, "we, being rescued from the hands of our enemies, might serve him [God] without fear" (Luke 1:74).

A modified *devotio* analogy is not strange. The notion that a person can accept evil in order to keep the evil away from another person is widespread. The ancient Greek playwright Euripides used this notion as the basis for his drama, *Alcestis*. As the drama opens, a king named Admetus has learned that he will die, but the fates have promised that if someone else is willing to die in his place, he will live. His wife, Alcestis, has agreed to die in her husband's place, and the drama proceeds from that point. (In the end Herakles/Hercules saves everyone.) The mythical story of Alcestis was ancient, going back hundreds of years before Euripides wrote his drama, but the notion endured and was still current in early Christian times. Versnel gives us a number of examples of stories on this general theme from the first century of our era.[33] According to this line of thought, the sin or curse which Christ accepted was not simply his becoming human, and not simply his being crucified, but was a decision to make an exchange on our behalf. This conclusion is consistent with our general understanding of the incarnation and is thoroughly consistent with the idea of flesh being sin and the cross being a curse, but framing it in terms of *devotio* is a further indication that the *devotio* analogy is consistent with the New Testament.

The Logos Became Flesh

There is more that can be said in favor of seeing the crucifixion as an inspirational example. John's Gospel identifies Christ as the Word of God (*Logos*). "Logos" is a word with multiple and complex referents and possible translations and it has been a highly evocative word from about 500 BCE until the present. It can be traced etymologically to both "word" and "reason." Beyond these two words conceptual connections have related it from "word" to "speech," "saying," "story," "oracle," "conversation," "dialogue," "definition," etc. . . . and from "reason" to "mathematical ratio," "proportion," "order," "argument," "theory." Most of these words will be found as standard translations of "*logos*" into English, and all of them relate conceptually to "*logos*." Taking all of this together, we can see how "wisdom" (*sophia* in Greek) is conceptually related to *logos*.

Beyond the matter of translation is cultural context. Around 500 BCE a mystical Greek philosopher/poet named Heraclitus left us some evocative aphorisms about the nature of Logos. He related "*logos*" both to the soul and to the cosmos, saying of the soul: "You would not discover the limits of the soul although you traveled every road: so deep a *logos* does it have."[34] Then he said, "The soul has a self-increasing *logos*."[35] Regarding the cosmos, he said, "The *kosmos*, the same for all . . . it was always and is and shall be: an ever-living *fire* being kindled in measures and being extinguished in

---

33. Versnel, "Two Types of Roman *Devotio*," 391–92.
34. Frag. 45.
35. Frag. 115.

measures."³⁶ Heraclitus considered fire to be the material form of *logos* (a thought that prefigured Stoicism). He also said, "Listening not to me but to the *logos*, it is wise to agree that all things are one."³⁷ De Beer interprets Heraclitus as meaning that "Due to the presence of the *logos*, the becoming and change that characterize the world do not occur in a chaotic manner."³⁸ Wisdom is incompatible with chaos.

All of this was background for what John wrote at the beginning of his Gospel. John was using this conceptually complex word to explain the complexity of Christ becoming human.

Why would Christ become human? All New Testament authors concur in the answer to this question, which was stated pithily by the author of Hebrews: "Long ago God spoke to our ancestors in many and various ways by the prophets, but in these last days he has spoken to us by a Son" (Heb 1:1–2). The best way to teach a skill is to give a demonstration with an explanation. If God wanted us to learn how to live, the best way to teach us would be to live among us, show us, and explain the demonstration. This would be the sense in which Christ is the "Word of God."

It is interesting to ponder this "Word of God" as example in the First Epistle of Peter. We are told, "Christ also suffered for you, leaving you an example, so you should follow in his steps." (2:21.) The word translated here as "example" is thought-provoking. It is *hupogrammon*, derived from the word for "writing." The literal reference is to a sample of writing given to students for instruction. When they are learning to form letters, they are to look at the example and imitate it. We can all remember the letter-charts posted at the top of the walls in our early elementary classrooms. The point of the text is that those to whom the epistle is addressed are beginners. They are to imitate Jesus as their model.

This epistle clearly affirms the notion of sacrificial blood atonement (1 Pet 1:19; 2:24), but the epistle's real concern is Christian behavior. The readers are told to live a life of morality, humility and good citizenship in spite of persecution. (The epistle may be addressed to Christians in the region from which the younger Pliny wrote to Emperor Trajan asking how to treat Christians.) The concern for morality and ethics starts in 2:11 and is carried to the conclusion of the epistle. How are people to do this? By following the example of Jesus Christ who was moral and humble and was

---

36. Frag. 30.
37. Frag. 50.
38. de Beer, "Cosmic Role of the Logos," 15.

also persecuted to death. We find this especially in 2:21–23; 3:14–18; and 4:1–6. This emphasis is worth noting because the epistle could as easily have focused on sacrificial blood atonement encouraging people by saying that, since the execution of Jesus has saved them, their behavior is of no consequence.

Paul sees things a bit differently and doesn't speak of Jesus as an example, but speaks repeatedly of Christians being "in Christ" and of Christ being in them. Paul is a poet and routinely chooses the "in Christ" metaphor which speaks of living inside Christ or of putting on Christ as one puts on a garment. As a matter of fact, in addition to speaking of being "in Christ," he also speaks explicitly of putting on Christ (Gal 3:27). This sounds a lot like "example." Paul does not specify the crucifixion as an example and this is likely because persecution and martyrdom were not part of the world in which Paul evangelized. Certainly Paul, himself, suffered many things (2 Cor 11:23–29, etc.), but his suffering was not part of any organized persecution. The congregations he organized (prior to Emperor Nero) had little worry about government-sanctioned brutality. Paul recognized the need for an inspirational example but spoke of it as coming directly from God through God's Spirit (Rom 8:14, etc.). The "Word of God," which we find in John, was not part of his mental/verbal toolbox.

Paul and John did share the concept of "love" (*agape*). Paul's great poem on love, 1 Corinthians 13, may have defined *agape* for later Christians, including John. People had witnessed God's love displayed in the life of Jesus, and throughout the Old Testament there are examples of God's "steadfast love" (*hesed*), but Paul's poem summarized what people had found in Jesus and it differentiated God's love from pagan discussions of love (*eros*). John took this idea and preserved Jesus's explanation of how love starts with God and ends in our relationship with one another: "This is my commandment, that you love one another as I have loved you. No one has greater love than this, to lay down one's life for one's friends" (John 15:12–13). In other words, we learn to love by watching the example of Jesus.

Our point is that the Bible affirms the role of Jesus Christ as our inspirational example. It is appropriate to see this as the defining element in Christianity. We recognize that the Bible also affirms the prospect of eternal salvation through the atonement made by Jesus Christ when he submitted to execution, thus becoming a human sacrifice offered to God Almighty. However, we have tried to make clear that the notion that Jesus's crucifixion as a sacrifice was almost inevitable because of a complex set of ancient expectations. The surprising element is that the New Testament does not uniformly teach this. In any case, the ancient expectations are no longer a part of our understanding of the cosmos or of God. Our argument is that the sacrificial blood atonement can and should be eliminated from Christian discussion.

9

Where Do We Go from Here? How to Sing a Different Song

> We conceive a given reality in this way or in that, to suit our purpose, and the reality passively submits to the conception. . . . Which may be treated as the *more* true depends altogether on the human use of it.
>
> —WILLIAM JAMES[1]

Recap

IF we are correct, why has the notion of sacrificial blood atonement persisted? Part of the answer is that it is clearly within the New Testament. Because it is in the New Testament, it is affirmed in all churches in the liturgy of the Eucharist/Holy Communion/Lord's Supper. The relevant New Testament Eucharistic passages (which we quoted in chapter 5) simply say what they say, but it would make sense for us to understand them as ancient expressions of ideas that now need to be expressed in different ways, perhaps with theological development deriving from Athanasius, perhaps development deriving from Roman *devotio*, perhaps some other theological development. There are many biblical words, customs, and beliefs that we now pass by, understanding that they were part of ancient understanding but do not apply today.

---

1. James, *Pragmatism and Other Essays*, 110–11.

In the first chapter we indicated another reason for the persistence of sacrificial blood atonement: we are mechanically oriented. Humans want to know how things work. We want to know how salvation "works," and sacrificial blood atonement is a mechanical explanation. Without it we cannot easily understand how God manages eternal salvation. Without this explanation we have to depend on faith. In the first chapter we saw that desire for a mechanical explanation goes back at least to Ignatius, who wrote: "[You are] carried up to the heights by the engine of Jesus Christ, that is the cross, and using as a rope the Holy Spirit. And your faith is your windlass and love is the road which leads up to God."[2]

The desire for a mechanical explanation became much more intense in the eighteenth-century with the (mechanical) industrial revolution and the (mechanical) scientific revolution. We observed in the first chapter that the rise of pietism and its appropriation of the blood atonement coincided with the work of Isaac Newton and other physicists who discovered the basic mechanical laws of nature. The cultural impact of the discovery of a massive number of mathematical laws governing our world was profound. We can sense the impact from Alexander Pope's couplet:

> Nature and Nature's laws lay hid in night:
> God said, *Let Newton be!—and all was light.*

The scientists seemed to be discovering that God is a systematic mechanic. If so, humanity might draw several different theological conclusions. One such conclusion was the Deist notion of a "watchmaker" God who had wound up the cosmos and is leaving it to tick out eternity on its own. Another of the several conclusions is that if God organized the physical world mechanically, certainly God must also have organized the metaphysical/spiritual world mechanically. If the spiritual world is mechanical, we should be able to discern the mechanism.

This may be why, in the first chapter, we found the eighteenth-century hymns strongly expressing belief in the sacrificial blood atonement. The execution of Jesus as a sacrifice is the mechanism of eternal salvation. Of course this notion didn't suddenly arise in the eighteenth-century. For 1700 years Christians had been puzzling and debating about the details.

Where is the problem in all of this? The problem is in our prideful notion that we must be capable of figuring out the mechanics of salvation. Grace doesn't seem to be sufficient for us. (We likewise mechanize grace

---

2. Ignatius, *Eph.* 9.1.

when we split it into several categories.) We require a mathematical formula, or at least a literal prose narrative that explains grace as well as salvation.

In the twenty-first century, natural science is much more humble than it was in the seventeenth century. Today when we look at the cosmos we understand a great deal, more than humans have ever understood, but we also have become aware that there are aspects of the cosmos that humanity will never understand. Chaos theory tells us that we will never be able to absolutely predict weather systems and similarly complex phenomena. When we look at subatomic particles we understand a great deal, but we have become aware that there are aspects of the structure of our material world that we will never understand. Werner Heisenberg, in his Gifford Lectures (1955–56), recalled early conversations with Niels Bohr after which he asked himself, "Can nature possibly be as absurd as it seemed to us in these atomic experiments?"[3] Heisenberg and the other early giants of atomic physics ultimately found peace with the notion that we can know a great deal, but we cannot know everything with deterministic certainty. We understand enough to make wonderful tools, but these tools are often based on physical and chemical principles that we don't really understand.

In the twentieth and twenty-first centuries, physicists and mathematicians have pondered and discussed at length the fact that we can use mathematical equations to model the physical world. One of the philosophical problems is that the mathematical models that work so well seem to be a bit arbitrary. To take a familiar example, although Ptolemy's earth-centered model of cosmic workings is considerably more complicated than our heliocentric model, Ptolemy's complicated model could be used in our explorations of the solar system. It would be possible to use Ptolemy's model to land a rocket on an asteroid.[4]

Shouldn't theologians be at least as humble as physicists? If the theologian feels a profound need to explain the mechanism of salvation, shouldn't the theologian be open to considering a variety of models for that mechanism?

As we have pointed out, there were alternatives. There were biblical alternatives. There was the Roman notion of *devotio*. There was the possibility offered by Athanasius based on a metaphysical exchange of "substance" for "substance." There was the possibility offered by Abelard of salvation through thanksgiving to God. None of these appeared as contentious

---

3. Heisenberg, *Physics and Philosophy*, 42.
4. Kline, *Mathematics*, 412–19.

debate alternatives. They were simply offered as ways to explore the meaning of Christ becoming incarnate and the meaning of the judicial execution of that Son of God.

It is the presumption of this book that not only is blood sacrifice an artifact of ancient history that no longer makes sense, but also that we don't need to understand the mechanics of salvation.

More Thought about the Eucharist

Today, many Christians learn that affirming the blood atonement is basic to Christian belief because of the way Eucharistic liturgy is expressed. If the liturgy emphasized a different interpretation of the significance of Jesus's death, the common presumptions about the blood atonement might fade. Consider our earlier reference to the twentieth-century conservative Protestant theologian, W. T. Conner. He considered the Eucharist to be subject to individual interpretation. In his view (based on John 6), the Eucharist is mystical and thus *subjective*. Independently of this, he considered that the crucifixion, as penal substitution and necessary to salvation, is an essential *objective* element in Christian faith.

If a theologian teaches that the Eucharist is somehow objective, rather than mystical, then that teaching can buttress the mechanical explanation of redemption. (Even if the connection is not based on logic, the rhetorical effect of the connection is powerful.) Otherwise redemption is open to other explanations, as we shall see. We cite Conner as a common example of conservative approaches to atonement. We are not objecting specifically to Conner. Conner, along with others, did not address the disconnect between his understanding of the Eucharist as subjective and blood atonement as objective. Ultimately he could only *assert* that penal substitution is the mechanical explanation of redemption.

We have said that there is nothing to be done about the texts on which the Eucharist is based, but we can modify our understanding. Across the world and among Christian denominations, the liturgy of the Eucharist echoes the earliest liturgies of which we have records, and these records come from the fourth century and later, a time when sacrificial blood atonement had become the normative interpretation of the execution of Jesus. To delve into the history and theology of the liturgy is outside the scope of this book, but we will make a simple observation: *not everything in the traditional liturgies is oriented toward blood sacrifice.*

In the English Mass, the minister introduces the breaking of bread as follows:

> Minister: The bread which we break, is it not a sharing in the body of Christ?
>
> People: Because there is one bread, we who are many are one body, for we all partake of the one bread.
>
> Minister: The wine which we drink, is it not a sharing in the blood of Christ?
>
> People: The cup which we bless is the communion in the blood of Christ.

This call and response serves to refresh people's memory of 1 Corinthians 10:16, where "sharing" or "participation," or "communion" is *koinonia*, sometimes translated as "spiritual fellowship." In this passage Paul speaks of "body" and "blood," but it is in reference to fellowship, not in reference to blood sacrifice.

The ontological teachings of Irenaeus (the elements of communion transform us so we become Christlike) and of Athanasius (the substance of Christ purges our substance of sin), both of which are independent of sacrificial blood atonement, show up in the liturgy. In the English Mass, during the Thanksgiving (shortly before the Breaking of Bread) the minister says a prayer that includes:

> Grant that all who share the communion of the body and blood of our Savior Jesus Christ may be one in him, and remain faithful in love and hope until that perfect feast with him in joy in his eternal kingdom.

In this prayer, "share the communion" evokes 1 Corinthians 10:16 about "participation" (*koinonia*) in the body and blood. As such, the prayer that participants "may be one in him" likely refers to unity within the congregation; however, the prayer might also refer (in the spirit of Irenaeus and Athanasius) to the individual being transformed. In any case, the prayer that they "remain faithful in love and hope" certainly has to do with ontological transformation away from sinful humanity into union with Christ. All of this is quite different from blood sacrifice.

Quite some time before this prayer, the people affirm:

> Dying you destroyed our death,
> Rising you restored our life.
> Lord Jesus come in glory.

In this affirmation we have the theology of Athanasius pure and simple.

In the late twentieth century (after the Second Vatican Council) many Protestant denominations adjusted their Eucharistic liturgy to be consistent with the ancient liturgy of the Mass. This was largely because many who had not been able to understand Latin now saw that the Mass was not "strange," but reflected much about which there is broad agreement. Protestants realized that they could accept much of the liturgy even if they did not accept the theology of the "real presence." Thus what we have quoted, although highly selective, indicates possibilities for a broadly accepted interpretation of the Eucharist apart from the notion of sacrificial blood atonement.

Eucharist as Living Memory

Recall that our earliest witness to the Eucharist, Saint Paul, referred to it as a memorial. The Rev. Robin Meyers of Mayflower Church in Oklahoma City, in his Easter Sunday sermon on April 1, 2018, reminded the congregation that one way in which the Roman judicial system punished people was wiping away the memory of the crucified individual. Crucifixion was so shameful that families and friends would simply forget the crucified one. The early Christians defeated the Roman authorities by refusing to forget Jesus as well as by refusing to forget the martyrs of the first three centuries. It makes sense to take Jesus's instruction, "Do this in remembrance of me," as the theme for Eucharist.

A tricky question is "What, exactly, are we remembering?" If we were to survey twenty-first-century Christians in any typical congregation, we would find a variety of answers. Some remember the infant Jesus, "meek and mild." Some remember the one who taught the crowds, especially the Sermon on the Mount. Some remember the healing of physical ailments. Some remember how Jesus loved the wealthy young man (without remembering the serious instruction Jesus gave this young man). Some remember how Jesus washed everyone's feet at the Last Supper. Some remember Jesus saying, "Do this in remembrance of me." Some remember Jesus's death. Some remember the post-resurrection appearances. The point is that people remember different things about Jesus, and what we remember depends on our personal psychological makeup. This fact about us leads to difficulties when we insist that memories of Jesus other than ours are inauthentic.

One could argue that theological disputes are disputes over what we should remember about Jesus.

One influential memory movement has been "theological liberalism." In the nineteenth and twentieth centuries a movement called "theological liberalism" was prominent in the United States among what were called "mainline denominations." The essence of this movement was an emphasis on the moral/ethical teachings of Jesus with the claim that if we were to follow these teachings we would, indeed, construct the kingdom of God. This movement, in other words, said that we need to remember Jesus as a great moral teacher. In general, this movement ignored or denied the miraculous content of the Gospels and held great uncertainty about Easter and the resurrection. Needless to say, the doctrine of sacrificial blood atonement was not favored among proponents of that "liberal" movement.

We need to speak a word of caution: When we speak of theological liberalism we are not speaking about the ordinary political liberal-conservative debate. Within religion "liberalism" is found in many forms, and likewise there are many forms of "conservatism."

Theological liberalism lost favor after the Second World War. Some blamed theological liberalism for the rise of Nazism, not because it promoted or justified Nazism, but because liberal clergy and congregations were not thought to have fought against Nazism. One of the great opponents of theological liberalism, Karl Barth, became famous for speaking strongly against Nazism, and his outspoken opposition to the Nazis was commonly seen as an aspect of his outspoken opposition to liberalism. Things are not so simple. Regardless of whether Barth was right or wrong about liberalism, there is no logical connection between his opposition to Nazism and his opposition to liberalism.

Students in any introductory course in statistical analysis learn as a mantra: "Correlation is not causation." Students of logic learn about the "post hoc" fallacy, the fallacy of concluding that when one phenomenon comes after another, the first must have caused the second. These two principles share a great deal, and both apply here. Barth's two objections (against Nazism and against theological liberalism) are independent of one another.

What we can say is that theological liberalism ignored a large portion of the Gospels. In particular, half of the Gospel material speaks of the arrest, trial, execution and resurrection of Jesus Christ. We should not attempt to ignore Jesus's execution and the events surrounding it, including the resurrection. Independent of Karl Barth's complaint, we understand today that theological liberalism was inadequate theology.

There are some who simply identify theological liberalism with objection to the notion of sacrificial blood atonement. They say that anyone who objects to blood atonement as the explanation of the significance of Jesus's execution must be a theological liberal and must subscribe to all of the shortcomings of that movement. Not so. We can remember the Last Supper, the arrest, the trial, execution, burial, and resurrection apart from the notion of blood atonement. We can worship the risen Christ without advocating penal substitution or anything similar. The question for this book: how might we see the Gospel accounts of the last days of Jesus in terms of anything other than sacrificial blood atonement?

Extraordinary Deaths that Change Lives

In the last chapter we spoke extensively about ways to see the arrest, trial, and execution as inspirational example. Let's look briefly at three more examples:

Auschwitz and Athanasius

Jürgen Moltmann has written a dense monograph titled *The Crucified God: The Cross of Christ as the Foundation and Criticism of Christian Theology*.[5] This book, which has been called "a Christian theology after Auschwitz," wrestles with the contradiction between the ancient Greek notion of god as passionless and impotent and the Hebrew notion of God as passionately involved with humanity.[6] Moltmann quotes from Elie Wiesel's *Night* a horrifying incident from Auschwitz. The prisoners were assembled and three were hung in their presence. One, a teen, survived, struggling and suffering, for half an hour, and someone in the group asked, "Where is God?" Wiesel, in his own mind, answered that God is there, hanging from the rope. Moltmann responds, "Any other answer would be blasphemy."[7]

Moltmann notes that there is some truth in the platonic notion of a passionless god, because passionless objectivity provides God with freedom. (Moltmann ignores the fact that the god of *Timaeus* is impotent, making

---

5. Moltmann, *Crucified God*.
6. Moltmann, *Crucified God*; see the preface, ix–xii.
7. Moltmann, *Crucified God*, 273–74.

that god's freedom useless.) Moltmann then notes that God Almighty is more than passionless. God's passion, exemplified in the cross, is how God "takes upon himself the eternal death of the godless and the godforsaken, so that all the godless and the godforsaken can experience communion with him."[8]

Moltmann has restated the opaque metaphysical theology of Athanasius, interpreting it through twentieth-century existentialism.[9] As such it is a theology of Christ as example. This is not to say that the boy on the gallows had intended to be an example, but for the person attempting to make sense of the boy's suffering and death, the horrible event has led to contemplation of the event in terms of God suffering with humanity when God cannot change humanity. Prior to Moltmann, another German theologian, Emil Brunner, affirmed a similar understanding without elaborating it.[10] This is quite different from understanding the cross as sacrificial blood atonement.

Roman crucifixion was horrible. Examples that reflect on the crucifixion are also likely to be horrible.

Goho among the Head Hunters

In 1923, Owen Rutter, a British traveler, told the Royal Geographic Society about Goho. We have to ask about the historicity of this story, because "*goho*" also means "fate" or "karma" in Japanese. However, as Rutter told the story, Goho was a Chinese diplomat assigned to Taiwan (known to Owen as "Formosa"). In those days the island was divided among various warring tribes, and at least some of them were headhunters and cannibals. The human heads taken in battle were thought effective in guaranteeing

---

8. Moltmann, *Crucified God*, 276.

9. Moltmann, *Crucified God*, acknowledges Athnasius on page 88: "[God] took on transitory, mortal being, for that which is transitory and mortal to become intransitory and immortal." When Moltmann says this he provides an endnote citing Athanasius, *Apoll.* 54. See also Moltmann, *Crucified God*, 228.

10. Brunner, *Christian Doctrine of Creation and Redemption*, 295–96: "The Atoning death of His Son is a 'sign' that God . . . gives us a 'proof of his righteousness' [Rom 3:25] but this 'proof' is not—as with Anselm—something objective . . . it is effective as this 'proof of righteousness' only where man, in faith, *identifies himself with Christ the Crucified*, and understands that it is really he who ought to be condemned to death and executed as a criminal, and that Christ is suffering in his stead, and bearing the penalty which he had deserved" (italics added). Brunner never references Athanasius.

crop production. Goho attempted to convince them to stop hunting for human heads, and had success in convincing them to substitute animal heads. As it happened, a season came that was especially bad for crops, and the tribal elders came to Goho and explained that they needed to go after a suitable human head, just as they had done in former days. Finally Goho instructed them that if they went to a certain place at a certain time they would find someone whose head they could use. At the designated place the elders found a man wearing a veil or sack over his head. They killed him, took his head, removed the veil and found that it was Goho, himself.

The Geographic Society article concludes with Rutter saying, "It is said, and I believe it is a matter of official history, that these people were so horrified that they took an oath to stop head-hunting and human sacrifice, and they have kept that oath to this day. A high official of the Japanese government placed on Goho's tomb an inscription which, being rendered into English, means: 'A candle by consuming itself gives light to others.'"[11]

Anglican Monks in the Solomon Islands

A similar story is told by Thomas Breidenthal. In the late 1990s and early 2000s there was a longstanding deadly struggle between two groups native to a region in the Solomon Islands. As the groups tried to destroy each other, society in the region was "divided and paralyzed," until a 2002 disarmament agreement which almost settled things down, but not quite. The Melanesian Brotherhood, a community of Anglican monks, decided their Christian call was to mediate. They sent one of their number to the dissident group to try to convince them to disarm, but he did not return, so they sent six more emissaries. All seven were tortured and killed: surely they were working on behalf of the other side.

Ultimately everyone realized that the monks were not working on behalf of either side, and this realization led to an effective peace agreement "which the surviving brothers helped to broker." Today an icon of the Melanesian martyrs is displayed in Canterbury Cathedral. Breidenthal says, "And rightly so. Their blood literally made peace."[12]

---

11. Hogarth, "Formosa: Discussion," 285–87.

12. Breidenthal, "Blood of Abel," 124. For more information see: https://en.wikipedia.org/wiki/Melanesian_Brotherhood; also http://www.anglican.org.nz/content/download/4231/22681/file/Melanesian%20Martrys%20FAS.doc.

Icon remembering the Melanesian martyrs. Photo by Fwalz2, Aug. 3, 2008. Photographer has released the photo to public domain on Wikimedia Commons, https://commons.wikimedia.org/wiki/File:Icon_Cathedral_3.jpg#filehistory.

Breidenthal is speaking about atonement. He is seeking to explain to twenty-first-century readers how the execution of Jesus is atonement. He is working from the Old Testament book of Genesis and the New Testament book of Hebrews, particularly Hebrews 12:24: "[You have come] to Jesus, the mediator of a new covenant, and to the sprinkled blood that speaks a better word than the blood of Abel." He goes on to say, "There is no avoiding the notion that for the author of Hebrews the death of Jesus was a blood sacrifice. This passage forces us to determine whether any satisfactory proclamation of the Good News can omit this feature."

What, then, as Breidenthal reads Hebrews, does crucifixion-as-sacrifice mean? How, in light of Hebrews, does he relate the witness of the monks in the Solomon Islands to the execution of Jesus? Speaking of the monks, he went on to say, "This is a reminder to us of how Jesus's blood has made peace, speaking a better word than vengeance." Then, expanding the matter, he says that Hebrews teaches that reconciliation of humans with other humans is a category of atonement.

Not only does Breidenthal argue that reconciliation is a part of atonement, but he also denies the traditional notion that atonement should be identified with any individual Christian's salvation:

> An atonement between humankind and God, achieved through the blood sacrifice of Jesus . . . would leave Jesus alone as high priest before the mercy seat, offering his blood to God in atonement for the rest of us . . . is the traditional reading. But Hebrews suggests something very different. Jesus's death on the cross is not a blood sacrifice.[13] Rather, Jesus, as the "pioneer and perfecter" of our faith, leads us into the holy place . . .

Breidenthal relates this to the "great cloud of witnesses" in Hebrews 12:1. The "holy place" to which Jesus leads us is the site where these witnesses are gathered. Specifically he cites Hebrews 12:22–24, which speaks of the assembly of angels, the firstborn, and the spirits of the righteous, along with Jesus. Note that Jesus is not alone in this place. Hebrews 12:24 says that this heavenly holy assembly place is where we find the sprinkled blood of Jesus, the atoning blood. But his point is that this is the place of reconciliation. Members of the "cloud of witnesses" have been reconciled to one another, and that's why they can come together in one holy place. The crucifixion of Jesus brings brothers and sisters together. It is, says Breidenthal, "an atonement between human and human, set in motion by the Incarnation, brought to perfection on the cross (even if this were not the only possible means of perfection) and vindicated in the resurrection."[14]

What, then, does "atonement with God" look like to Breidenthal? It does not look like ancient blood sacrifice that somehow pleases God or that makes God pay attention to our problems. It does not look like a payment of ransom to the devil. It does not look like God Almighty appearing in the robes of an appellate court judge who limits his review to the structure of the law. It also does not look like the "mimetic violence" discussed by followers of René Girard. It looks to me like Breidenthal is illustrating the "inspirational example":

---

13. Breidenthal's article is clearly homiletical, not an academic lecture. He evidently uses two different senses of the term "blood sacrifice" or "sacrifice" without clarifying the distinction. His use of "blood sacrifice" at this point seems to be a reference to the traditional, ancient understanding of temple sacrifice, and he seems to be relying more on its connotation than its denotation.

14. Breidenthal, "Blood of Abel." All of this is found on page 125.

> His blood is not primarily about blood sacrifice or mimetic violence. . . . the shedding of blood must be about witness—the ultimate refusal to accede to any social order grounded in collusion and violence. But such shedding of blood has real consequences, arising out of the very principles that govern the dynamics of atonement. Jesus' death on the cross, without recrimination or call for redress, broadcasts the power of his forgiveness in every direction, and belies all the forces that would deny the economy of mercy and grace, which he both preached and embodied.[15]

Breidenthal's story of the Anglican monks should spark a memory in the reader. Jesus told a story about a landowner sending servants to collect rent, but one after another they were beaten up. Finally the landowner sent his son, who was killed (Mark 12:1–12; Matt 21:33–41; Luke 20:9–19). The Gospels tell us that Jesus told this story as a warning. Certainly in many cases good people are injured and killed with no good result. Even so, there are many cases where injury and death ultimately lead to repentance and atonement on a human level . . . and we judge that God is at work in the process, so atonement between humanity and God is also at work in these cases.

When Jesus affirms that Eucharistic wine is his blood and says that we should drink it in his memory, it makes sense in the twenty-first century to remember all of the following: (a) his teaching about forgiveness, etc., (b) the consistent theme of his miracles: that he wants health and welfare for all, and (c) his resurrection as "the first fruits of those who have fallen asleep": earthly life is the beginning, not the end.

Another Eighteenth-Century Hymn

We began this book by looking at hymns (or spiritual songs—we will not force a distinction between these terms), so it seems appropriate to look at hymns again. There are many hymns that don't force the singer to espouse sacrificial blood atonement. In 1910, Henry Sloane Coffin and Ambrose White Vernon edited an intentionally liberal hymnal, *Hymns of the Kingdom of God*, that attempted, among other things, to avoid hymns that advocated belief in sacrificial blood atonement. They were not entirely

---

15. Breidenthal, "Blood of Abel," 124.

successful, but they demonstrated that Christians have options. Christians don't have to sing songs about blood atonement.[16]

There is a particularly interesting story that relates to John Wesley and Isaac Watts, both of whom we cited in the first chapter as strong eighteenth-century proponents of the notion of sacrificial blood atonement. One of the hymns by Watts, to which Wesley made additions, is "I'll Praise my Maker while I've Breath." We are told that

> John Wesley gave out this hymn just before preaching for the last time in City Road Chapel, Tuesday evening, February 22, 1791. The following Monday afternoon, though very ill, he amazed the friends at his bedside by singing the hymn throughout in a strong voice. The next night, his biographer, Tyermann, tells us, he tried scores of times to repeat the hymn, but could only say I'll praise— I'll praise—. And with praise for his Maker on his lips and in his heart he passed to that life where "immortality endures."[17]

Given this story, the hymn is worth a careful examination:

> I'll praise my maker while I've breath,
> And when my voice is lost in death,
> Praise shall employ my nobler powers;
> My days of praise shall ne'er be past,
> While life, and thought, and being last,
> Or immortality endures.

This first stanza is a vow combined with a hope: a hope that praise will be possible after our earthly death.

> Why should I make a man my trust?
> Princes must die and turn to dust;
> Vain is the help of flesh and blood:
> Their breath departs, their pomp, and power,
> And thoughts, all vanish in an hour,
> Nor can they make their promise good.

---

16. Coffin and Vernon, *Hymns of the Kingdom of God*. In their words, hymns "which express a normal and healthy spiritual experience, contain no divisive theology, and are specifically Christian in religion." Unfortunately they did not totally achieve their goal. As one example of editorial failure, hymn no. 65, "My Lord, My Master, at Thy Feet Adoring," is especially inappropriate. It not only affirms the necessity of the blood atonement, but it also blames the Jews for the Roman execution of Jesus.

17. Price, *One Hundred and One Hymn Stories*, 70.

This stanza is not sung today, even though its wisdom remains true.

> Happy the man whose hopes rely
> On Israel's God: He made the sky,
> And earth, and seas, with all their train:
> His truth forever stands secure;
> He saves th' oppressed, He feeds the poor,
> And none shall find His promise vain.

The writer of Ecclesiastes assures us that "all is vanity," and "vain" means "worthless" or "empty." The hymn assures us that God's promise is not worthless. We know that because of what God has already done, both in creation and in speaking on behalf of the oppressed and poverty stricken. We cannot create as God creates, but we can imitate God in helping the oppressed and the poor.

> The Lord has eyes to give the blind;
> The Lord supports the sinking mind;
> He sends the laboring conscience peace;
> He helps the stranger in distress,
> The widow, and the fatherless,
> And grants the prisoner sweet release.

Again, God has given us a model to follow. We may not be able to heal blindness, and we struggle with mental illness and dementia (the "sinking" or "fainting" mind), but we can certainly follow God in helping the stranger, the widow, the orphan, the prisoners, along with the spiritually blind who forget their creator.

> He loves His saints, He knows them well,
> But turns the wicked down to hell;
> Thy God, O Zion! ever reigns:
> Let every tongue, let every age,
> In this exalted work engage;
> Praise Him in everlasting strains.

Like the second stanza, this stanza is no longer sung, but it is worth contemplation even by those who have theological disagreement with it.

> I'll praise Him while He lends me breath,
> And when my voice is lost in death,

> Praise shall employ my nobler powers;
> My days of praise shall ne'er be past,
> While life, and thought, and being last,
> Or immortality endures.

Finally, the hymn concludes with a repeat of the vow and hope expressed in the first stanza.

Notice that this hymn shows no concern for blood atonement. Salvation is for those who are not "wicked." No payment to God is required to receive the immortality that endures. This is a hymn about the essence of Christianity being seen in following the teaching and example of Jesus: help the oppressed, the poor, the stranger, the widow, the orphan, and even the prisoner.

Appendix I

Thirty Pieces of Silver in Our World

JESUS might or might not have had one traditional sacrificial attribute: depending on how one looks at it, he might have been "expensive." Actually, in terms of secular economy, he was less expensive than a slave. Judas was paid thirty pieces of silver to betray Jesus (Matt 26:15) and thirty pieces of silver was the penalty required by the Torah assessed against the owner of an ox that gores a slave. In addition, the ox was to be stoned (Exod 21:32). Since the ox is not bled out, apparently no one was to eat the meat, so the animal was a total loss in addition to the money forfeited. Jesus was also less expensive than a young woman. According to the Torah, if a man was convicted of raping a virgin, he was required to pay fifty shekels to the woman's father, and was also required to marry her with no possibility of divorce (Deut 22:28–29).

How much was thirty pieces of silver? Let's think about slavery in nineteenth-century United States of America. Williamson and Cain, determined that the purchase price for a healthy male slave, ages twenty to forty, in 1850 Louisiana, translated into 2016 US dollars, would be around $23,000. However the price varied greatly. Fifty years earlier, the price (in 2016 dollars) was around $5,000. Their raw data compares well with the raw data for the purchase price of slaves in South Carolina provided by Mancall, Rosenbloom, and Weiss. Thus the thirty-pieces-of-silver purchase price of a slave can be compared to some figure between $5,000 and $23,000.[1]

Since we've started this line of financial speculation, let's carry it one step further to see if we have a good comparison. If the slave owner had not purchased a slave, but had hired someone to do the slave's work, how much would it have cost?

---

1. Williamson and Cain, "Measuring Slavery"; Mancall et al., "Slave Prices."

APPENDIX I

We start on this question by asking about the value of one piece of silver in terms of 2016 US dollars. For the sake of argument, pick a number for the purchase price of a slave between $5,000 and $23,000. Again, for the sake of argument, let's consider $10,000. Divide thirty into $10,000, and we find that one piece of silver should be worth approximately $300 to $350. (It would actually be $333.33, but remember that our $10,000 figure is speculative, not a precise number.) The "piece of silver" was probably a Tyrian shekel, known for its purity. This was worth about four Roman obles, and an ordinary worker earned one or two obles per day. Let's assume the worker earns one oble, and let's assume the worker gets paid for 300 days per year. (Romans didn't have weekends off, but they had lots of religious holidays.) Our speculative worker would earn 300 obles per year, or seventy-five pieces of silver. 75 x $300 = 22,500, which was close to what an unskilled worker would be paid in the United States in 2016. A more highly skilled worker would receive two obles per day, and using the same assumptions, 150 x $300 = $45,000 per year. Again, this is not an unreasonable figure. A slave (for $5,000 to $23,000) in most cases cost less than wages paid to a hired worker.

Such financial reasoning is "slippery" because the economic base today is nothing like it was two thousand years ago, yet it is very interesting that we come up with numbers that are not wildly unrealistic when we engage in such speculation. We do get a reasonable sense of the value of thirty pieces of silver, and we see that slave ownership made economic sense, even considering that the owner was responsible for food and other life necessities for the slave. (We also find thirty pieces of silver referred to in relation to wages in Zechariah 11:12. It was apparently not a good wage.)[2]

Should we be worried about a disparity between economic realities when Exodus was written and when Jesus lived? In answering this question we need to remember that the Torah was still law in the first century. The rabbis would have assessed the same fines for the same infractions and not taken into account any possible change in monetary value.

At thirty pieces of silver, Jesus was not expensive. A good sacrifice should be expensive, and Jesus was less expensive than a slave killed by an ox as well as less expensive than a virgin young woman. His price might

---

2. For what it's worth, John Wesley, in 1754, calculated the value of thirty pieces of silver and determined that it worked out to three pounds, fifteen shillings of British silver. (Wesley, *Notes on the New Testament*, 88.) The point of observing Wesley's curiosity about this matter is to show that the economics around thirty pieces of silver has been interesting to many people.

purchase an inexpensive automobile in 2016. In what way would he be seen as an "expensive" sacrifice? There is only one measure that makes him "expensive." He was the son of God, and one's own child is always of surpassing value. The reasoning is that, even though his execution met none of the ordinary criteria for a sacrifice, God Almighty must have accepted him as a sacrifice because, in God's eyes, Jesus was more costly than any other possible sacrifice. Even today, that is the only reason advocates of sacrificial blood atonement can give for Jesus being an appropriate sacrifice. No person is as important to God as God's incarnate Son. (See the parable of the son going to the vineyard and being murdered: Mark 12:1–11 = Matt 21:33–43 = Luke 20:9–18.)

Appendix II

Love as Emotion

IN popular imagination we often think of "emotion" as an extreme reaction to a stimulus, and it is usually a negative reaction such as rage or terror. Robert Plutchek has suggested that, at their extreme, all emotions fuse into a generalized response. In artistic terms, Edvard Munch's 1893 painting "The Scream" might exemplify this generalized response. This is what many would call the "fight or flight" reaction that is independent of rational cognition.[1]

It is worth recognizing (a) that all emotions have manifestations that are not extreme, (b) there are emotions that don't seem to have any extreme manifestation, and (c) there certainly are positive emotions.

We have the vocabulary to speak of gradations of certain emotions: unease → fear → terror; irritation → upset → anger → rage. We are most sensitive to the extreme manifestations, but everyone recognizes (at least within themselves) the early, less extreme manifestations. People can more easily mask these less extreme manifestations than the extreme ones, so it is more difficult to recognize that someone is irritated than that they are in a state of rage, but irritation is truly an emotional response.

Not all emotions are graded. Contempt is a negative emotion which seems to have limited gradation. At any rate, we do not have a common vocabulary that allows us to speak about gradations of contempt.

It seems that the positive emotions are less graded than the negative emotions, or our vocabulary for positive emotional gradations is less well-developed than for negative emotions. Perhaps this is because the consequences of not recognizing negative emotional escalation can be very

---

1. Plutchik, "Circumplex As a General Model"; Plutchik, "Nature of Emotions," fig. 6. See also Lambert, "Plutchik Emotion Circumplex."

serious, even leading to deadly conflict. Positive emotional escalation is not serious in the same way. Because we lack the extensive vocabulary we are less likely to recognize positive emotion than negative emotion.

Ancient depiction of facial expression of emotion. These four pictures illustrate the thesis that the ancients were willing to depict emotion in the faces of humans and other creatures, but not in deities. Clockwise from upper left: Satyr of Vienne, second century, CE (Louvre Ma528); Woman with ivy in her hair. We might guess that she was a devotee of Dionysus. Her dilated pupils evince arousal of some sort. c. 300 BCE (British Museum GR1859.2-16.2, Terracotta D196); Zeus on Olympus. He is in the act of throwing a thunderbolt, but shows no emotion. c. 450 BCE (Louvre Me 33); Persian warrior in terror. c. 400 BCE (British Museum GR1849.6-20.12, Vase E791).

APPENDIX II

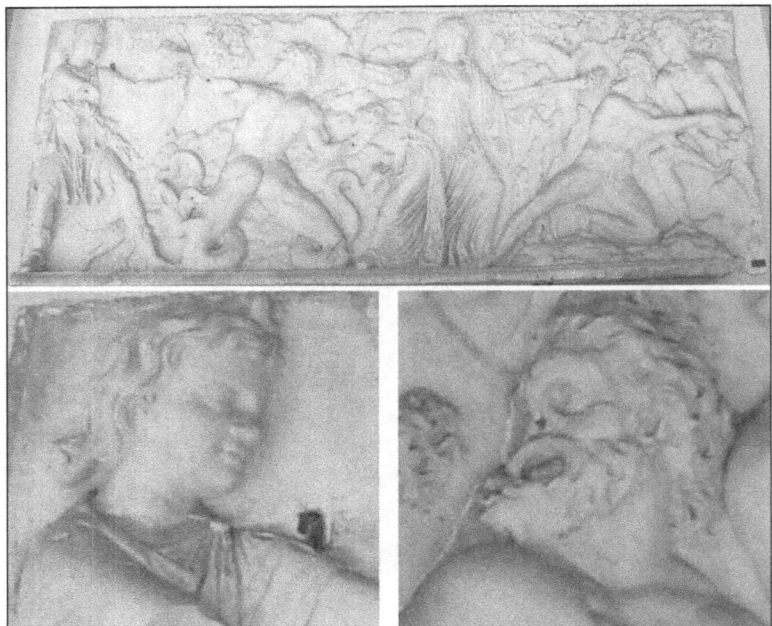

Case study of ancient emotional depiction. This fragment of a frieze from second-century-CE Rome depicts the primordial battle between the gods and the titans. Here we see Artemis/Diana and her mother Leto/Latona vanquishing titans. Even though the frieze is not in perfect condition, it shows us that the divine goddesses show no emotion, even though they are fighting for their very lives. In contrast, the despised titans (who were cast to the bottom of the pit of Tartarus) show great fear. Vatican Museums.

Are there positive emotions? Certainly. A major way of recognizing emotional response in others is via facial expression, something that psychologists have studied seriously for at least a century and a half.[2] Long before the age of modern psychological science the ancients understood the importance of facial expression and were expert at sculpting faces that displayed both negative and positive emotions such as fear, joy, and ecstasy. Apart from the implicit depiction of emotion by sculptors, there were also explicit ancient discussions of facial expression of emotion. As Cicero said, "everything depends on the face."[3]

2. Darwin, *Expression of the Emotions*.
3. Cicero, *De or.* 3.221, quoted at length in Fögen, "*Sermo corporis*," 29. See also note 37 on that page with another citation to Cicero and a quotation from Quintilian.

One such positive emotion is "love," however framed. It is well-known that, in New Testament times and beyond, Greek vocabulary labeled three concepts that English vocabulary groups under one term: "love." Of these three, "*eros*" is graded from "attraction" to "passion." The other two, brotherly or family love (*philia*) and divine love (*agape*), don't have a commonly recognized vocabulary of gradation. Are they emotions?

Think about grief. Everyone recognizes that grief is emotional response to loss. We don't have a popular vocabulary for the gradations of grief, but everyone recognizes that there are gradations. Professional psychologists use a variety of (sometimes complex) terms to label gradations of grief. We experience grief when we lose a bit of money from our wallet, but it is a low level of grief. We experience extreme or profound grief when we lose a spouse, especially when the loss is from death and the marriage has been long.

Love and grief are related. Consider the love of one for another in a marriage that has lasted for many years. There are times in the marriage when the partners seem to take each other for granted, and that is why some assert that love is a rational decision, not an emotion. However, human experience from ancient times until now shows that when one partner is lost, the other partner grieves profoundly. If grief is an emotion, so is love.

At this point, we need to recognize the limitations of our discussion. A full discussion would require a book. Cairns has presented a useful analysis of the issues and problems related to discussion of emotion.[4] However I believe what I have just presented serves our purposes well. Sokolon provides a good abstract statement that encompasses the approach in this essay: "An understanding of emotion based on Aristotle's theory emphasizes emotions as innate, physiological and psychological processes that assess environmental and cultural circumstances and are somewhat plastic in response to individual circumstances."[5]

Now we must ask about the theological implications of what we have said. There are two essential questions: (a) is God subject to emotional response, and (b) is divine love (*agape*) an emotional response?

As we have seen, Plato did not allow God to display emotion. What about the Hebrew understanding of God?

---

4. Cairns, "Look Both Ways."
5. Sokolon, *Political Emotions*, abstract.

We will take for granted that words such as "wrath" (used in relation to God throughout the Old and New Testaments) make reference to emotion. Thus we will take for granted that God, as understood in the Old and New Testaments, can display emotion.

An objection to this might be that what humans see as emotion might be rationally controlled from God's perspective. That is, God has rational control over divine emotion, just as humans can sometimes use their rational mind to overcome an emotional response. To this we can say, if God controls divine emotion, it is still emotion, just as humans experience emotional response even when they overcome it through rational thought.

In theology there is a danger in anthropomorphizing God, but any discussion of God's rationality inevitably gets us involved in anthropomorphizing. Thus, if we can speak of God's rationality, we can also speak of God's emotion.

If we assent that God is sometimes manifested in terms of emotion, we can ask if the divine love (*agape*) that defines God (1 John 4:8, etc.) is emotion. I have discussed this question with several theologically alert individuals, and some deny that God's love is emotional. Their contention is that love is a decision, love is therefore rational. We need not think of God as being subject to nonrational emotion.

Consider as Isaiah 63:9, speaking of God's relation to the people of Israel: "In all their distress he too was distressed" (NIV) or "In all their affliction he was afflicted" (KJV). This distress or affliction is emotional. The Bible consistently depicts God Almighty as vulnerable, even though this same God is creator and judge. The emotion of *agape* is the basis of vulnerability. The only one who is invulnerable is the one who has no commitments.

Consider also 1 Corinthians 13 in homiletical terms. From a human point of view, *agape* is given its Christian definition in 1 Corinthians 13. Verse 5 speaks in negative terms, saying that *agape* is not irritable or resentful. Verse 6 speaks of rejoicing. Verses 8 and 9 contrast *agape* with knowledge and prophecies. "Irritation," "resentfulness," and "rejoicing" seem to be words associated with emotions. *Agape*, as contrasted to an emotion, would be another emotion. "Knowledge" and "prophecies" are not emotions. What, then, is a cognitive contrast with these two cognitions? Verse 9 speaks of the imperfection or limitation of "knowledge" and "prophecies," so we are looking for a positive contrast. Verse 9 says that *agape* is the contrast, but for our discussion we need a synonym for *agape* that is clearly cognitive. I know of none, so it seems to make more sense to contrast *agape* as an emotion with "knowledge" and "prophecies," even though these are cognitive. Emotion and cognition are related because both are aspects of mind.

We can continue our homiletical exploration of *agape* by noting the tears of Jesus, the Son of God. In Luke 19:41 we find that Jesus wept because he recognized the disastrous future of Jerusalem and understood that the city could change in such a way as to avoid the disaster. (His emotion and cognition were related.) Here we see Jesus in grief that must reflect the grief of God Almighty. As we have said, we can recognize love through grief. John 11:35 tells us that Jesus wept when confronted by the death of his good friend, Lazarus. This could not have been anything other than an expression of grief.

Certainly emotion and rationality work together. As Sokolon said, emotions are "somewhat plastic in response to individual circumstances." In a long-term relationship the love can sometimes become thin, so that the relationship depends on rational decision, but in the end, love is emotional. If God is characterized by love, God is characterized emotionally. God's love must be in addition to or beyond rationality.

Appendix III

A List of Comparisons between Hercules and Christ

I HAVE spent a great deal of time in archaeological museums, paying close attention to items from several centuries before and after Jesus. I have become more and more amazed at the number of votives (of many kinds) to Hercules or Herakles. In our own popular culture Hercules is something of a buffoon, and in Greek/Roman mythology Hercules is simply a demented thug who murders his family and does many other evil things. Would anyone really worship him as a god?

In fact, for whatever reason, they would and did worship him. Furthermore, in the first Christian centuries ordinary people could examine the stories of Hercules and Jesus in order to convince themselves that Hercules was just as good a savior as Jesus. What follows is, without much elaboration, a set of comparisons ordinary pagans *could have made* between Hercules and Jesus.

We need to remember that, unlike in our day, religious conversation was common in the Roman world. When Christians and pagans engaged in conversation, Hercules would become a topic. No one is likely to have invoked all of these points in such conversation, but the points of comparison were available.

1. Zeus fathered Hercules through Alcmene when her husband was on a trip. When her husband discovered her pregnancy, he attempted to immolate her, but Zeus sent a rainstorm to put out the fire. God Almighty fathered Jesus through Mary who was betrothed to Joseph. When Joseph discovered her pregnancy he thought about rejecting her, but an angel convinced Joseph to stay with Mary. In both cases the true father was a deity, and in both cases the mother almost suffered severe punishment.

A LIST OF COMPARISONS BETWEEN HERCULES AND CHRIST

2. Mythology is often not consistent. There is also a story that when Alcmene's husband returned he fathered another child in her, so that Hercules was a twin. (The twin's name was Iphicles.) There was a legend among Christians (especially among gnostics) that the Thomas of the Gospels ("doubting Thomas") was the twin of Jesus.

3. When Hercules was an infant, someone (maybe Zeus's wife, Hera) put snakes in his bed, attempting to kill him. When Jesus was an infant, Herod attempted to kill him.

4. The seer, Tiresias, gave the parents magic to protect young Hercules. The angel of the Lord led the parents of Jesus to Egypt where he would be under God's protection.

5. Infant Hercules killed the snakes, a demonstration of who he really was. Folklore also gave Jesus a "demonstration" story. A document called "The Gospel of Thomas" (not the well-known collection of teachings) tells about Jesus and his young friends making mud pies, except that precocious Jesus was making clay sparrows instead of mud pies. An adult chastised them for doing "work" on the Sabbath, so Jesus blew on his clay sparrows and they flew away chirping, thus demonstrating who he really was.

6. The adolescent Hercules was met at a crossroad by two women, each of whom wanted to accompany him. One called herself Eudaimonia ("happiness") and the other called herself Arete ("virtue"). Arete offered him a hard road of effort, while Eudaimonia an easy road of endless pleasure. On being questioned, Eudaimonia admitted that many called her Kakia ("vice"). Hercules is said to have considered carefully and chosen Arete as his companion. (Given his subsequent behavior, we have to question this story, but the story stands.) The adolescent Jesus went to Jerusalem to visit the temple and became engaged in a three-day conversation with the temple priests. Thus we know that he was naturally wise. A pagan could have seen these two stories of early discernment as being similar.

7. Hercules found himself in Egypt where he entered battle with a group of Egyptian priests. One vase painting of this story emphasizes the circumcision of the priests in contrast with the more powerful uncircumcised Hercules. Circumcision was not an issue for Jesus, but it was for Saint Paul, who argued that Christians should not be circumcised.

APPENDIX III

Paul was not arguing that circumcision had anything to do with personal power, but pagans might have seen a connection.

8. Hercules, while travelling through Italy, encountered a group of women celebrating a women's religious festival. He asked for a drink of water, and, on religious grounds, they refused him. Hercules retaliated by decreeing that no woman would ever be permitted to swear in his name. Jesus likewise asked for a drink of water, and, on religious grounds, the Samaritan woman of Sychar refused him. Jesus did not curse the woman or her city, but turned the refusal into an opportunity for teaching.

9. In his drama, *Alcastes*, Euripides tells about a family in which a wife has agreed to suffer death in her husband's place. About that time, Hercules visits them and is welcomed, but he detects that there is sadness in the household. When he discovers the source of the sadness, he pursues Death, who has just taken the wife, and wrestles Death until the woman is released. The followers of Jesus celebrated his ability to revive the dead: the daughter of Jarius, the son of the widow at Nain, and Lazarus.

10. Among the famous twelve labors, Hercules was required to capture Cerberus, the three-headed watchdog of Hades. He went down to Hades and arranged to borrow the dog. While he was there, he found Theseus, the great hero of Athens, tied to a chair, released him and brought him back. (He was unable to release Theseus's companion, Peleus.) Christian tradition holds that between Jesus's crucifixion and resurrection, he visited the underworld, broke down the gates of hell, and freed many, many people. Even though Hercules freed only one, many could see a comparison here between Hercules and Jesus.

11. Hercules was killed in a fire and almost immediately escorted to Mount Olympus where he became a god. Christians claimed that Jesus had always been equivalent to God, so his ascension to heaven was different from pagan apotheosis, but pagans would have seen this as a point calling for serious discussion.

12. The ancient mythologist Apollodorus tells us that when Hercules was cremated, a cloud settled beneath him and raised him to heaven. This is similar to what is described in Acts 1:9, "he was lifted up, and a cloud took him out of their sight."

Appendix IV

Blood Atonement Is Not Confirmed by Chains of Biblical References

WE turn to some relatively recent arguments defending the notion of sacrificial blood atonement. John MacArthur gives us chains of biblical references. One such chain is: 2 Corinthians 5:21 → Isaiah 53 → Daniel 9:24–27 → Zechariah 13:1, 7 → John 1:29, 36 → John 11:50–51 → Acts 4:10 → Romans 3:25 → Romans 5:8–11 → Galatians 1:4 → 1 Thessalonians 1:10 → 1 Timothy 2:5–6 → 1 Peter 1:11, 20 → 1 John 2:2 → 1 John 4:10 → Revelation 13:8.[1]

First a general comment and then we will look at them in sequence. Although most of these are from the writings of Saint Paul, we also find Old Testament prophets, Johannine literature, and a reference to Saint Peter. The clear assumption is that all of these biblical authors share one view of salvation. Furthermore, chronology makes no difference: we can easily move from the first century CE back to the eighth century BCE, etc. Without speaking specifically of these references, we should note that the Bible includes a variety of views. In the Old Testament there is a clear difference of opinion between Ezra and Ruth about God's will. In the New Testament, Luther found a clear difference of opinion between Galatians and James. Thus we need to examine any mixture of references carefully.

2 Corinthians 5:21—This must be considered in the context of Paul's overall teaching that the "flesh" is sinful. If "flesh" is sinful, then Christ becoming incarnate means that Christ inevitably encountered sin. Note that this is the beginning of MacArthur's argument.

---

1. MacArthur, *MacArthur Bible Handbook*, 385.

APPENDIX IV

Isaiah 53—This is part of the fourth "servant song," which Christians from earliest times have seen as a prediction of the coming of Christ. It says: "He was wounded for our transgressions . . . it was the will of the Lord to bruise him . . . he makes of himself an offering for sin . . ." (Isa 53:5, 10). We don't know who Isaiah used as a model or inspiration for this great poem. Perhaps it was strictly from divine revelation, or perhaps Isaiah knew someone who was righteous and suffered unjustly. No matter why Isaiah wrote it, it is a lens through which Jesus can be viewed. Keep in mind, however, that it is poetry, not a literal statement.

Daniel 9:24–27[2]—In chapter 9, Daniel offers a prayer of confession for the sins of his people and reflects on the Babylonian exile that resulted from these sins. Then the angel Gabriel comes to him and offers a vision of the future which includes: "an anointed one shall be cut off, and shall have nothing; and the people of the prince who is to come shall destroy the city and the sanctuary" (Dan 9:26). After the Jerusalem temple was destroyed in 70 CE, it became possible to see Daniel 9:26 as predicting that destruction. The "anointed one" in this verse might be Jesus or any of a number of people who claimed to be the messiah in those years. This can be read in terms of the work of Christ, although it is not necessarily a personal blood sacrifice such as death on the cross. In any case, being "cut off" is simply evidence of injustice, and has nothing to do with sacrifice or atonement. MacArthur wants it to follow logically from Isaiah 53:10, but it doesn't.

Zechariah 13:1—Chapters 12, 13 and 14 form a unit of prophecy about the reinstitution of a righteous Jerusalem. Zechariah 14 suggests that this prophecy is eschatological rather than within history. When Zechariah 12:10 refers to God being "pierced," the context makes it seem that the "piercing" is a metaphor for the unrighteous worship of idols. We can see how some Christians would understand Zechariah 13:1 poetically as a reference to Christ: "a fountain shall be opened." However, when we consider 13:1 in relation to 14:8, which is part of the same prophetic monologue, we see that the "fountain" is a fountain of water inside the heavenly Jerusalem. This is very similar to the vision of heavenly Jerusalem in Revelation 22:1–2.

Zechariah 13:7—This relates to a shepherd who is probably a prophet. As we have said, Ezekiel 34 is also relevant at this point. In Ezekiel's vision, God Almighty decides to assume the role of shepherd since the human

---

2. Scholars have concluded that the Book of Daniel was written perhaps a hundred years before the birth of Jesus, not during the Babylonian exile, but this conclusion is not relevant to our discussion.

BLOOD ATONEMENT NOT CONFIRMED BY BIBLICAL REFERENCES

shepherds God has appointed have not fulfilled their commitment. In Zechariah 13:7, the wrath of God Almighty is exercised against the shepherd, so this seems an odd text to apply to a discussion of atonement.

John 1:29, 36—In these verses John the Baptist testifies that Jesus is the "lamb of God who takes away the sins of the world." This is evidently a metaphorical reference to the Passover lamb, but that lamb was not sacrificed for sin. The Baptist's reference is obscure. Is it or is it not a prediction of Jesus's death? In any case, this has nothing to do with Zechariah 13. The chain is definitely broken here.

John 11:50–51—This is the ironic statement by Caiaphas that we discussed in chapter 7. John 11:51–52 suggests God's purpose in allowing the death of Jesus was either to gather together the Jews, or to gather together all the people of the world. In either case, this is atonement only in the exemplary sense.

Acts 4:10—Peter is being questioned by Caiaphas about a healing he has performed, and he tells Caiaphas and his associates the healing happened through the name of Jesus, who was raised from death, the very man Caiaphas talked about in John 11:50. The point is that even the name of Jesus is powerful. This has nothing to do with sacrifice or atonement.

Romans 3:25—"Since all have sinned and fall short of the glory of God, they are now justified by his grace as a gift, through the redemption that is in Christ Jesus, whom God put forward as a sacrifice of atonement by his blood" (Rom 3:23–25). This passage is one of Paul's clearest statements of his belief in sacrificial blood atonement. We have an extended discussion of it in chapters 7 and 8.

Romans 5:8–11—This continues Paul's exposition of sacrificial blood atonement.

Galatians 1:4—"The Lord Jesus Christ, who gave himself for our sins to set us free from the present evil age, according to the will of our God and Father" (Galatians 1:3–4). Once again, as Paul begins this letter, he affirms his belief in sacrificial blood atonement.

1 Thessalonians 1:10—This is a statement about the second coming of Christ (apparently a major concern for Christians in Macedonia; see 4:16–17), and Paul appends an affirmation that Christ can save us from the terrible events to come as the world ends. Even though we have seen that Paul sincerely believes in the notion that Jesus sacrificed himself as atonement, this passage has nothing to do with that belief. The "theology of the cross" didn't fit the purpose of this particular letter.

1 Timothy 2:5–6—This passage affirms that Jesus gave himself as a "ransom." It is clearly consistent with Paul's belief in sacrificial blood atonement, even though scholars debate whether Paul or someone else wrote this letter to Timothy. This is apparently a quotation from a hymn that follows (or implies) the "exalted—humiliated—exalted" theme of all the early Christian hymns we know about. Even if Paul didn't write this letter, he may have written the hymn. The hymn also could have been written earlier. In any case, this expression of sacrificial blood atonement is probably earlier than this letter to Timothy.

1 Peter 1:11, 20—This passage, when seen in the context of verses 3–21, is specifically referenced to enduring martyrdom, noting that Jesus suffered so you should endure suffering. Jesus came to glory, so you will come to glory. As they relate to the suffering and glorification of Christ (a theme of John's Gospel), these two verses have nothing to do with sacrifice or atonement. There is one point of contact with the blood atonement: "you were ransomed . . . with the precious blood of Christ, like that of a lamb" (vv. 18–19). If we carry over from Paul the presumption that Peter (or whoever wrote this letter) also believes firmly in the sacrificial blood atonement, then we can fit this passage into that belief, but we don't have evidence that Peter and Paul agreed on this matter.

1 John 2:2—"We have an advocate with the Father, Jesus Christ the righteous; and he is the atoning sacrifice for our sins, and not for ours only but also for the sins of the whole world" (1 John 2:1–2). As we saw in chapter 7, this is a clear statement of belief in sacrificial blood atonement. Scholars debate who wrote this letter.

1 John 4:10—God sent Christ (his Son) as an atoning sacrifice for our sins. This is consistent with 1 John 2:2.

Rev 13:8—This is a reference to the Lamb that was slain. As with the Baptist's pronouncement in John 1:29 and 36, this has nothing to do with sacrifice or atonement.

We conclude that this list of references does not constitute an argument in favor of sacrificial blood atonement. This list does not show that the Bible affirms the theological necessity for believing in the sacrificial blood atonement. Instead we have the affirmations of Saint Paul (which we expected), the First Epistle to Timothy (which we have not looked at), and the First Epistle of John (which we have looked at briefly). As far as the other references are concerned, if one already accepts the theological necessity of sacrificial blood atonement, then that person can read that notion into them, but they don't support the notion by themselves. Summary of

BLOOD ATONEMENT NOT CONFIRMED BY BIBLICAL REFERENCES

this chain: Romans 3:25; Galatians 1:4; 1 Timothy 2:5-6; 1 Peter 1:18-19; 1 John 2:2; and 1 John 4:10 are the references that specifically teach that Jesus was sacrificed as an atonement for our sin. Regarding OT prophecy, Isaiah 53 comes closest to a prophecy of an atoning messiah.

Here are some other references MacArthur cites in other chains defending sacrificial blood atonement: John 15:13; Acts 4:12; Romans 8:2; Titus 2:14; Hebrews 10:14; 1 Peter 3:18.[3]

John 15:13 is the "no greater love" text. It could equally relate to the Roman practice of *devotio*. (Saint Augustine recognizes that many in Roman history were willing to lay down their lives for their "friends."[4]) The context of John 15 suggests that Jesus is encouraging the disciples to active love, to the level of martyrdom if necessary. There is no blood atonement here.

Acts 4:12 says "there is salvation in no one else." The mechanism of salvation is not mentioned. Yes, Jesus was crucified and raised (v. 10) but it is not necessarily a blood sacrifice. In ancient pagan belief, others who had died were claimed as saviors, especially Hercules. Acts 4:12 differentiates between Christ and Hercules, an issue we have taken up in Appendix III.

Romans 8:2 has nothing to do with sacrifice.

Titus 2:14—"He it is who gave himself for us that he might redeem us from all iniquity and purify for himself a people of his own." This could also reference *devotio*.

Hebrews 10:11-14 is clearly blood atonement, a special theme of Hebrews, as we have seen.

1 Peter 3:18—"Christ suffered for sins." This is blood atonement.

Conclusion: Hebrews 10:11-14 and 1 Peter 3:18 are clearly teaching blood atonement.

Does the New Testament require us to affirm the notion of sacrificial blood atonement? The question does not yield a simple "yes" or "no." Not even a "maybe." The answer is that (a) some biblical passages support the blood atonement, (b) some passages support other interpretations of the crucifixion, (c) some of the passages often cited in support of the blood atonement are not really clear, and (d) some of the passages often cited in support of blood atonement simply do not support it. Just as we gave a brief overview of hymns, so we can only give a brief overview of the biblical evidence. A full biblical study would require a very long book.

---

3. MacArthur, *MacArthur Bible Handbook*, 453.
4. Augustine, *Civ.* 5.18.

Bibliography

Anselm. *Cur Deus Homo*. In *Saint Anselm: Basic Writings*, translated by S. N. Deane, 171–288. 2nd ed. LaSalle, IL: Open Court, 1962.
Aristotle. *Magna Moralia*. In *The Complete Works of Aristotle*, edited by Jonathan Barnes, 2:1868–921. Bollingen Series 71. Revised Oxford Translation. Princeton: Princeton University Press, 1984.
Augustine. *City of God*. In *A Select Library of the Nicene and Post-Nicene Fathers of the Christian Church, First Series: St. Augustine's City of God and Christian Doctrine*, edited by Philip Schaff, translated by Marcus Dods, 2:1–511. Edinburgh: T. & T. Clark, 1886.
Barr, James. *The Semantics of Biblical Language*. London: Oxford University Press, 1961.
Barth, Karl. *The Epistle to the Romans*. Translated by Edwyn C. Hoskins. New York: Oxford University Press, 1933.
Bauer, Walter, et al. *A Greek-English Lexicon of the New Testament and Other Early Christian Literature*. Chicago: University of Chicago Press, 1955.
Behm, J. "*diathēkē*." In *TDNTA* 157–61.
Benko, Stephen. *Pagan Rome and the Early Christians*. Bloomington: Indiana University Press, 1984.
Bernard, J. H. *A Critical and Exegetical Commentary on the Gospel according to St. John*. Vol. 1, *John 1–7*. International Critical Commentary on the Holy Scriptures of the Old and New Testaments. New York: Scribner's, 1929.
Bohak, Gideon. *Joseph and Aseneth and the Jewish Temple in Heliopolis*. Atlanta: Scholars, 1996.
Boman, Thorlief. *Hebrew Thought Compared with Greek*. Translated by Jules L. Moreau. Philadelphia: Westminster, 1960.
Bookidis, Nancy, and Ronald S. Stroud. *Demeter and Persephone in Ancient Corinth*. Princeton: American School of Classical Studies at Athens, 1987.
Bray, Gerald, ed. *Ancient Christian Commentary on the Scripture*. Vol. 6, *Romans*. Downers Grove: InterVarsity, 1998.
Breidenthal, Thomas E. "The Blood of Abel: Atonement and the Neighbor." *Sewanee Theological Review* 54.2 (2011) 111–25. http://s3.amazonaws.com/dfc_attachments/public/documents/1529/Breidenthal_1.pdf.
Brewer, David Josiah, et al., eds. *The World's Best Orations: From the Earliest Period to the Present Time*, Vol. 1. N.p.: Kaiser, 1899.

BIBLIOGRAPHY

Brooke, A. E. *A Critical and Exegetical Commentary on the Johannine Epistles*. International Critical Commentary on the Holy Scriptures of the Old and New Testaments. New York: Scribner's, 1928.

Brunner, Emil. *The Christian Doctrine of Creation and Redemption*. Vol. 2, *Dogmatics*. Translated by Olive Wyon. Philadelphia: Westminster, 1962.

Büchsel, F. "Iýō." etc. In *TDNTA* 543–47.

Bultmann, Rudolf. "New Testament and Mythology." In *Kerygma and Myth: A Theological Debate*, by Rudolf Bultmann et al., 1–44. New York: Harper, 1961.

Burriss, Eli Edward. "The Nature of Taboo and Its Survival in Roman Life." *Classical Philology* 24.2 (1929) 142–63.

Cairns, Douglas. "Look Both Ways: Studying Emotion in Ancient Greek." *Critical Quarterly* 50.4 (2008) 43–62.

Calvin, John. *The Epistles of Paul the Apostle to the Romans and to the Thessalonians*. Translated by Ross Mackenzie. Grand Rapids: Eerdmans, 1960.

Case, Robert A., II. "Will the Real Athanasius Please Stand Up?" *Journal of the Evangelical Theological Society* 19 (1976) 283–95.

Clay, Jenny Strauss. "Immortal and Ageless Forever." *The Classical Journal* 77.2 (1981) 112–17.

Coffin, Henry Sloane, and Ambrose White Vernon, eds. *Hymns of the Kingdom of God, with Tunes*. New York: Barnes, 1910.

Conner, W. T. *Christian Doctrine*. Nashville: Broadman, 1935.

Crossan, John Dominic. *The Birth of Christianity*. San Francisco: HarperSanFrancisco, 1998.

Darwin, Charles. *The Expression of the Emotions in Man and Animals*. Reprint, Chicago: University of Chicago Press, 1965.

Davies, Richard E. *St. Paul in Macedonia: What the People Heard*. Morrow, GA: Ina and Elsie Memorial, 2013.

Day, Leslie Preston. "Dog Burials in the Greek World." *American Journal of Archaeology* 88.1 (1984) 21–32.

de Beer, Vladimir. "The Cosmic Role of the Logos, as Conceived from Heraclitus until Eriugena." *Greek Orthodox Theological Review* 59 (2014) 13–39.

Digeser, Elizabteh DePalma. *A Threat to Public Policy: Christians, Platonists, and the Great Persecution*. Ithaca: Cornell University Press, 2012.

Dio, Cassius. *Historiae Romanae* [*History of Rome*]. Translated by Earnest Cary. Loeb Classical Library. New York: Harvard University Press, 1914–27. http://penelope.uchicago.edu/Thayer/E/Roman/Texts/Cassius_Dio/home.html.

Duke, Paul D. *Irony in the Fourth Gospel*. Atlanta: Westminster John Knox, 1985.

Edmonds, J. M. *Lyrica Graeca: Being the Remains of all the Greek Poets from Eumelus to Timotheus excepting Pindar, Vol. 1*. Loeb Classical Library. New York: Putnam's, 1922.

Edwards, James R. "Archaeology Gives New Reality to Paul's Ephesus Riot." *Biblical Archaeology Review* 42.4 (July/August 2016) 24–32.

Eisenbaum, Pamela. "A Remedy for Having Been Born of Woman: Jesus, Gentiles, and Genealogy in Romans." *Journal of Biblical Literature* 123.4 (2004) 571–702.

Ensor, Peter. "Clement of Alexandria and Penal Substitutionary Atonement." *Evangelical Quarterly* 85.1 (2013) 19–35.

BIBLIOGRAPHY

Euripides. "Hippolytus." In *Great Books of the Western World: Aeschylus, Sophocles, Euripides, Aristophanes*, edited by Mortimer J. Adler et al., translated by Edward P. Coleridge, 5:225–36. Chicago: Encyclopedia Britannica, 1952.

Eusebius of Caesarea. *Church History*. In *Nicene and Post-Nicene Fathers*, edited by Philip Schaff and Henry Wace, translated by Arthur Cushman McGiffert, 1:81–387. Edinburgh: T. & T. Clark, 1890.

———. *Praeparatio Evangelica [Preparation for the Gospel]*. Translated by E. H. Gifford. N.p., 1903. https://is.muni.cz/el/1421/podzim2012/RLB295/um/Eusebius_of_Caesarea_-_Praeparatio_Evangelica.pdf.

Fögen, Thorsten. "*Sermo corporis*: Ancient Reflections on gestus, vultus and vox." In *Bodies and Boundaries in Graeco-Roman Antiquity*, edited by Mireille M. Lee and Thorsten Fögen, 15–44. Berlin: De Gruyter, 2009.

Frazer, James George. *The Magic Art and the Evolution of Kings, Vol. 2*. 3rd ed. Reprint, London: Macmillan, 1963.

Gardner, John, and John Maier. *Gilgamesh: Translated from the Sîn-leqi-unninnī Version*. New York: Vintage, 1984.

Garland, Robert. *The Greek Way of Death*. Ithaca: Cornell University Press, 1985.

Grant, Edward. *Physical Science in the Middle Ages*. New York: Wiley, 1971.

Grant, Frederick C. *Hellenistic Religions: The Age of Syncretism*. Indianapolis: Bobbs-Merrill, 1953.

"Great Martyr Irene." https://oca.org/saints/lives/2016/05/05/101297-greatmartyr-irene-of-thessalonica.

Hartman, Lars. "Is a Crucified Christ the Center of a New Testament Theology?" In *Approaching New Testament Texts and Contexts: Collected Essays II*, edited by David Helholm and Todd Fornberg, 57–67. Tübingen: Mohr Siebeck, 2013.

———. "Is a Crucified Christ the Center of a New Testament Theology?" In *Text and Logos: The Humanistic Interpretation of the New Testament*, edited by Theodore W. Jennings Jr., 175–88. Atlanta: Scholars, 1990.

Heisenberg, Werner. *Physics and Philosophy: The Revolution in Modern Science*. World Perspectives 19. New York: Harper, 1958.

Hiestand, Gerald. "Not 'Just Forgiven': How Athanasius Overcomes the Under-realised Eschatology of Evangelicalism." *Evangelical Quarterly* 84.1 (2012) 47–66.

Hodges, Henry. *Technology in the Ancient World*. New York: Barnes & Noble, 1970.

Hogarth, et al. "Formosa: Discussion." *The Geographical Journal* 70.3 (1927) 285–87.

Homer. *The Iliad of Homer Translated into English Blank Verse*. Translated by William Cowper. New York: Appleton, 1860. http://www.gutenberg.org/files/16452/16452-h/16452-h.htm#page_105.

———. *The Odyssey*. Translated by Robert Fagles. New York: Penguin, 1996.

Hyginus. *Fabulae*. In *Apollodorus' Library and Hyginus' Fabulae: Two Handbooks of Greek Mythology*, edited by R. Scott Smith and Stephen M. Trzaskoma, 95–182. Indianapolis: Hackett, 2007.

James, Montague Rhodes. *The Apocryphal New Testament*. Oxford: Clarendon, 1924.

James, William. *Pragmatism and Other Essays*. New York: Washington Square, 1963.

Keel, Othmar. *The Symbolism of the Biblical World: Ancient Near Eastern Iconography and the Book of Psalms*. Translated by Timothy J. Hallett. New York: Seabury, 1978.

Kidner, Derek. "Sacrifice: Metaphors and Meaning." *Tyndale Bulletin* 33 (1982) 119–36.

Kline, Morris. *Mathematics: The Loss of Certainty*. Reprint, New York: Fall River, 2011.

Lake, Kirsopp, trans. *The Apostolic Fathers*. 2 vols. Loeb Classical Library. Cambridge: Harvard University Press, 1912–13.

Lambert, Brent. "The Plutchik Emotion Circumplex and the 8 Primary Bipolar Emotions." *FEELguide*, June 7, 2011. https://www.feelguide.com/2011/06/07/the-plutchik-emotion-circumplex-and-the-8-primary-bipolar-emotions/.

Lefebure, Leo D. *Toward a Contemporary Wisdom Christology*. Lanham: University Press of America, 1988.

Leith, Mary Joan. "Creating Woman." *Biblical Archaeology Review* 42.2 (March/April 2016), 58–61.

Lietzmann, Hans. *A History of the Early Church*. 4 vols. Translated by Bertram Lee Woolf. Cleveland: World Publishing Company, 1953.

Lindström, Harald. *Wesley and Sanctification: A Study in the Doctrine of Sanctification*. Translated by H. S. Harvey. Nashville: Abingdon, 1950. http://www.holypig.com/cotor/E-Books/holiness/Sanctification/Wesley%20and%20Sanctification.pdf.

MacArthur, John. *The MacArthur Bible Handbook*. Nashville: Nelson, 2003.

MacCulloch, Diarmaid. *Christianity: The First Three Thousand Years*. New York: Penguin, 2009.

Magie, David, trans. *The Scriptores Historia Augusta, Vol 1*. Loeb Classical Library. Cambridge: Harvard University Press, 1921. https://archive.org/stream/scriptoreshistor01camb/scriptoreshistor01camb_djvu.txt.

Magness, Jodi, et al. "Inside the Huqoq Synagogue." *Biblical Archaeology Review* 45.3 (May/June 2019) 24–38.

Mancall, Peter C., et al. "Slave Prices and the South Carolina Economy, 1722–1809." *The Journal of Economic History* 61.3 (2011) 616–39.

Marenbon, John. *Pagans and Philosophers: The Problem of Paganism from Augustine to Leibniz*. Princeton: Princeton University Press, 2015.

Methodist Church. *The Methodist Hymnal: Official Hymnal of the Methodist Church*. Nashville: Methodist Publishing House, 1939.

Metzger, Bruce M. "Considerations of Methodology in the Study of the Mystery Religions and Early Christianity." *The Harvard Theological Review* 48.1 (1955) 1–20.

Meyer, Marvin, ed. *The Nag Hammadi Scriptures: The International Edition*. New York: HarperOne, 2007.

Moltmann, Jürgen. *The Crucified God [Der gekreuzigte Gott : Das Kreuz Christi als Grund und Kritik christlicher Theologie]*. Translated by R. A. Wilson and John Bowden. Minneapolis: Fortress, 1991.

Montgomery, Helen Barrett. *The New Testament in Modern English (Centenary Translation)*. Philadelphia: Judson, 1952.

Nutt, Roger W. *General Principles of Sacramental Theology*. Washington, DC: Catholic University of America Press, 2017.

Pagels, Elaine. *The Gnostic Gospels*. New York: Random House, 1979.

Paley, William. *Natural Theology or Evidences of the Existence and Attributes of the Deity*. N.p., 1802.

Paton, W. R. *The Greek Anthology*. Vol. 1. Loeb Classical Library. New York: Putnam's, 1916.

———. *The Greek Anthology*. Vol. 5. Loeb Classical Library. New York: Putnam's, 1918.

Patterson, Stephen J. "Platonism and the Apocryphal Origins of Immortality in the Christian Imagination, or Why Do Christians Have Souls that Go to Heaven?" In

The Apocryphal Gospels within the Context of Early Christian Theology, edited by Jens Schröter, 447–76. Leuven: Peeters, 2013.

Pausanias. *Description of Greece*. Translated by W. H. S. Jones. Loeb Classical Library. Cambridge: Harvard University Press, 1918. http://www.perseus.tufts.edu/hopper/text?doc=Perseus:text:1999.01.0160.

Philostratus. *Life of Apollonius of Tyana, The Epistles of Apollonius, and the Treatise of Eusebius*. Translated by F. C. Conybeare. 2 vols. Loeb Classical Library. London: Heinemann, 1912. Vol. 1 is available at: https://archive.org/details/lifeofapollonius01phil.

Plutchik, Robert. "The Circumplex As a General Model of the Structure of Emotions and Personality." In *Circumplex Models of Personality and Emotions*, edited by R. Plutchik and H. R. Conte, 17–45. Washington, DC: American Psychological Association, 1997.

———. "The Nature of Emotions." *American Scientist* 89.4 (2001) 344–50.

Price, Carl Fowler. *One Hundred and One Hymn Stories*. New York: Abingdon, 1923.

Quintus Smyrnaeus. *Quintus Smyrnaeus: The Fall of Troy*. Translated by A. S. Way. Loeb Classical Library. Harvard University Press, 1913.

Ramsay, W. M. *The Cities of St. Paul: Their Influence on His Life and Thought*. New York: Armstrong, 1908.

Ray, John. *The Wisdom of God Manifested in the Works of the Creation*. London: Smith, 1691.

Reasoner, Mark. "Divine Sons: Aeneas and Jesus in Hebrews." In *Reading Religions in the Ancient World: Essays Presented to Robert McQueen Grant on His 90th Birthday*, edited by David E. Aune and Robin D. Young, 149–75. Leiden: Brill, 2007.

Ritchie, A. *Matter and Manner for Christian Workers with Special Reference to Sabbath School Work*. Cincinnati: Western Tract and Book Society, 1871.

Roberts, Alexander, and James Donaldson, eds. *Ante-Nicene Fathers*. 10 vols. Buffalo: Christian Literature, 1885–97.

Rogers, Guy MacLean. *Alexander: The Ambiguity of Greatness*. New York: Random House, 2004.

Rosenberg, Stephen G. "The Jewish Temple at Elephantine." *Near Eastern Archaeology* 67.1 (2004) 4–13.

Runesson, Anders, et al. *The Ancient Synagogue from its Origins to 200 CE: A Sourcebook*. Leiden: Brill, 2007.

Sandy, William and Arthur C. Headlam. *A Critical and Exegetical Commentary on the Epistle to the Romans*. 11th ed. International Critical Commentary 32. New York: Scribner's, 1906.

Schaff, Philip, ed. *A Select Library of the Nicene and Post-Nicene Fathers of the Christian Church, First Series*. Translated by Marcus Dods. Edinburgh: T. & T. Clark, 1886.

Schaff, Philip, and Henry Wace, eds. *A Select Library of the Nicene and Post-Nicene Fathers of the Christian Church, Second Series*. 7 vols. Edinburgh: T. & T. Clark, 1892.

Schmitz, Leonhard. "Ver Sacrum." In *A Dictionary of Greek and Roman Antiquities*, edited by William Smith. London: Murray, 1875. http://penelope.uchicago.edu/Thayer/E/Roman/Texts/secondary/SMIGRA*/Ver_Sacrum.html.

Seligmann, Kurt. *The Mirror of Magic*. New York: Pantheon, 1948.

Shoberg, Gerry. *Perspectives of Jesus in the Writings of Paul*. Cambridge: Clarke, 2014.

Smith, Morton. *Jesus the Magician*. New York: Harper & Row, 1978.

Snyder, Graydon F. *Ante Pacem: Archaeological Evidence of Church Life before Constantine*. Macon: Mercer University Press, 1985.
Sokolon, Marlene Karen. *Political Emotions: Aristotle and the Symphony of Reason and Emotion*. PhD diss., Northern Illinois University, 2003. https://philpapers.org/rec/SOKPEA-2.
Sophocles. "Trachiniae." In *Great Books of the Western World: Aeschylus, Sophocles, Euripides, Aristophanes*, edited by Mortimer J. Adler et al., translated by Richard C. Jebb, 5:170–81. Chicago: Encyclopedia Britannica, 1952.
Srejović, Dragoslav. *Museums of Yugoslavia*. Great Museums of the World. New York: Newsweek, 1977.
Stevens, Marty E. *Temples, Tithes and Taxes: The Temple and the Economic Life of Ancient Israel*. Grand Rapids: Baker Academic, 2006.
Stowers, Stanley. *A Rereading of Romans: Justice, Jews, and Gentiles*. New Haven: Yale University Press, 1994.
Suetonius. *The Deified Vespasian*. In *Lives of the Caesars*, translated by J. C. Rolfe, 2:281–321. Loeb Classical Library. Cambridge: Harvard University Press, 1914.
Turcan, Robert. *The Cults of the Roman Empire*. Translated by Antonia Nevill. Oxford: Blackwell, 1996.
United Methodist Church. *The United Methodist Hymnal: Book of United Methodist Worship*. Nashville: United Methodist, 1989.
Versnel, H. S. "Two Types of Roman *Devotio*." *Mnemosyne* 29.4 (1976) 365–410.
Wesley, John. *Explanatory Notes on the New Testament*. New York: Soule & Mason, 1818.
Williamson, Samuel H., and Louis P. Cain. "Measuring Slavery in 2016 Dollars." www.measuringworth.com/slavery.php
Willis, Wendell. "The Koinonia of Christians—and Others." In *Eucharist and Ecclesiology: Essays in Honor of Dr. Everett Ferguson*, 172–88. Eugene, OR: Pickwick, 2017.
Wirth, Albrecht. *Danaë in christlichen Legenden*. Vienna: Tempsky, 1892.
Wright, F. A. "The Food of the Gods." *The Classical Review* 31.1 (1917) 4–6.
Yeats, William Butler. *Fairy and Folk Tales of Ireland*. Reprint, New York: Galahad, 1996.
Zanker, Paul. *The Power of Images in the Age of Augustus*. Translated by Alan Shapiro. Ann Arbor: University of Michigan Press, 1990.

Index of Subjects

Abelard, xvii, 102, 123, 124, 140
Abraham, 30, 63, 65, 67, 92–95
Achilles, 26, 55, 65
Acrisius, 40
Adoptionism, 117
Aeneas/Aenaeus, 22, 38
Aeneid, 22
Agamemnon, 26
Agape, 129, 136, 161–163
Ahab, 56
Alcastes or *Alcestis*, drama, 49, 133–134, 166
Alcmene, 164–165
Alexander the Great, 19–20, 25
Ampère, Andre-Marié, 5
Anastasis icon, 131, 133, 166
Anchises, 22, 38
Andromeda, 40
Anselm, xvii, 76, 111, 117, 122, 123, 124, 146
Antioch, 4, 46, 47, 80
Apollo, 16, 20, 29, 49, 117
Apollodorus, 166
Apollonius of Tyana, 23, 49, 54–55
Arete, 165
Aristotle, 4, 30, 45, 54, 118, 161
Aristotle (Pseudo), 28
Arnobius, 1, 89, 116–117, 124, 125
Artemis (see also Diana), 26, 29, 160
Athanasius, xvii, 39, 83, 96, 117–120, 122, 124, 132, 138, 140, 142–143, 145–146
Athena, 65
Attis, 52

Augustine of Hippo, xvii, 117, 126, 127, 171
Auschwitz, 145

Bacchus, 22
Baker, Henry W., 122
Barr, James, 29
Barth, Karl, 124, 144–145
Bede, Venerable, 2
Benko, Stephen, 83
Bernard of Clairvaux, 9
Bernard, J. H., 74, 75, 91
Bernoulli, Daniel, 5
Boehm, Anthony W., 9
Bohr, Niels, 140
Boman, Thorlief, 28–29
Boyle, Robert, 5
Breidenthal, Thomas, 90, 147–150
Brooke, A. E., 91
Brunner, Emil, 146
Bultmann, Rudolph, 12
Burriss, Eli Edward, 52–53, 66, 71

Caduceus, 69
Caiaphas, 109–110, 169
Cain, Louis, 155
Cairns, Douglas, 161
Caligula (Gaius), Emperor, 58, 71
Calvin, John, 124
Campground, 79
Cassius Dio, 58
CCLI licensing agency, 1
Celsus, 46, 57
Cerberus, 166
Chalcedon, Council, 116

INDEX OF SUBJECTS

Cicero, 160
Circumcision, 65–66, 93, 165–166
City of God, 127
Clement of Alexandria, 3, 84, 116, 124, 130
Coffin, Henry Sloane, 150
Commodus, Emperor, 57
Conner, W. T., 75–76, 106, 141
Constantine, Emperor, 43, 117, 128, 132
Constitution of the Holy Apostles, 78
Copernicus, 5, 6
Corinth/Corinthian congregation, 18, 54, 60, 72, 91, 103, 113
Covenant, 30, 63–67, 71–72, 88, 89, 93, 148
Crimea, 26
Croly, George, 10
Crosby, Fanny, 12
Cupid (see also eros and love), 40
Curse tablets, 18
Curtius, 126–127
Cybele, 52, 56
Cyncus, 55

Danaë, 39–43
Decius/Decii, 127–129, 131
DeBeer, Vladimir, 135
Deiphobus, 65
Deism, 7–8, 139
Delphi, 117
Devotio, xvii, 99, 108–109, 112, 127–134, 138, 140, 171
Dialogue with Trypho, 115
Diana (see also Artemis), 29, 160
Didache, 60, 73, 78–80, 82, 102
Diognetus, Letter to, 3, 122
Dionysus, 50, 72, 159
Diocletian, Emperor, 84
Docetism, 45–48, 58, 75, 81–82, 117
Domitian, Emperor, 58
Dwight, Timothy, 11

Earnest money, 65
Eisenbaum, Pamela, 14, 66, 67, 92–94, 95
Eli, 42
Emanation, 34–38, 39, 44

Emmaus, 60, 111
Emotion, 30, 34–39, 158–163
Ephesus, 58
Ephrem the Syrian, 23
Eros, 40, 136, 161
Eucharist, 16, 47, 55, 60–85, 87, 110, 111, 112, 119, 120, 138, 141–145, 150
Eudaimonia, 165
Euripides, 4, 26, 87, 133–134, 166
Eusebius, 55, 128
Expiation, 14, 88, 94

Faustina, 57
Flamen Dialis, 71
Frazer, James, 39–40

Gabriel, angel, 168
Gaius Caligula, Emperor, see "Caligula"
Galileo, 5
Gilgamesh Epic, 24, 53
Girard, René, 149
Gladiator, 57, 71
Goho, 146–147
Goltzius, Hendrik, 41
Gnosticism, 34, 35, 36, 38, 43, 46, 48, 75, 81, 165
Graham, Franklin, 1–2
Gregory of Nyssa, 115, 121–122

Hades, 53, 54–55, 128, 130, 166
Hadrian, Emperor, 56
Hartman, Lars, 103, 107, 113
Hecate, 26
Hector, 55, 65
Heisenberg, Werner, 5, 140
Helen of Troy, 38
Hera, 39, 165
Heraclitus, 134–135
Hercules/Herakles, 48–52, 57, 58, 119, 134, 164–166
Herod, King, 165
Hesiod, 20
Hiestand, Gerald, 120
Hippolytus, drama, 4, 87
Historia Augusta, 57
Hoffman, Elisha A., 56
Homer, 21, 22, 24, 46, 54, 65

INDEX OF SUBJECTS

Human sacrifice, 3, 26

Ichor, 21, 22, 38, 46, 48, 52, 57, 58
Ignatius of Antioch, 4, 47–48, 70, 71, 79, 80–82, 83, 84, 108, 139
Iphigenia, 26
Iphicles, 165
Iliad, 21, 65
Irenaeus, xvii, 39, 83, 113, 118, 119, 120, 142
Irene, Saint, 42–43

Jacobi, John C., 9
James, Protevangelium, 42
James, William, 138
Jeremiah, 63–64, 97
Jericho, 127
Jezebel, 56
Joseph, husband of Mary, 15, 66, 92, 164
Joshua, 128
Jove, 39
Jupiter, 49, 50
Julius II, Pope, 43
Julius Caesar, 20, 58
Justin Martyr, 21–22, 24, 72–73, 80, 82–83, 84, 115

Kakia, 165
Karpile Babbia, 18, 23
Kepler, Johannes, 5
Kidner, Derek, 89, 90

Leibniz, Gottfried, 5
Leto/Latona, 160
Lietzmann, Hans, 68–70, 118
Leonidas (tutor of Alexander the Great), 19
Liberalism, 144–145
Logos (see also Word of God), 32, 35, 117–119, 134–135
Love, 4, 28, 30, 33, 38, 40, 47, 79, 80, 81, 90, 98, 99, 104, 105, 109, 114, 123, 124, 126, 136, 139, 142, 143, 158–163, 171
Livy, 13, 69, 127, 129
Luther, Martin, 56, 124, 133, 167

MacArthur, John, 167–171
Magic, 15, 57, 71, 83–85, 124, 165
Mancall, Peter C., 155
Marcus Aurelius, 57
Mars, 39
Martyrs, Christian, 46–48, 52, 58, 80–81, 84, 99, 100, 108–109, 126, 129, 136, 143, 147–148, 170, 171
Mary, Blessed Virgin, 8, 15, 39–43, 66, 92, 164
Meander River, 40
Medusa, 40
Melanesian Brotherhood, 147–148
Melito of Sardis, 13, 19
Memnon, 55
Menoeceus, 126
Mercury, 49
Mercy seat, 89
Meyers, Robin, 143
Mime drama, 14–15, 20
Mithraism, 56
Moltmann, Jürgen, 145–146
Moses, 30, 32, 63, 66, 105–108
Munch, Edvard, 158

Nazism, 144
Nero, Emperor, 136
Neptune (see also Poseidon), 29
Newton, Isaac, 5, 6, 139
Nicene Creed, 117, 119
Nissus, 49
Noah, 24, 63
Nominalism, 76–77

Octavian (Augustus Caesar), 20
Odysseus, 54–55
Ohm, Georg Simon, 5
Omphale, 51
Onione, 51
Orazio Gentileschi, 41
Origen, 3, 46, 50, 59, 86, 117, 123, 126
Orpheus, 52
Osiris, 52

Pagels, Elaine, 48, 81
Paley, William, 6
Pantera, 41
Paris (Alexander the Trojan), 51

INDEX OF SUBJECTS

Patterson, Stephen J., 81
Peleus, 166
Penelope, 42–43
Perseus, 40
Peter, Gospel, 130
Peter, Saint, 114, 167, 169, 170
Phaedo, 54
Phaedra, drama, 87
Philia (love), 161
Philippi/Philippian congregation, 49, 100
Philo of Alexandria, 58
Philostratus, 54
Pindar, 54
Plato, 29–38, 43, 45, 54, 76, 118, 161
Pliny the Elder, 27
Pliny the Younger, 18–19, 135
Plutchek, Robert, 158
Pope, Alexander, 139
Porphyry, 55, 84
Poseidon (see also Neptune), 19, 20
Prometheus, 20–21, 53
Propitiation, 55, 83, 90, 92, 115, 129
Prudentius, 56
Ptolmey, 140
Pythagoras, 23, 125

Quintilian, 160

Ray, John, 6
Realism, 76–77
Remus, 39
Res Gesta, 20
Ritchie, A., 125
Robinson, Robert, 11
Roddenberry, Gene, 33
Rolfe, J. C., 26
Romulus, 39
Rutter, Owen, 146–147

Sacrifice industry, 16–19
Samuel, 42
Sandal exchange as sign of covenant, 64
Sappho, 23, 25
Scamander River, 40
Scream, The (painting), 158
Second Vatican Council, 143
Semiotics, 64

Seneca, 87
Sermon on the Mount, 111, 143
Servius Tullius, 39
Shurtlrff, Ernest W., 11
Simon of Cyrene, 26
Sixtus V, Pope, 116
Smyrna, 47
Sokolon, Marlene Karen, 161, 163
Solomon Islands, 147
Soul (*pseuche*), 2, 31, 32, 54, 56, 71, 76, 82, 94, 115, 119, 121, 122, 127, 130, 134
Spock (TV character), 33
"Star Trek," 33
Stowers, 94
Sychar, 166
Suetonius, 26

Tabernacle, 79
Taiwan/Formosa, 146
Tarsus, 40
Taurobolium, 56
Temple, Jewish, outside Jerusalem, 13–14
Tertullian, 36–38, 103–104
Thayer, 26
Thebes (Greek), 126
Theodosius, Emperor, 132
Theogony, 20
Theseus, 166
thirty pieces of silver, 27, 155–157
Thomas (doubting Apostle), 165
Thomas, Gospel of, 165
Thysia, 60, 69, 100, 102
Timaeus, 31–35, 36, 145
Timothy, 43
Tiresias, 54–55, 126, 165
Titan, 50, 160
Titian (artist), 41
Trajan, Emperor, 18, 47, 80, 135
Trojan War, 26, 51, 55, 65
Tyrian shekel, 156

Vače, Slovenia, 24
Varro, 37
Venus, 38
Vernon, Ambrose White, 150
Versnel, H. S., 127, 134

INDEX OF SUBJECTS

Vespasian, Emperor, 26, 58
Vestal Virgins, 39
Virginal conception (legends), 39–40
Volta, Alessandro, 5

Watts, Isaac, 9, 151
Wesley, Charles, 9–10
Wesley, John, 6, 7–8, 151, 156
Wiesel, Elie, 145
Williamson, Samuel H., 155

Word of God (see also *Logos*), 32, 35, 36, 38, 39, 65, 75, 82, 88, 107, 113, 123, 133, 134, 135, 136
World War Two, 144

Yeats, W. B., 122

Zeus, 20–21, 28, 38–41, 53, 57, 159, 164–165

Index of Scripture

Genesis

8:21	24
15:7–21	65
17:1–14	65, 67
18:22–33	30

Exodus

3:1–6	30
20:5	32
21:32	155
29	22
29:21	22
30	27
33:23	30

Leviticus

12:6	92
12:8	15
14:1–32	22
16	93, 97
16:6–28	22
17:3–4, 7	21
17:10–14	75
17:10–16	22
17:11, 14	44, 53, 111
19: 5–6	21
19:26	22, 75
21:22	20

Numbers

18–19	22
21	105
21:8–9	107

Deuteronomy

5:9	32
10:16	66
12:16, 23–4	75
14:3–20	75
14:21	22
21:22–23	133
22:28–29	155
28:53–57	75
30:6	66

Joshua

6:21—7:26	128

Ruth

4:7	64

First Samuel

1:22–28	42

INDEX OF SCRIPTURE

First Kings

22:38	56

Second Kings

3:16–18	110
18:4	105

Psalms

18	28–29
22	50
51:17	80

Isaiah

1:11	104
33:13–19	82–83
53	167, 168, 171
53:5, 10	3, 168
55:12	29
59:21	64
63:9	162

Jeremiah

1:4–10	97
3:16	63
4:4	66
9:26	66
31:31–33	64

Ezekiel

34	110, 168
43:18–27	22
44:7	66

Daniel

9:24–27	167, 168

Joel

2:12–13	66, 80
2:32	98

Amos

5:21–24	98
5:23–24	21

Zechariah

11:12	156
12:10	168
13:1	167, 168
13:7	110, 167, 168–169
14:8	168

Malachi

1:11, 14	80, 82

Matthew

1:18–25	35
3:16–17	35
5:23–24	80
10:28	127
10:38	112, 115
16:24	112, 115
20:28	67, 111, 122
21:33–41	150, 157
25:41, 46	116
26:15	155
26:26–29	62
26:28	67, 88
26:39, 42, 44	126
27	111

INDEX OF SCRIPTURE

27:37	25
27:52–53	130
27:66—28:4	42
28:11–15	42

Mark

1:10–11	35
5:40–42	114
8:34	112, 115
10:21	115
10:45	67, 111, 122
12:1–12	150, 157
14:22–25	62
14:24	88
14:35–36, 39	126
15:26	25

Luke

1:9	27
1:24	15
1:26–33	35
1:74	133
2:22–24	66, 92
3:21–22	35
9:23	112, 115
14:27	112, 115
18:9–14	25
19:41	163
20:9–19	150, 157
22:15–20	62
22:17–23	111
22:19	71
22:20	88
22:42	126
23:38	25
24:30–31	60, 111

John

1:1–2	32, 107
1:29, 36	167, 169, 170
1:32–33	35
3:13–18	105–109
3:16	109
4:7–15	75, 110
4:20	14
4:23–24	104
5:25, 28–29	130
6	75, 141
6:25–51	75
6:31–40	110
6:35	63
6:48–58	63
6:51–58	74, 75
6:53–56	88, 110
6:61–63	63
6:66	75
7:33	110
7:37–38	75, 110
8:21	110
8:28	108
10:11–17	108–109, 110
11:35	75, 163
11:50–52	109, 167, 169
12:34	108
13:15	114
13:34	114
14:19	110
15:12–13	126, 136, 171
15:18–21	110
16:5–7	110
16:16	110
17:12	110
18:14	109
19:19–20	25
19:30	75
21	126

Acts

1:9	166
4:10	167, 169
4:12	171
4:34–5:11	69
9–10	8
9:1–19	98
9:16	103
9:40–41	114
13:1	47

Index of Scripture

Romans

2:29	66
3:23–25	102, 123, 169
3:25	102, 115, 123, 124, 146, 167, 169, 171
4:24–25	95
5	96, 118
5:6–8	98–99
5:8–9	95–96
5:8–11	167, 169
5:9	99
5:12–18	96–97
5:16, 18	95–96
7:7–25	95
8:2	171
8:3–4	3, 91, 94
8:14	136
8:28–30	97
8—10	98
10	113
10:9–13	98

First Corinthians

1:17–18	91
2:8	87
8:4	66
10:14–22	68, 70
10:16	70, 88, 142
10:16–18	62
10:20	70
10:32	72
11:20–22	72
11:23–26	62
11:25	88
11:27	72
11:33	72
13	136, 162
15:3	91

Second Corinthians

1:5	103
5:16–21	94
5:21	95, 132, 167
8:1–7	102
11:23–29	100, 103, 136

Galatians

1:4	167, 169, 171
3:13	94, 133
3:27	136

Ephesians

1:7	91
2:1–7	129
2:5	94
2:11–19	94
2:13–16	91
4:9–10	128

Philippians

2	99
2:6–11	49–50, 52, 114
2:7	100
2:17	100, 101, 102
4:18–19	101

First Thessalonians

1:10	167, 169
4:16–17	169

First Timothy

2:6	111, 122, 167, 170, 171

Titus

2:14	111, 171

Hebrews

1:1–2	135
1:3	88
8:8–10	64
9:13–14	88
10:14	171
10:16	64
11—12	90
12:1–24	149
12:24	64, 71, 148
13:20	88–89

First Peter

1:3–21	170
1:11, 20	167, 170
1:15–19	115, 170, 171
1:19	135
2:5	103
2:11	135
2:21	114, 135
2:21–23	136
2:24	135
3:14–18	136
3:18	171
3:18–20	128
4:1–6	136
4:6	128

First John

1:7—2:2	90
2:2	167, 170, 171
4:7	90
4:8	162
4:10	90, 167, 170, 171
5:6–8	90–91

Revelation

1:18	130
4:4	11
7:13–14	57
8:3–4	27
13:8	167, 170
22:1–2	168

www.ingramcontent.com/pod-product-compliance
Lightning Source LLC
Chambersburg PA
CBHW062038220426
43662CB00010B/1554